IMAGES
of America
DELAWARE COUNTY

ON THE COVER: Cannonsville's final Old Home Day, celebrated July 4, 1956, featured a parade that crossed the bridge over the West Branch of the Delaware River. At the rear of the parade, five boys marched donning papier-mâché fish costumes, a poignant, if not-so-subtle comment on the fact that the 1956 event was to be the village's last. Soon after the day's festivities concluded, residents of Cannonsville had to gradually vacate their homes and businesses to make way for the construction of the Cannonsville Reservoir. Eventually, the village would become just a memory to former inhabitants, one of numerous "drowned towns" in Delaware County. When it was completed almost 10 years later, the reservoir would prove to be the last one constructed in the Catskills as part of the broader water supply system for New York City. (Courtesy of the Delaware County Historical Association.)

IMAGES
of America

DELAWARE COUNTY

Tim Duerden and Ray LaFever

ARCADIA
PUBLISHING

ISBN 978-1-4671-1691-6

Published by Arcadia Publishing
Charleston, South Carolina

Printed in the United States of America

Library of Congress Control Number: 2015960042

For all general information, please contact Arcadia Publishing:
Telephone 843-853-2070
Fax 843-853-0044
E-mail sales@arcadiapublishing.com
For customer service and orders:
Toll-Free 1-888-313-2665

Visit us on the Internet at www.arcadiapublishing.com

To the people of Delaware County, past, present, and future

Contents

ACKNOWLEDGMENTS

The authors would like to acknowledge and give thanks to the following people and organizations: earlier historians of the county and region whose research and writing informs our knowledge of Delaware County today, the hundreds of people who have donated archival material to Delaware County Historical Association (DCHA) over several decades, those volunteers who founded DCHA in 1945 in the months immediately following World War II, and those who have stewarded the organization through thick and thin down to the present day. Without those who came before, this volume would not have been possible.

All of the images included in this book are from the collections of the Delaware County Historical Association.

INTRODUCTION

The history of Delaware County has been affected by its location in the Catskill Mountains of New York State and by the perseverance of the people who have settled the county's upland terrain. Some early settlers farmed the rocky hillsides and valley bottoms, while others sought raw materials in the forests.

Before the mid-18th century, Mohawk tribes of the Iroquois Confederation called the region around the upper Delaware and Susquehanna Rivers home. However, beginning in the 1740s, settlers of European ethnicity moved into the area. For the most part, these new arrivals constructed log cabins in clearings in the forests and occupied themselves with hunting and trapping.

By the time of the American Revolution, most of the Catskills had been apportioned out in patents to wealthy speculators. Patent holders subsequently sold some of this land to pioneering settlers, while vast tracts, sometimes consisting of thousands of acres, continued to be owned by the likes of Dutchman Johannes Hardenburgh.

On the eve of the Revolutionary War, intrepid Scotch-Irish settlers began to find their way down the West Branch of the Delaware River and along the Susquehanna River, establishing tiny communities in Davenport, Kortright, Stamford, Harpersfield, and Sidney. But the Revolutionary War slowed the settlement of the future Delaware County; indeed, many settlers fled to the relative safety of more populated areas in present-day Otsego and Schoharie Counties.

After the war, survivors and new settlers returned to the region, among them Scotch-Irish and Germans. In addition, a great many of these pioneers made their way to the Catskills from lower New York State and New England.

As scattered communities grew, buildings of a more communal function joined the individual log cabins. One-room schoolhouses, churches, water-powered gristmills and sawmills, and, eventually, a general store here and there were constructed to fulfill the needs of a growing settlement.

By the 1790s, with war becoming a distant memory for younger pioneers, the population of the region had increased to the extent that the New York State Legislature was petitioned to establish a new county. In 1797, when enough support in the legislature had been secured, the region officially became known as Delaware County, breaking away from Ulster County in the south and Otsego County in north.

This new political entity was made up of six towns, and representatives of each town met in March 1797 to begin the work of constructing the county's necessary political and legal infrastructure. By October 1797, the first jury of the Court of Common Pleas began to meet at the home and tavern of Judge Gideon Frisbee, located at the spot north of the village of Delhi where Elk Creek joins the West Branch of the Delaware River. The building houses presently the Delaware County Historical Association. Court continued to be held at this site until construction of a new courthouse in the village of Delhi was completed in 1799.

Although the name and outline of the new county now began to appear on maps of the Catskills, Delaware County's mountainous terrain continued to pose significant barriers to the movement of people and goods in and out—a situation that was not to change much until the late 19th century.

As a result of their isolation, new settlers relied on a far-reaching subsistence economy in which most important commodities were produced locally, either within the household or at the hands of local artisans. These isolated communities frequently boasted cabinetmakers, joiners, tinsmiths, blacksmiths, and basket makers—craftspeople specializing in trades that farmers could not.

Some resourceful residents, however, utilized the region's waterways to transport their products out of the mountains. By the end of the 18th century and continuing on until the final decades of the 19th century, enormous rafts of floating timber were lashed together for transport southward along both branches of the Delaware River to Trenton and Philadelphia. Cargoes of bluestone, wheat, potash, wool, and whiskey were loaded onto the rafts for transport to the cities.

Men and women, and sometimes even children, shared equally in production in this small-scale economy. On local farms, men and boys tended to the larger livestock, while their female counterparts maintained the household and looked after the smaller animals. In addition to vegetables and grains, most households produced flax and wool, cut their own timber, and, in the spring, tapped the maple trees for their sap. Trees also provided the raw material for products such as potash and tannic acid.

Delaware County continued to attract new migrants through the first quarter of the 19th century. However, the rugged topography of the region, combined with accessibility problems, hindered any large-scale migration. After 1800 and the construction of the Jericho Turnpike (connecting Rhinecliff in the Hudson Valley with Bainbridge on the Susquehanna River) and the Catskill Turnpike (from Catskill in the east to Unadilla in the west), the county gained slightly easier connections to the outside world.

Still, population growth in the new county was slow. In 1800, the population stood at 10,000; some 60 years later it had reached 40,000, and it has continued to hover around this mark ever since. The opening of the Erie Canal to the north of the county in 1825, while providing an easier transportation route between the Hudson Valley and Buffalo, only served to divert trade and population growth away from the Catskills.

The rugged nature of the land also delayed the arrival of railroads into Delaware County. While other areas of New York State were becoming increasingly accessible by train, most towns in Delaware County had to wait until the 1860s and 1870s for regular service.

However, the advent of rail service when it came proved a boon to the region's dairy farmers. Now large quantities of milk and butter could be shipped in refrigerated cars rapidly and directly to urban markets. The creameries that received and shipped the milk from local farmers flourished in those communities along the rails. "Milk trains" departed early every morning bound for urban markets, and the dairy industry continued to be the mainstay of the local economy until well into the 20th century.

Rail transportation, and later the automobile, also provided the catalyst for a tourism industry in Delaware County. Only three or four hours from New York City by car and still less to Albany and the Hudson Valley, the summer and fall months saw throngs of urbanites flooding to the Catskills. Local boardinghouses, and later larger hotels, provided summer accommodations for vacationers seeking the cool of the mountains.

Newcomers, many paying their first visit to Delaware County as tourists, have continued to settle in the region. Today, Delaware County may be described as having a mixed population of "locals," many of whom are able to trace their lineage all the way back to the original pioneers, and the numerous "city folk," denoting the segment of the community that has arrived more recently.

Despite the increasingly heterogeneous nature of the county's population, one phenomenon remains indisputable: as the local dairy industry has declined during recent decades, the forests have once more spread their sylvan blanket over the hills and fields of Delaware County, returning this small corner of the world to an appearance much closer to a time before the arrival of the first European American pioneers.

One

Nineteen Towns

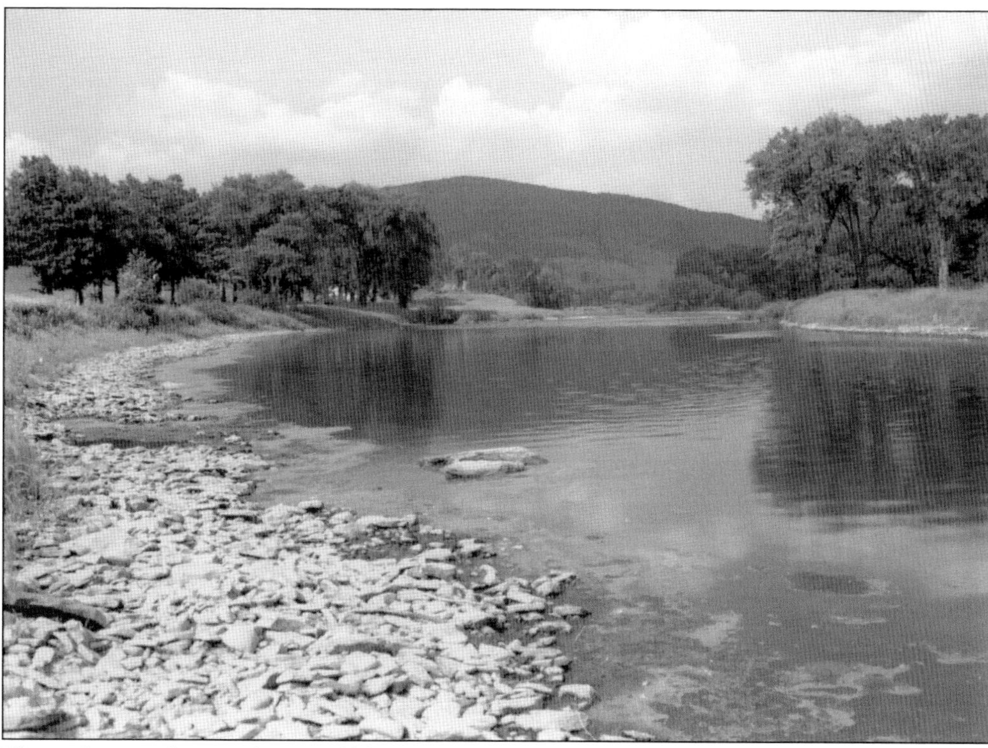

The earliest settlers to what would later become Delaware County were particularly attracted by the waterways the region had to offer. As well as the East and West Branches of the Delaware River and the Susquehanna River, the county boasted many streams, useful for fishing, milling, and traveling. The proximity to the Delaware River in the southwest part of the county made moving early goods, such as furs and logs, to markets in the East and South possible.

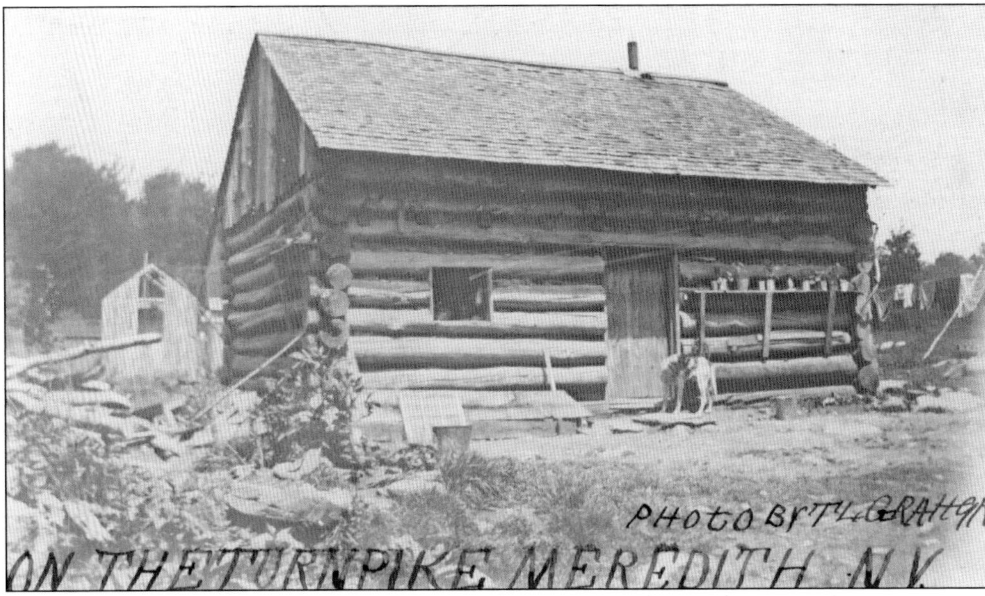

Utilizing the raw materials at hand, intrepid 18th-century settlers in the region first constructed rude log cabins, such as the one shown here on the Catskill Turnpike in the town of Meredith. Log cabins were usually the first permanent structures erected on the mountain frontier. Until well into the 19th century, numerous local families continued to inhabit such cabins.

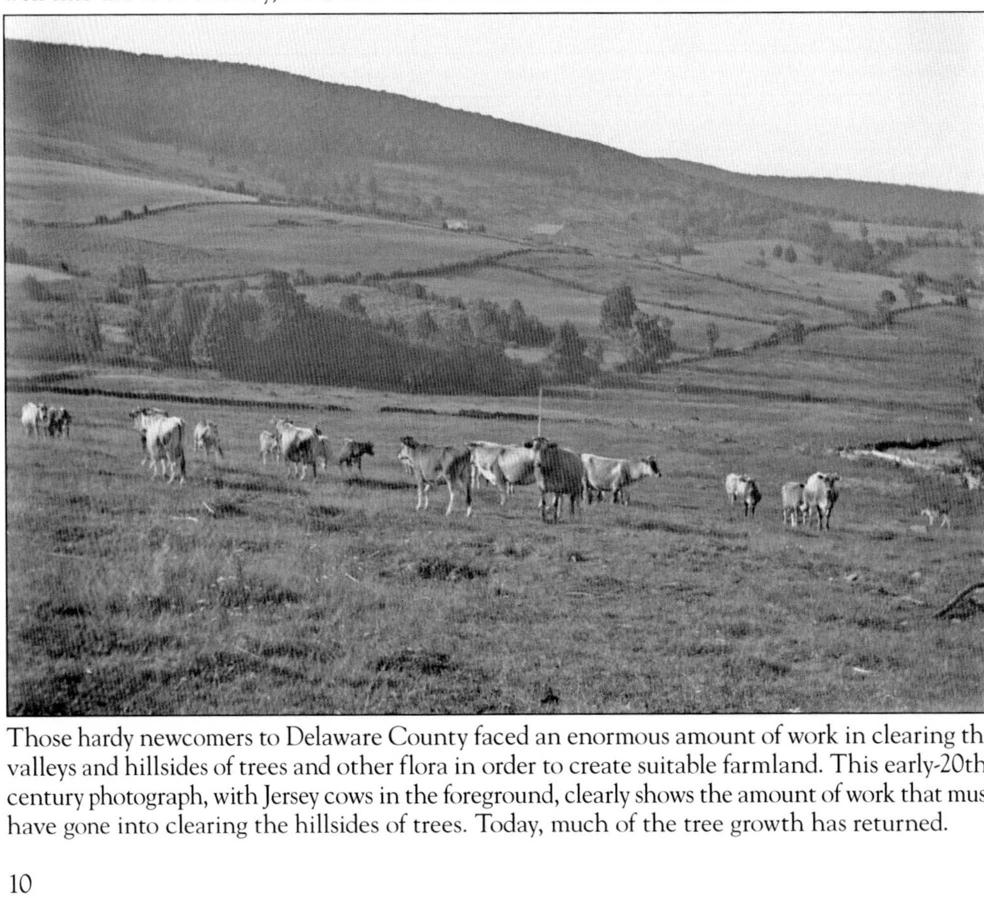

Those hardy newcomers to Delaware County faced an enormous amount of work in clearing the valleys and hillsides of trees and other flora in order to create suitable farmland. This early-20th-century photograph, with Jersey cows in the foreground, clearly shows the amount of work that must have gone into clearing the hillsides of trees. Today, much of the tree growth has returned.

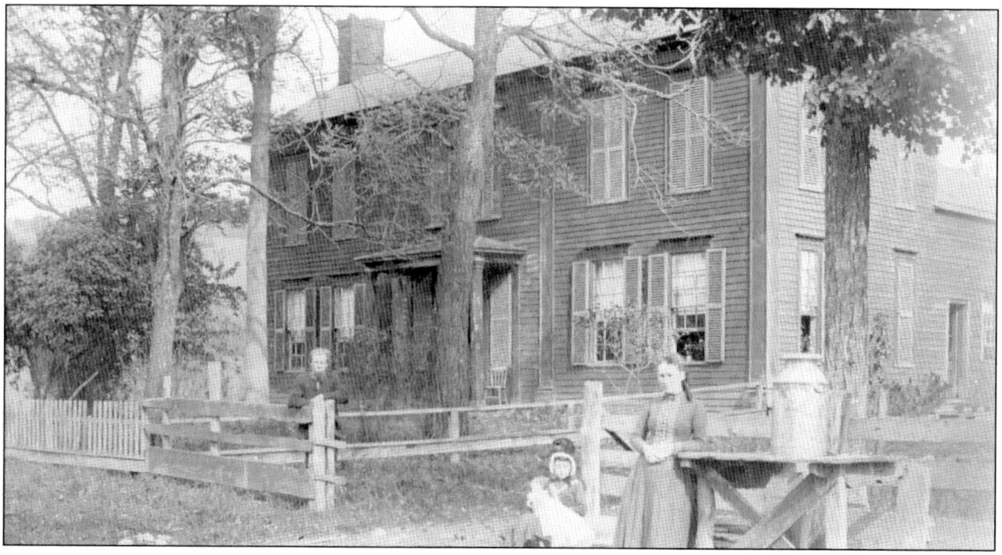

The 1797 Gideon Frisbee House is referred to as the "Birthplace of Delaware County." Throughout 1797, the house hosted the first meetings of the Delaware County Board of Supervisors, including the meeting at which Delaware County was formally established in May 1797. Frisbee's home also served the county as the first county court. This image is the earliest known of the house, taken about 1888. Pictured are James Frisbee and Nancy (McMullen) Frisbee and their daughter Jennie. The house is now a part of the Delaware County Historical Association in the town of Delhi.

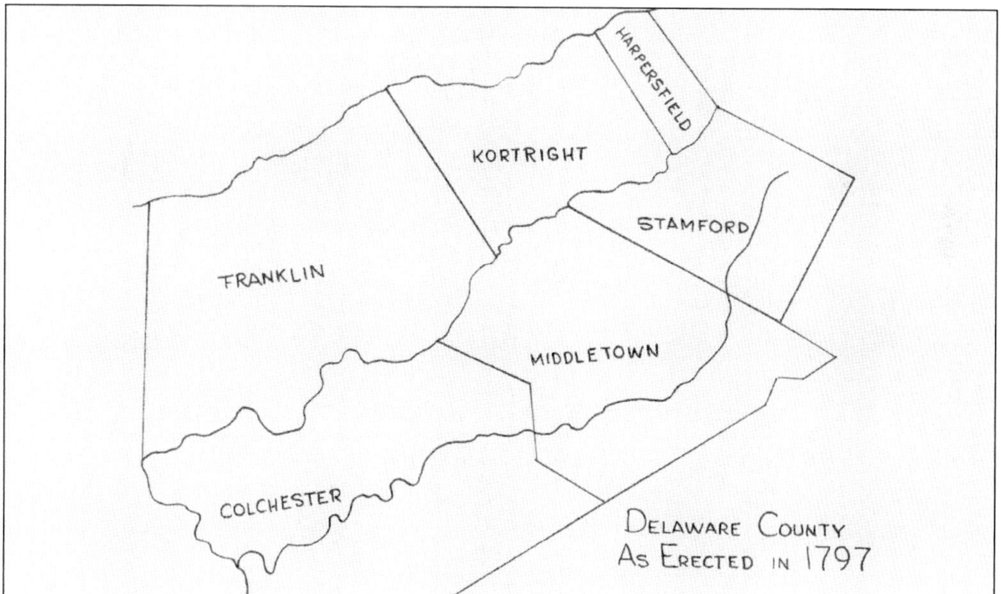

When Delaware County was created by an act of the state legislature in March 1797, it was created out of two existing counties, Otsego and Ulster. The West Branch of the Delaware River was the old Otsego/Ulster boundary. At the time of its creation, there were six towns. Franklin, Kortright, and Harpersfield came from Otsego while Colchester, Middletown, and Stamford came out of Ulster.

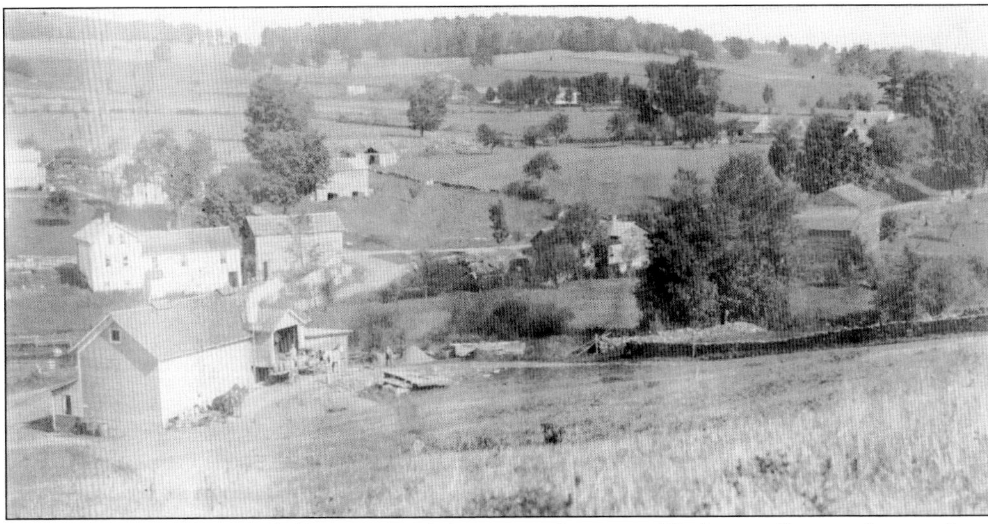

Created in 1788, Harpersfield was one of the original towns of Delaware County, having been part of Montgomery, then Otsego County before the creation of Delaware. The earliest settler, Col. John Harper, came in 1771. The settlers left during the American Revolution, when the region was contested territory, but returned after the end of the war. The community was one of the more populated settlements in the county during the 19th century.

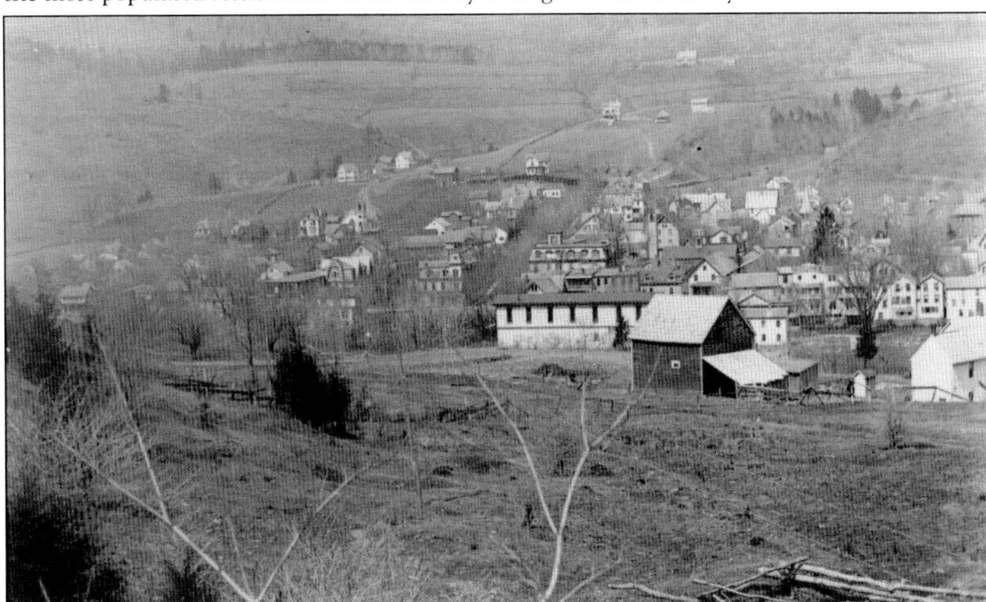

The town of Middletown was created in 1789 as part of Ulster County and was one of the original towns of Delaware County at its creation in 1797. It was so named due to its position midway between the Hudson, Susquehanna, and Delaware Rivers. The East Branch of the Delaware River goes through the town. The creation of the Pepacton Reservoir in the 1950s eliminated the hamlet of Arena, once known as Lumberville. The village of Margaretville (above) was incorporated in 1875 and the village of Fleischmanns in 1913, the latter created from the settlements of Griffin Corners and Fleischmann. Griffin Corners was named for Matthew Griffin, and Fleischmanns (originally Fleischmann) was named for Charles F. Fleischmann, founder of Fleischmann Yeast Company. Summer visitors began coming with the advent of the railroad in the 1870s.

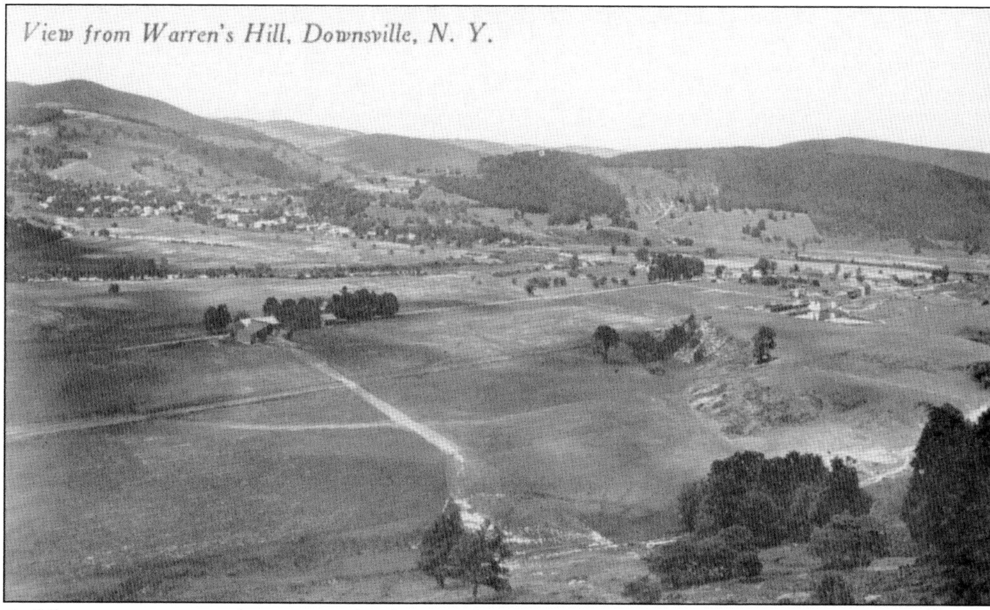

Colchester was created in 1792, the first settlers having arrived in 1776. The name came from Colchester, Connecticut. Portions of the town were later taken off for Hancock and Walton. As well as farming, the town was once noted for rafting, lumbering, and acid factories. In the 1950s, the Pepacton Reservoir was constructed, flooding the hamlet of Pepacton. The dam for the reservoir is just outside the hamlet of Downsville, the main commercial center of Colchester.

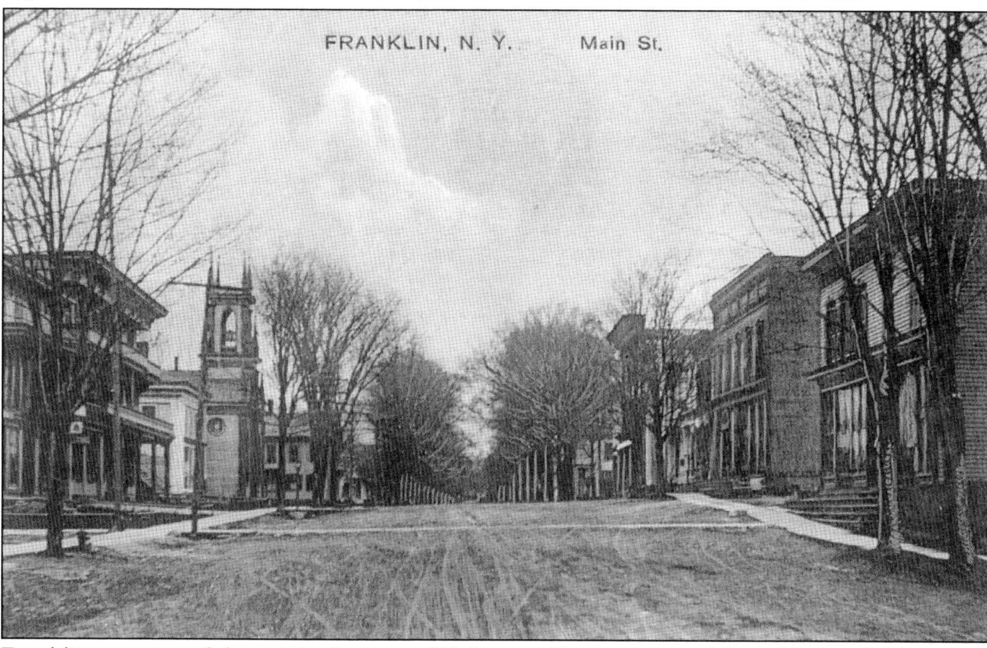

Franklin was one of the original towns of Delaware County, created from Harpersfield in 1792. Portions were later taken for Walton, Meredith, Sidney and the Otsego County town of Otego. First settled in 1787, the town was a leader in New York State for the production of wool. The town includes the hamlet of Treadwell, earlier known as Croton. The town also includes the village of Franklin, incorporated in 1836.

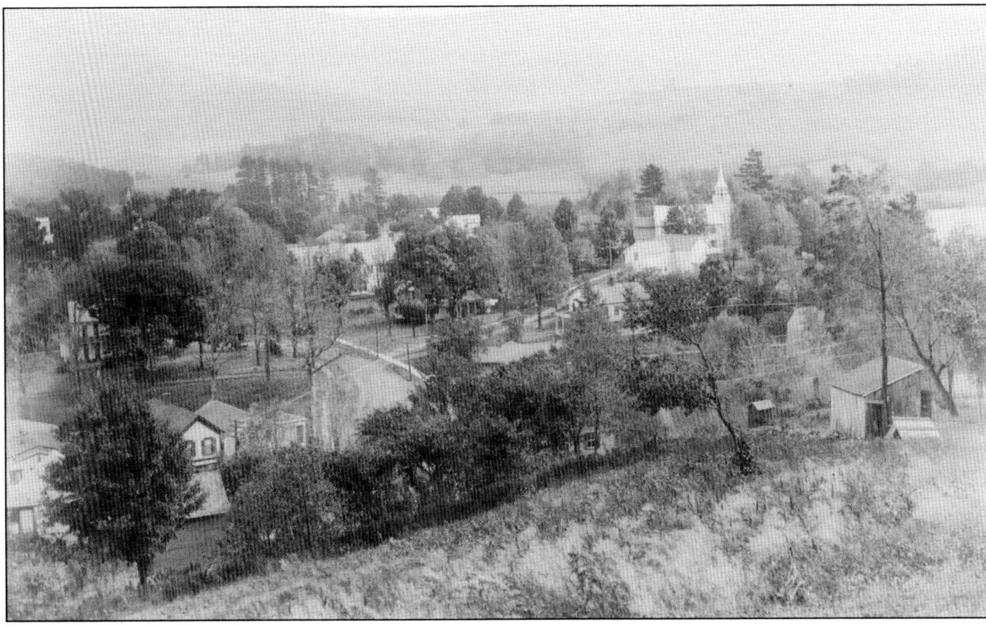

The town of Stamford was created in 1792 as part of Ulster County. It was one of the original towns of Delaware County at its creation in 1797. Settlers came in the 1780s, laying out the settlement of New Stamford. The railroad allowed for tourism and summer guests. Stamford has two villages, Hobart (shown above) and Stamford, as well as the hamlet of South Kortright. The village of Stamford was incorporated in 1870 and Hobart in 1888.

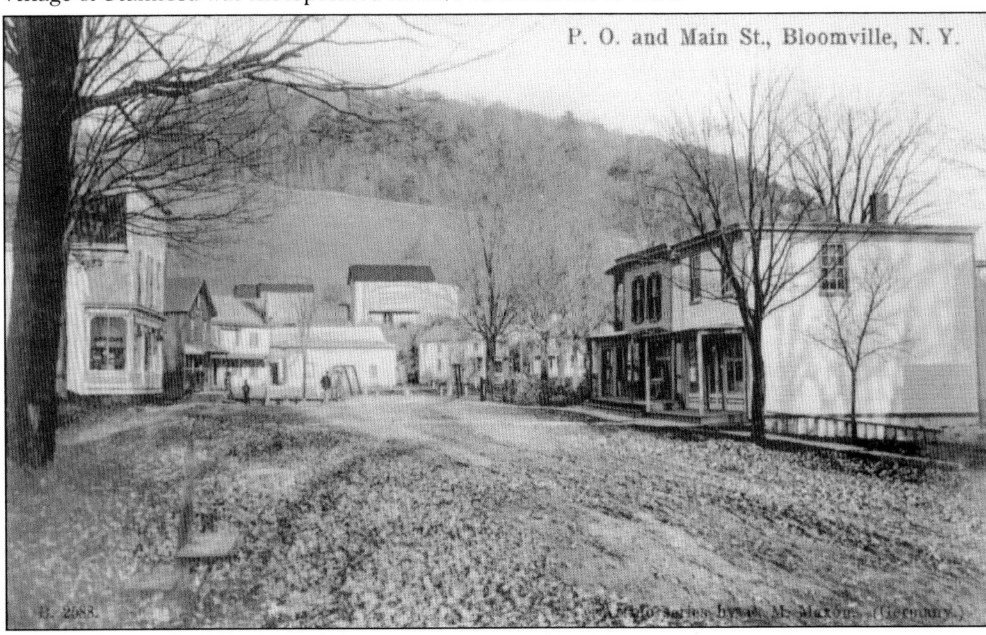

Kortright was first settled in 1774 by several Scottish families. Created in 1793 as part of Otsego County, it was one of the original towns of Delaware County. The two main centers were Kortright Center on the Susquehanna Turnpike and Bloomville, also known as Four Corners, or the Corners. In 1891, the Ulster & Delaware (U&D) Railroad reached Bloomville. Two years later, the Sheffield creamery was established for the pasteurization of milk.

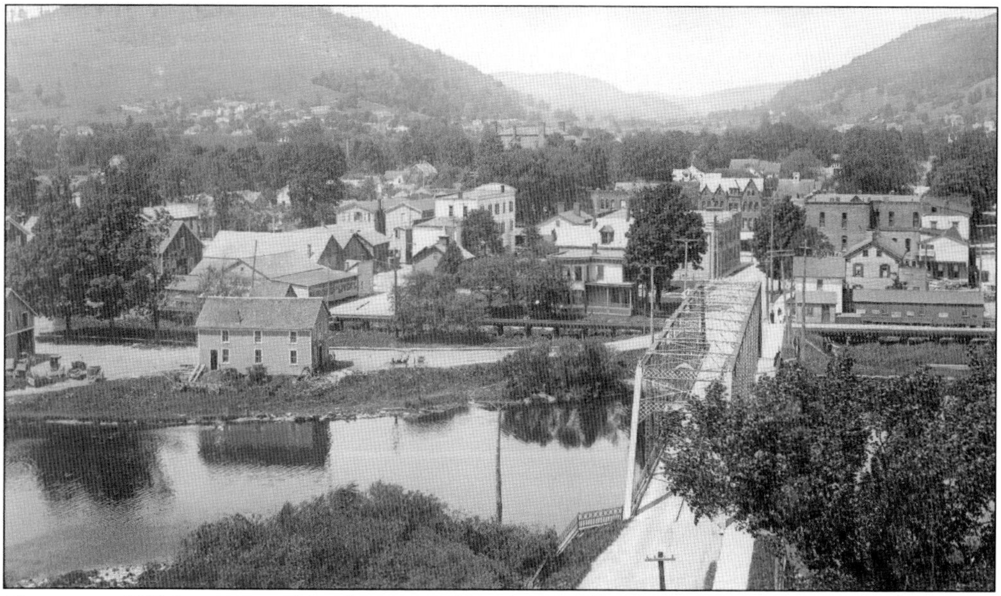

The town of Walton, named for the original land patent holder, William Walton, was created in 1797 out of the town of Franklin. First settled in 1785, the town's rapid growth was due to fulling and carding mills, quarries, tanneries, farming, and woodworking factories. The economy was further boosted by the Ontario & Western (O&W) Railway reaching the town in 1872. In 1851, the village of Walton was incorporated. The village once had a creamery and cheese factory and was the home of the Munn Piano Factory in the early 20th century. The Delaware County Fair moved to Walton in 1926 and has been held there ever since. The village includes the Ogden Free Library, founded in 1896 and endowed by the estate of William B. Ogden.

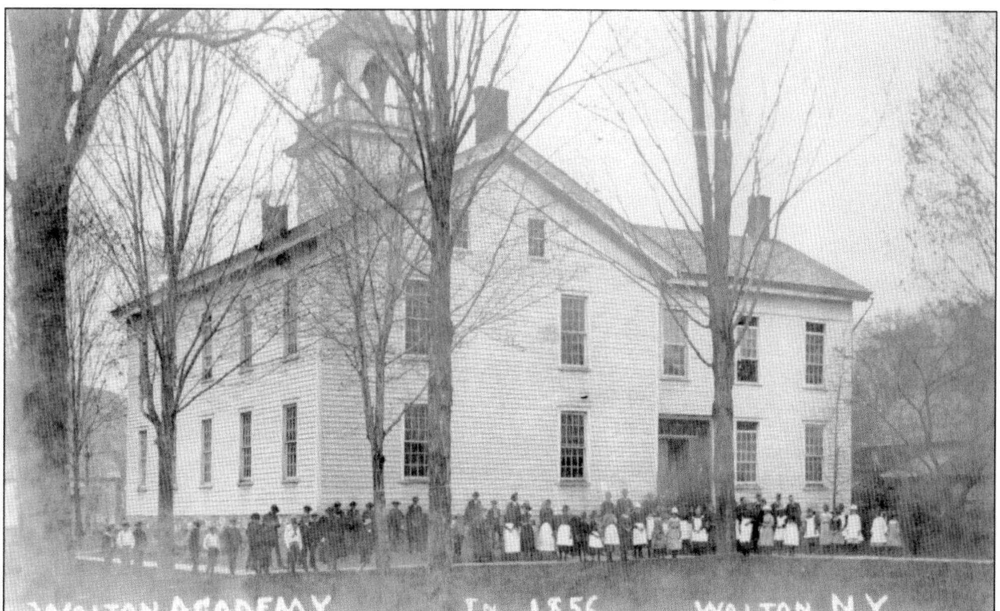

Walton Academy was created in the 1850s, with subscribers to the Academy Association helping to provide funds for the building. It functioned as a private academy until 1868, when it became a Union School run under the auspices of the local board of education.

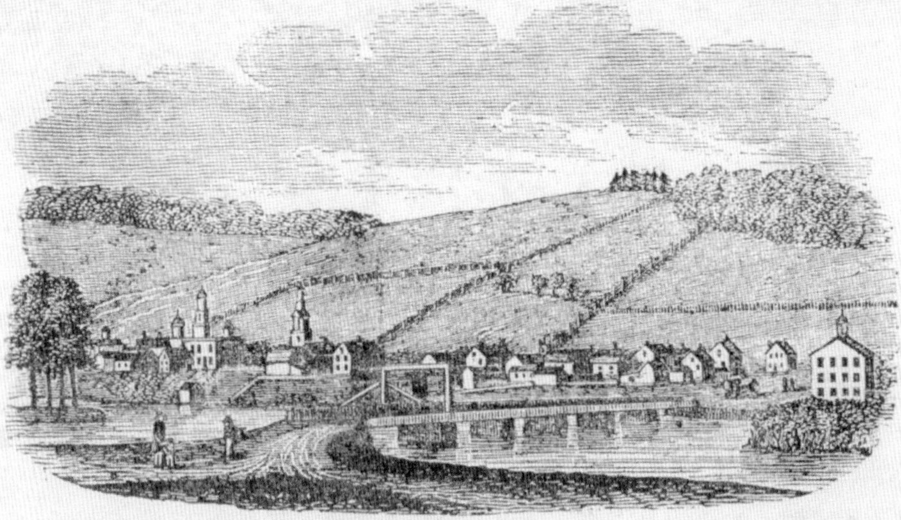

EASTERN VIEW OF DELHI VILLAGE. (Barber's Historical Collections 1841)
Principal Buildings right to left:
Factory, Episcopal Church, Presbyterian Church, Court House, Jail, Old Academy.

Delhi's first settlers came in 1785. The town was created in 1798 from the towns of Middletown, Kortright, and Walton (parts later were taken for the creation of Bovina and Hamden). Centrally located in the county, Delhi became the county seat. The West Branch of the Delaware River runs through the town. The village of Delhi was incorporated in 1821. The village is the home of Delaware Academy, created as a private literary school in 1819. The village also is home to the State University of New York at Delhi, created originally as the State Agricultural School and known in the 1960s and 1970s as Delhi Agricultural and Technical College. The Ontario & Western Railway came in 1872, and the village once had four hotels. Noted residents of Delhi have included textile artist Candace Thurber Wheeler (1827–1923) and journalist John W. Vandercook.

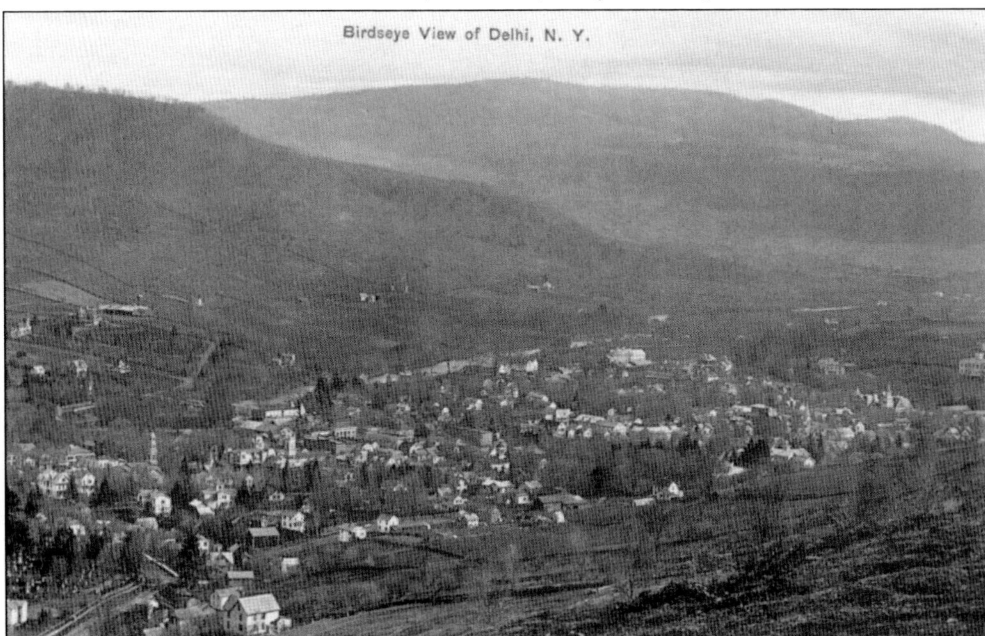

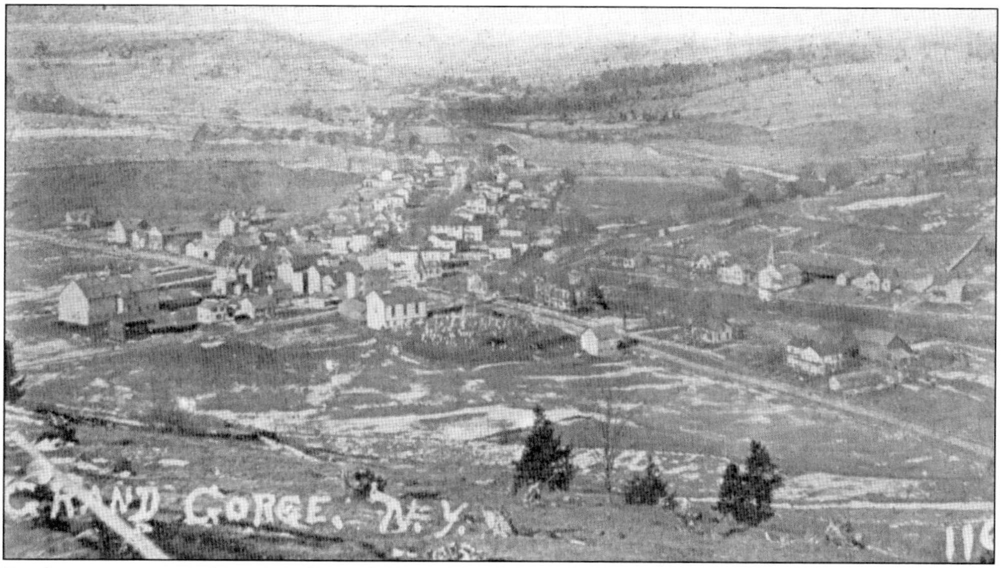

Roxbury was created in 1799 from the town of Stamford. John More was an early settler, coming in 1786 and creating what later became Grand Gorge. The town had tanneries, sawmills, and a distillery among other industries, as well as dairy farmers, taking advantage of the Windham Turnpike to bring their products to market. Two of the town's more famous native sons were financier Jay Gould and naturalist John Burroughs.

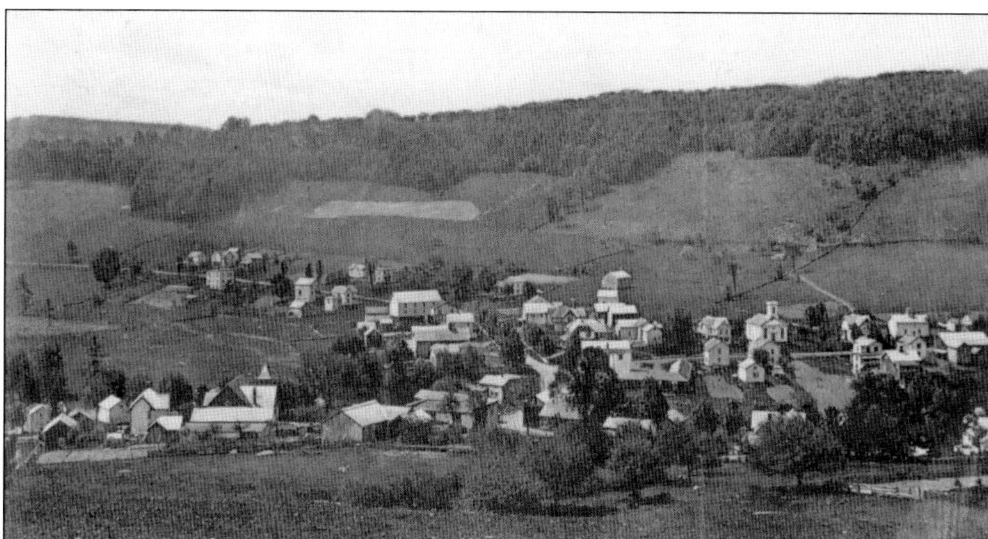

Created in 1800 out of parts of the towns of Delhi, Kortright, and Franklin, Meredith was named for Reese Meredith, the original patent holder. Meredith Square was laid out by Samuel Law when he settled in the area in 1797. Dairy farming was the main economic activity in Meredith, reaching its zenith with the establishment of Meridale Farms in 1888. The Ulster & Delaware Railroad came to East Meredith in 1900. Pictured here is Meridale.

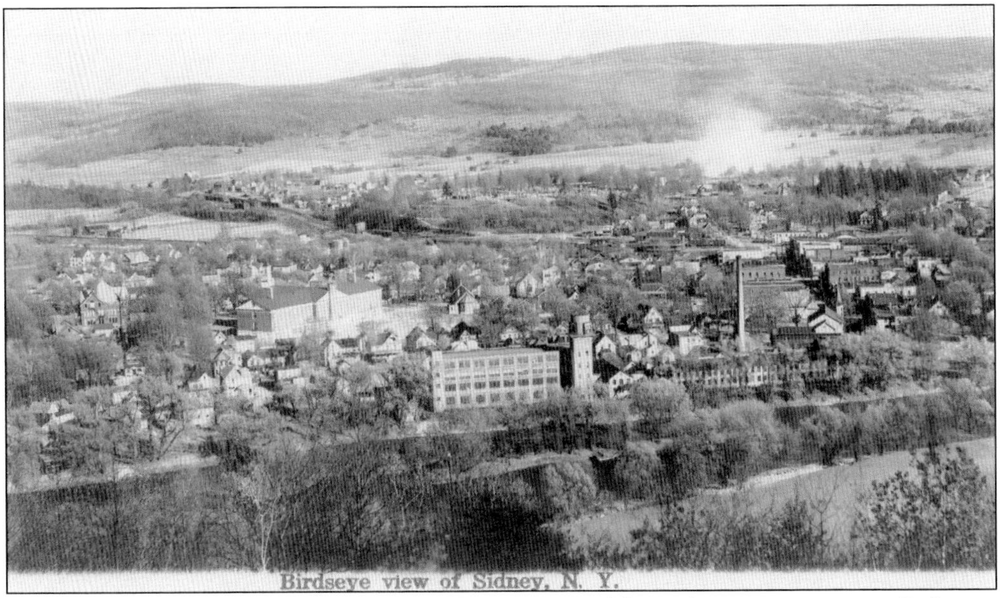

First settled in 1770 by William Johnston, Sidney was one of the earliest communities in Delaware County. The town of Sidney was created in 1801 from the town of Franklin. Development was enhanced by the Susquehanna Turnpike and then by the Delaware & Hudson (D&H) and New York, Ontario & Western Railroads. The town includes the village of Sidney, incorporated in 1888, pictured here in the 1930s. The village is the largest in Delaware County. Many factories flourished in the 19th and into the 20th century.

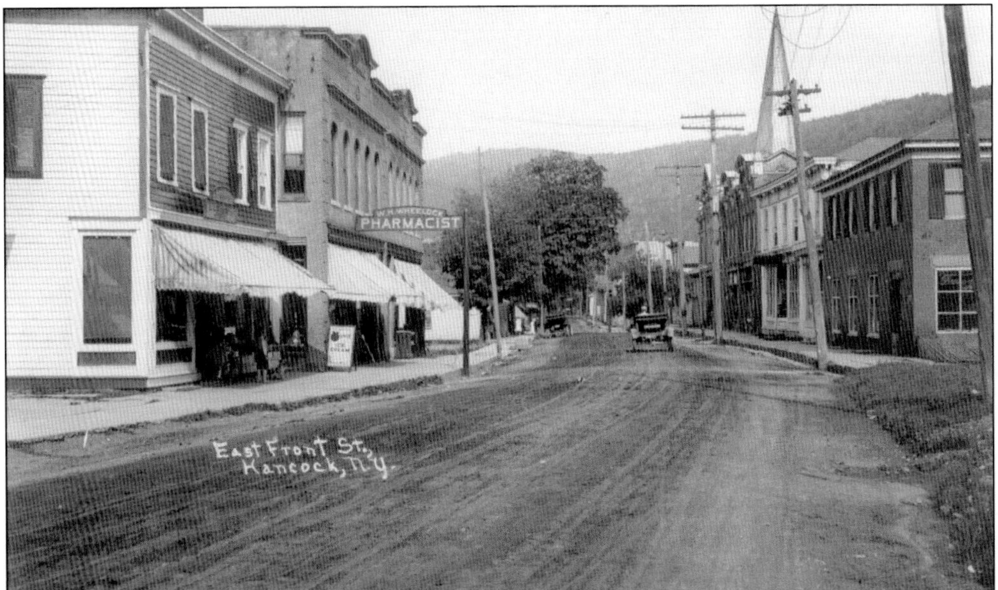

Hancock was created in 1806 by dividing the town of Colchester, located in the southwest corner of Delaware County. The town's 19th-century economy was fueled by tanning, quarrying, and acid factories. Lumbering and quarrying remain as business ventures today. The town includes the village of Hancock, incorporated in 1888 and located where the East and West Branches of the Delaware River meet on the New York–Pennsylvania border.

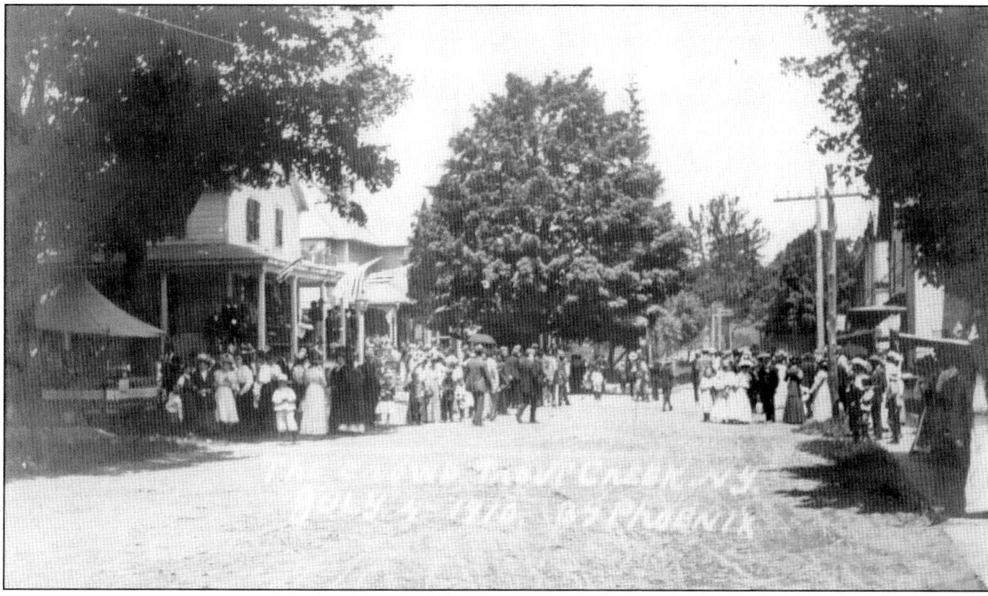

Created in 1806 from the town of Walton, Tompkins saw its first settlers in 1786. The town was originally named Pinefield but changed two years later in honor of Gov. Daniel D. Tompkins. Tompkins was the county's most populous town in 1875, but this changed with the creation of the town of Deposit in 1880. The construction of the Cannonsville Reservoir in the 1960s wiped out the communities of Cannonsville, Granton, Rock Rift, and Rock Royal. The hamlet of Trout Creek remains.

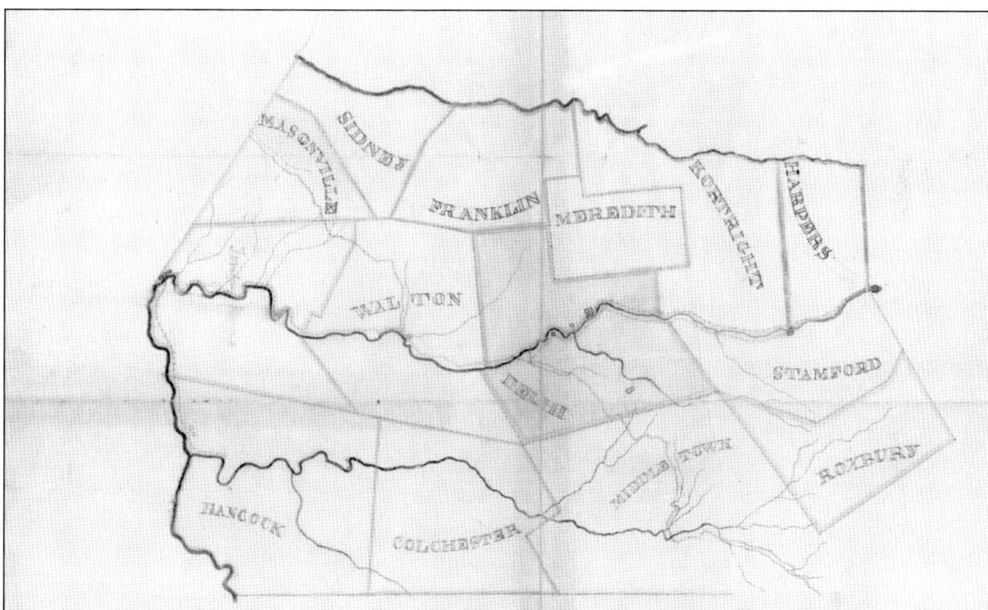

One of the earliest known maps of Delaware County was drawn around 1810 for local attorney (and future congressman) Samuel Sherwood. Fourteen towns existed at this time, including the recently created town of Tompkins in the western part of the county (note its name in faint pencil). Five more towns would be created after this map, and the last town was the town of Deposit in 1880.

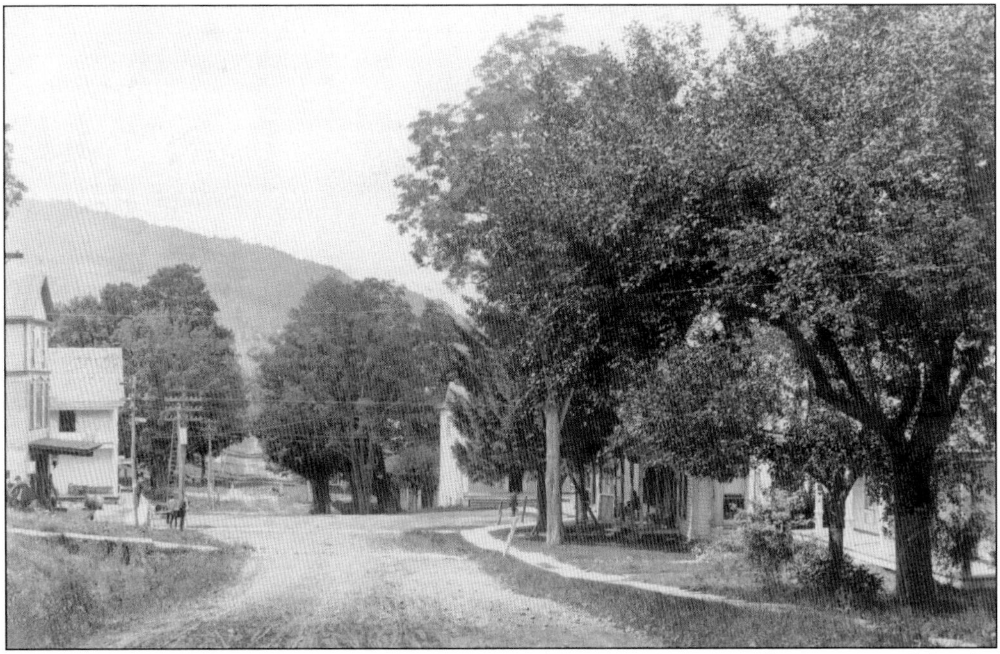

Created in 1811 by dividing the town of Sidney, the town of Masonville was named for the Reverend John M. Mason. The earliest settlers came in 1792. Lumbering was an early economic activity for settlers, later followed by dairy farming, which received a boost from the establishment of the railroads, specifically the Ontario & Western Railway.

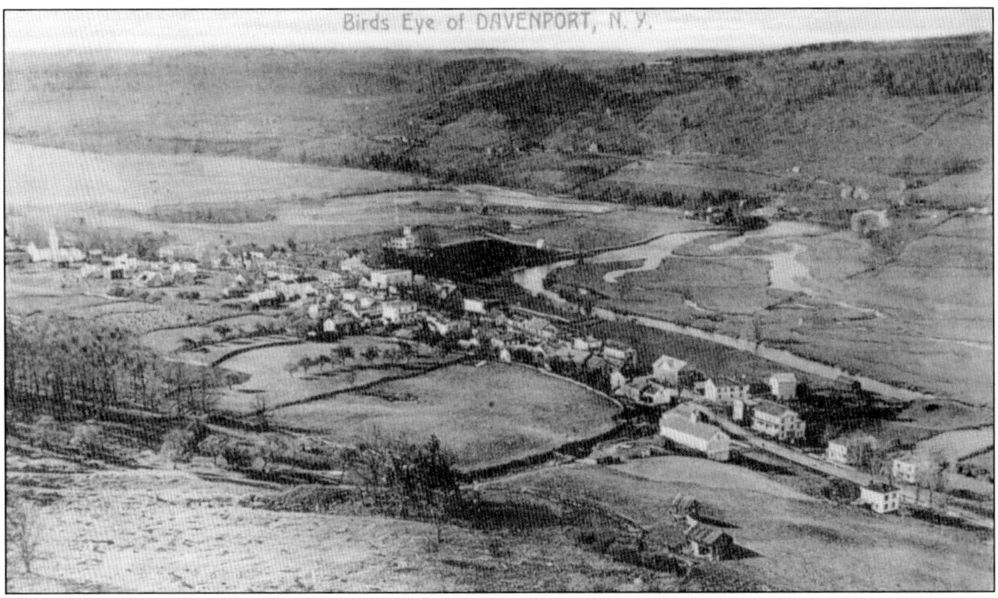

The first settlers came to what became Davenport in 1786. The town was created in 1817 from the towns of Kortright and Maryland (in Otsego County). The Charlotte River is the main body of water that flows through the town. Hamlets included Fergusonville, Davenport, Davenport Center, and West Davenport. Settlers took advantage of the water for gristmills and lumber and woolen mills. Today, State Route 23, the old Charlotte Turnpike, connects the town with Oneonta and Interstate 88.

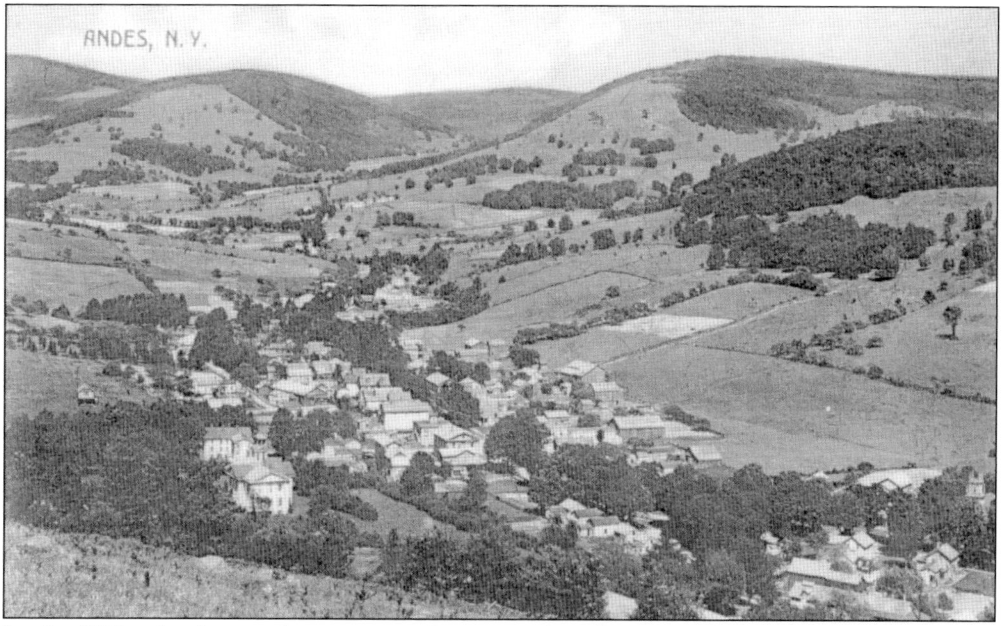

In the 1780s, the first settlers came to the town of Andes, created in 1819 from the town of Middletown. Andes included the hamlets of Cabin Hill, Shavertown, and Union Grove. The creation of the Pepacton Reservoir in the 1950s led to the elimination of Shavertown and Union Grove. The town of Andes also included the incorporated village of Andes, created in 1861. In 2003, the residents voted to disband the village, making what was the village into a hamlet.

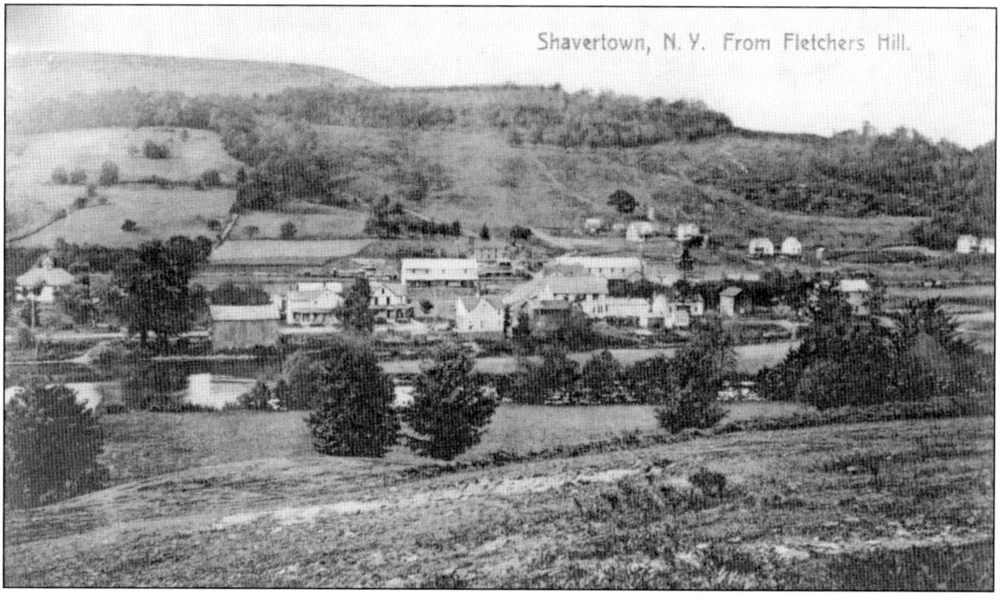

Shavertown was a hamlet in the town of Andes, settled in the early 19th century. The first post office was established in 1828. The hamlet was doomed when the decision was made to construct a reservoir for New York City's water system, the Pepacton Reservoir. Properties were sold, buildings were demolished or burned, and cemeteries were moved to make way for the water. The post office closed in 1954, and by the end of the year, the site of Shavertown was fast disappearing under the rising waters of the East Branch of the Delaware River.

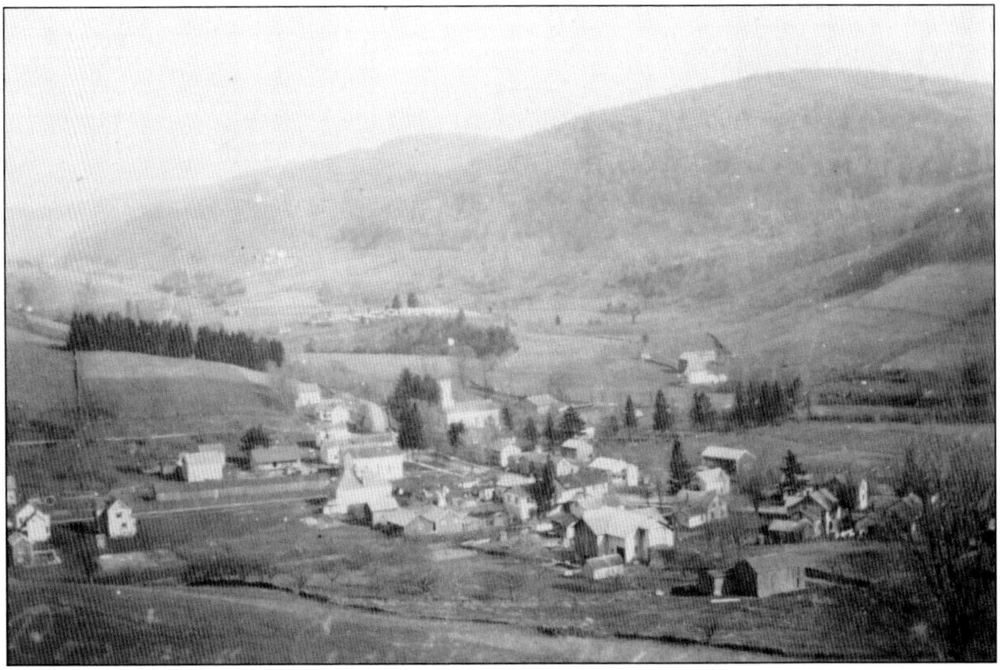

Created in 1820 from the towns of Delhi, Middletown, and Stamford, Bovina had its first European settlers arrive in 1792. The town had three population centers in its early days—the Huddle, now known as Bovina Center; Bovina hamlet, also referred to as the Butt End; and the Hook, also known as Lake Delaware. The town's name is credited to Erastus Root, who suggested the name due to the town's suitability for grazing.

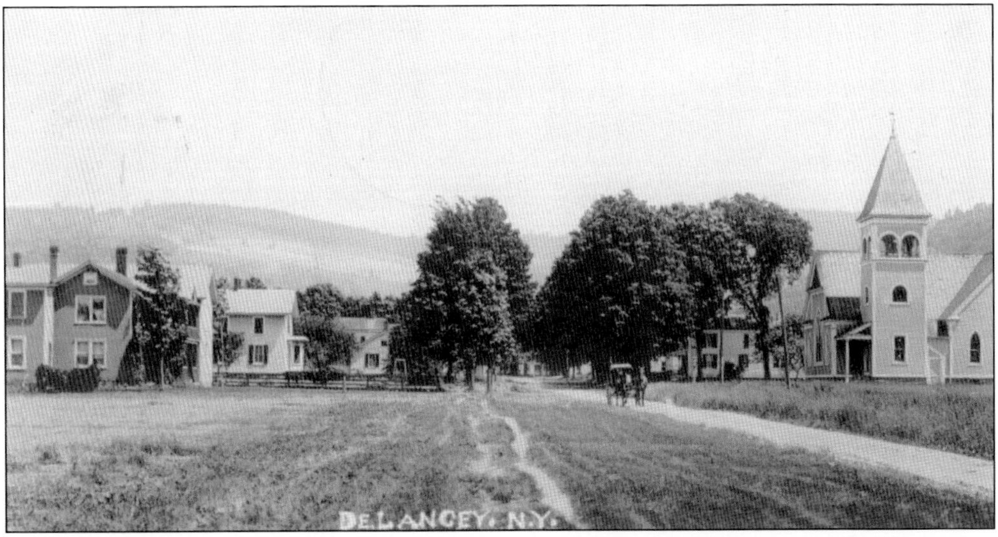

Created in 1825 from parts of the towns of Walton and Delhi, Hamden saw its earliest European settlers in 1779. They worked at lumbering, rafting, and dairy farming. Originally named Hampton, the name was changed to Hamden in 1826. The hamlet of Lansingville, settled in 1790, later became Delancey. The Hamden Inn, built in 1844, and the restored covered bridge, dating from 1857, still draw visitors to the area.

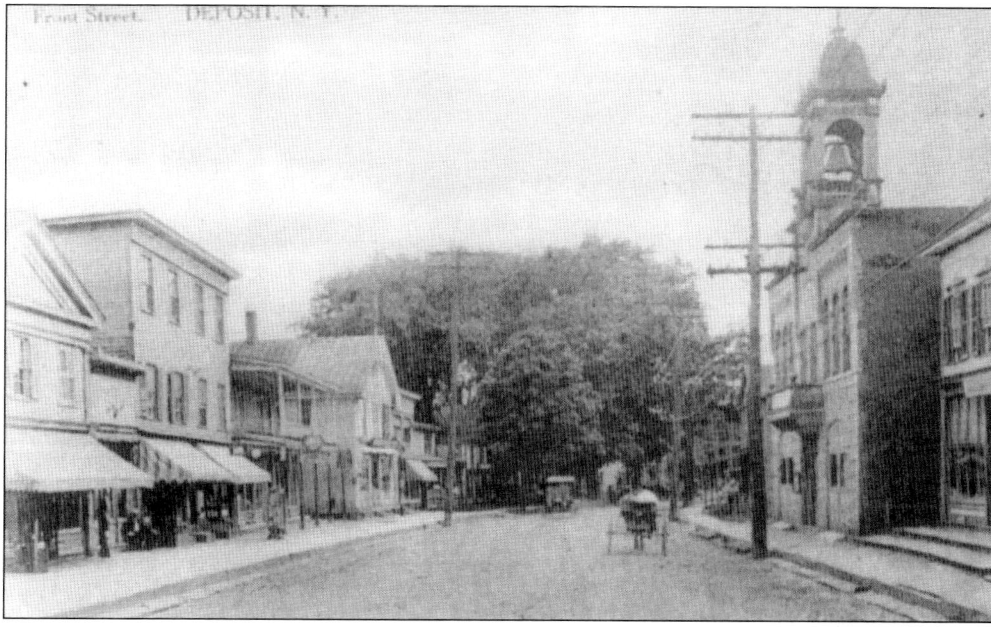

Created in 1880 from the town of Tompkins, Deposit was the last town created in Delaware County. Located on the West Branch of the Delaware River, it was known as a lumbering and rafting center. In fact, it was the rafting trade that gave the town its unusual name, as here timbers floated downriver were "deposited" en masse to be formed into the rafts. Some of the town was lost when the Cannonsville Reservoir was built in the 1960s. The town includes the village of Deposit, created before the town in 1811, the first incorporated village in Delaware County.

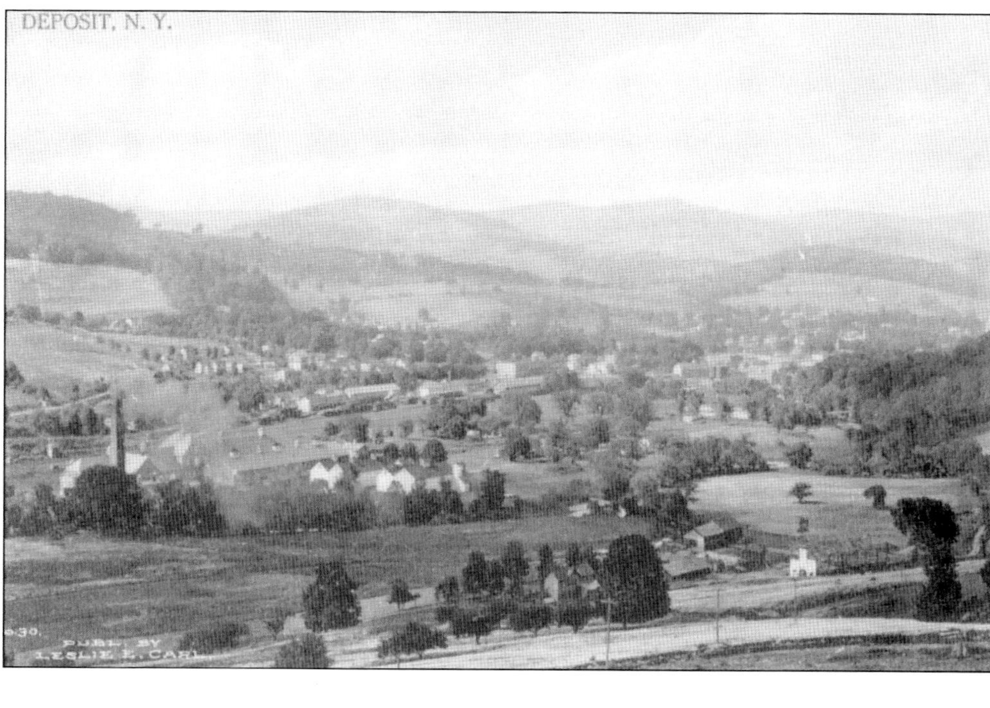

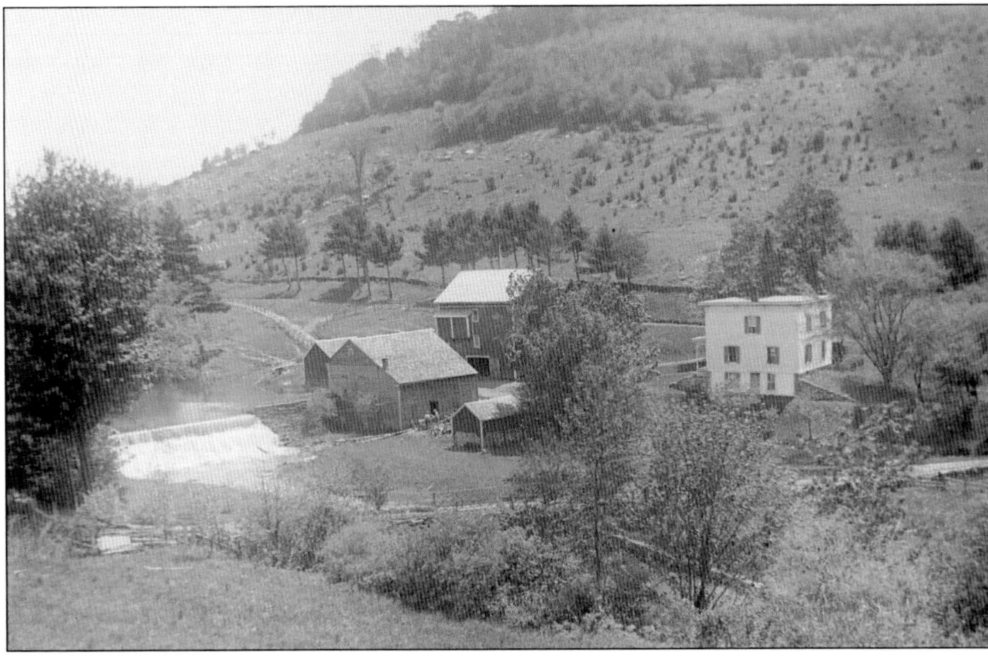

Early settlers cleared the land and built the infrastructure for survival and economic growth. In the late 18th and early 19th centuries, they began constructing houses and barns for farming, commercial buildings in the villages, and gristmills and sawmills. As this image from the town of Meredith shows, they also dammed the region's streams and rivers to provide power for the mills.

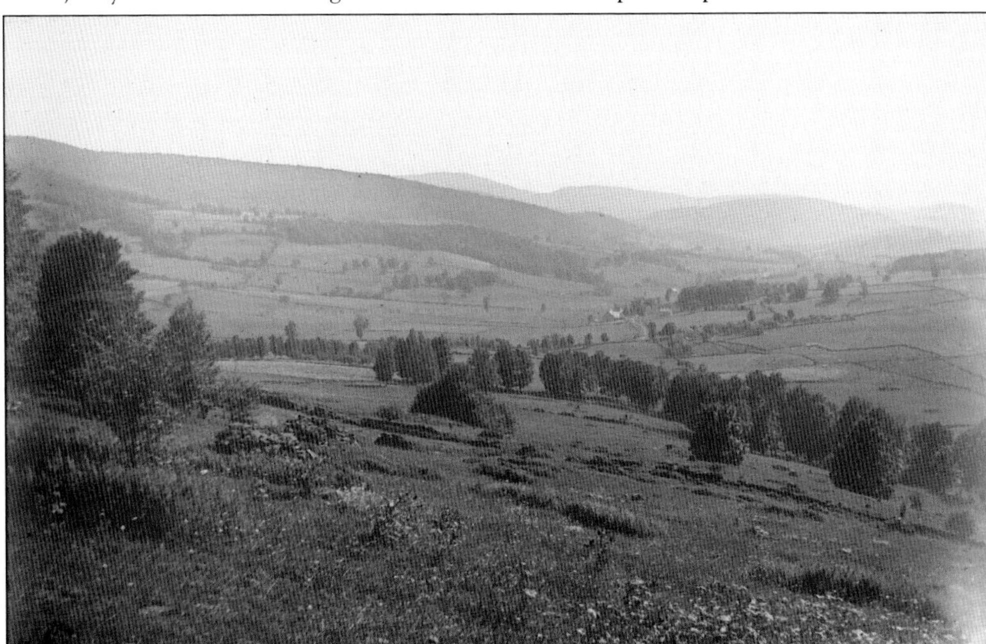

Many of the early settlers to Delaware County leased their land from what generally were absentee landlords. They nonetheless worked hard to clear the land and make it usable to support their families and pay the rent. Many of the leases continued for multiple generations, in most cases offering those working the land little or no hope of ever taking ownership of their farms.

The never-ending leases on land that farmers had worked for generations began to wear on them. In 1839, farmers in the Helderberg Mountains near Albany began to agitate for a change in the system. By 1844, this protest movement, commonly known as the "Anti-Rent War," came into Delaware County, splitting the county into "up-renters" (mainly in the western part) and "down-renters" (mainly in the east). As tenant farmers refused to pay their rent, the authorities began to force the sale of the farmer's various goods and chattels to pay the past due rent. This letter, sent to G.H. Edgerton of Delhi, threatened to "tar and feather" him if he continued to work with the landlords in collecting past due rents. "Calico Indians," usually men in disguise, would disrupt the sales.

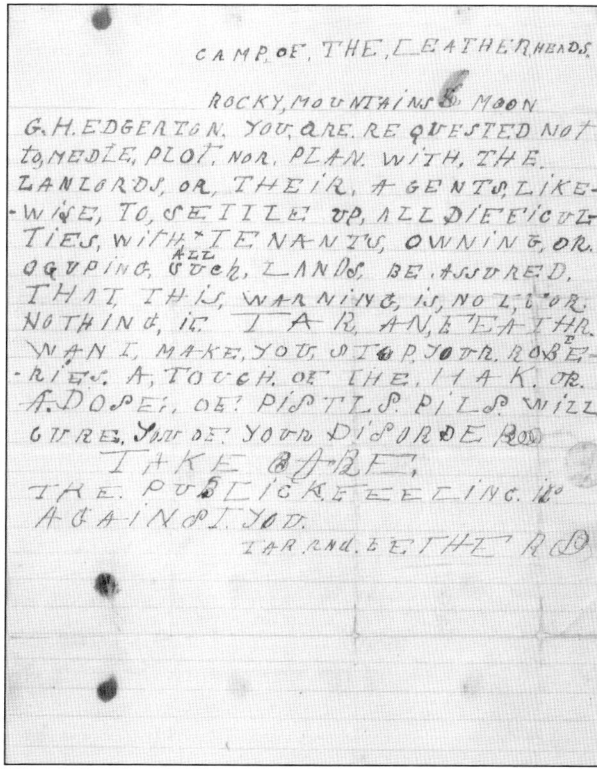
CAMP, OF, THE, LEATHERHEADS.

ROCKY, MOUNTAINS & MOON

G.H. EDGERTON, YOU, ARE. REQUESTED NOT TO, MEDLE, PLOT, NOR, PLAN. WITH, THE. LANLORDS, OR, THEIR, AGENTS, LIKE-WISE, TO, SETTLE UP, ALL DIFFICULTIES, WITH TENANTS, OWNING, OR. OCUPING, ALL SUCH, LANDS, BE ASSURED, THAT, THIS, WARNING, IS, NOT, FOR. NOTHING, IF TAR, AN, FEATHR. WANT, MAKE, YOU, STOP, YOUR. ROBBE-RIES. A, TOUCH, OF THE, HAK, OR. A DOSE, OF PISTLS PILLS WILL CURE, YOU OF YOUR DISORDER

TAKE CARE,

THE. PUBLICK FEELING IS AGAINST YOU.

TAR AND FETHERS

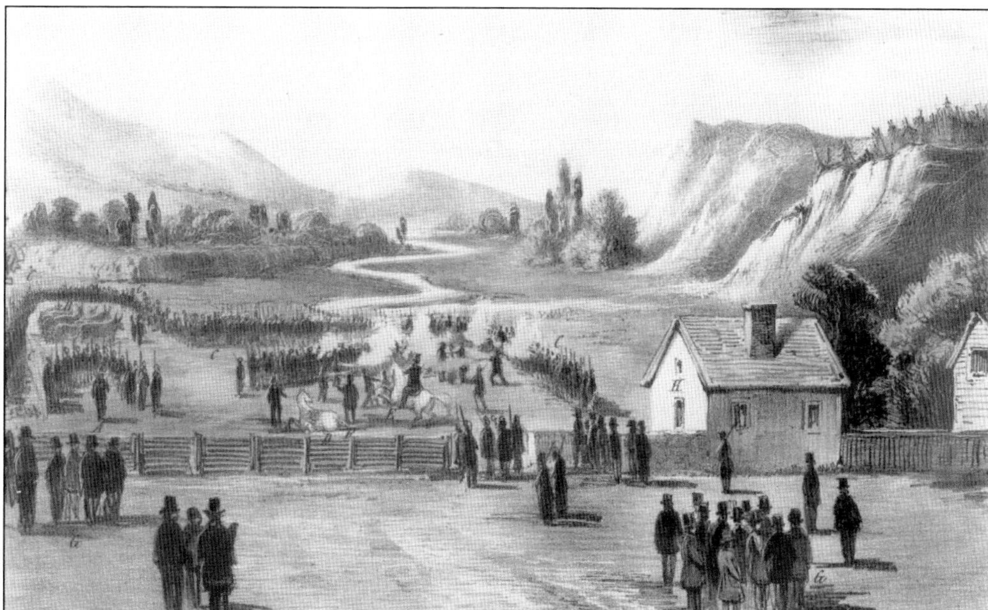
The shooting of Undersheriff Osman Steele at the farm of Moses Earle in Andes on August 7, 1845, was the climax of the Anti-Rent War in Delaware County. The attempt to sell some of Earle's assets for nonpayment of rent was met by a crowd of Calico Indians who tried to stop the sale. A volley of gunfire fatally struck Steele. The men scattered and went into hiding while the governor declared the county in a state of insurrection.

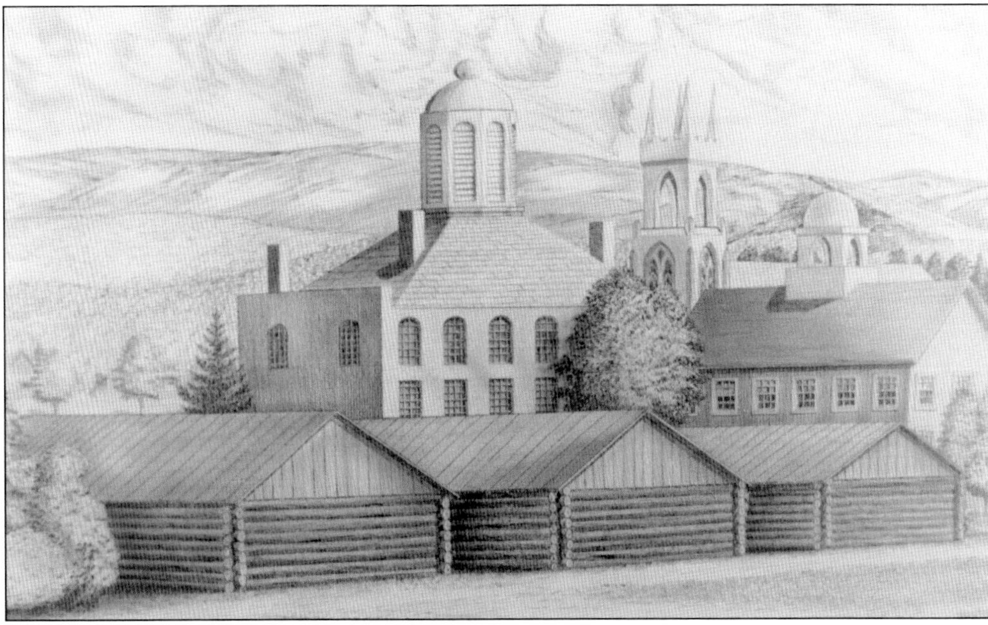

Most of the anti-renters were captured and brought to Delhi where they were incarcerated in specially built log jails. After trials had been held, 84 of them were ultimately convicted in the murder of Steele, including two who were given death sentences. However, within two years, all the prisoners, including those destined for the gallows, were pardoned by a new governor of New York.

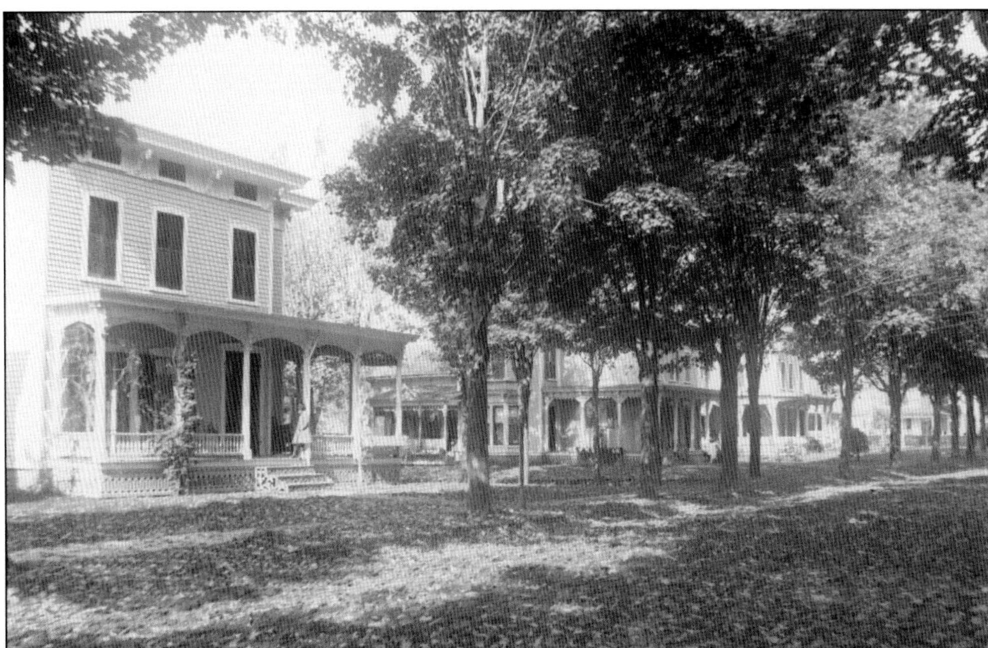

By the late 19th century, Delaware County could boast several established villages and smaller communities. As this image of Franklin's Center Street shows, no longer could the county be considered a "howling wilderness," as it had once been described in the late 18th century.

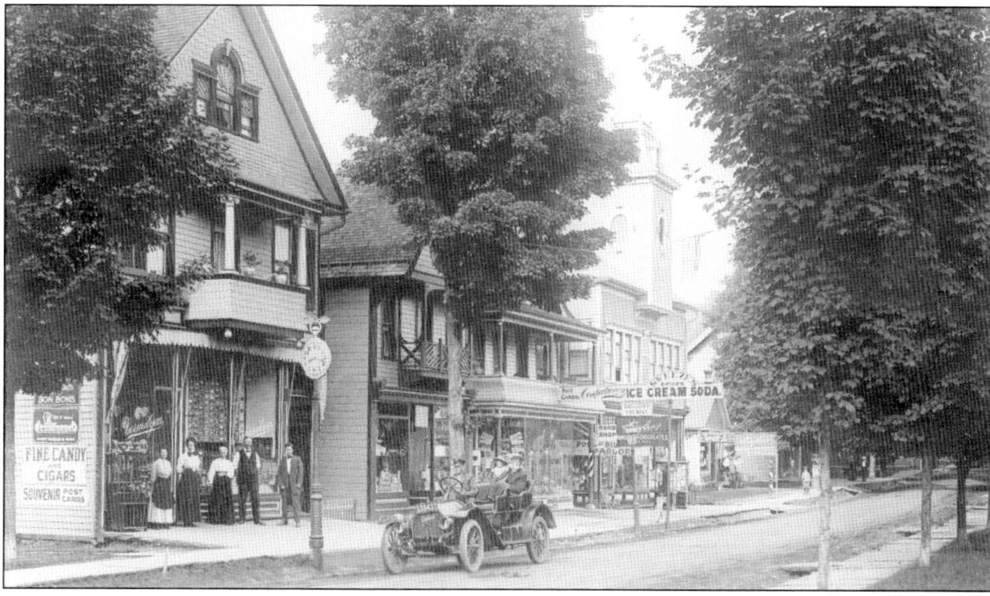

Griffin Corners in the town of Middletown was named for Matthew Griffin, an early settler in the area. The name later changed to Fleischmanns after Charles F. Fleischmann, founder of Fleischmann Yeast Company and a noted summer resident. In 1913, around the time this photograph was taken, the village of Fleischmanns was incorporated, created from the smaller settlements of Griffin Corners and Fleischmanns.

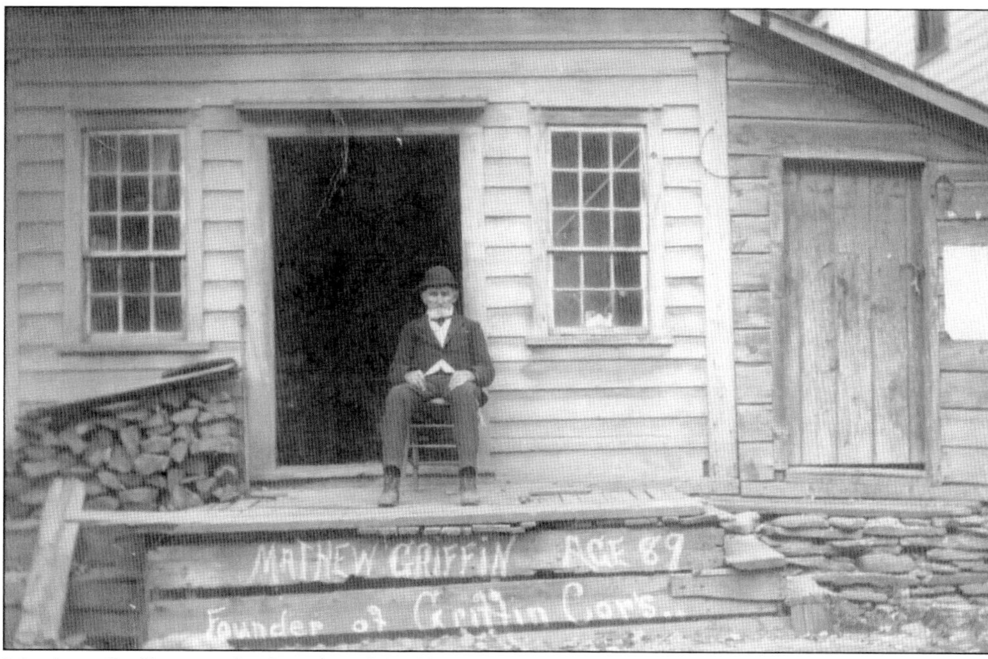

Matthew Griffin was the founder of Griffin Corners, which later became Fleischmanns. Born in 1810 in Dutchess County, New York, he came to Delaware County with his father when he was 12 years old. He became a noted businessman and lawyer. His diary, now at the Delaware County Historical Association, is an invaluable resource concerning the 1840s and 1850s in Delaware County. This photograph dates from about 1899. He died in 1903 at the age of 93.

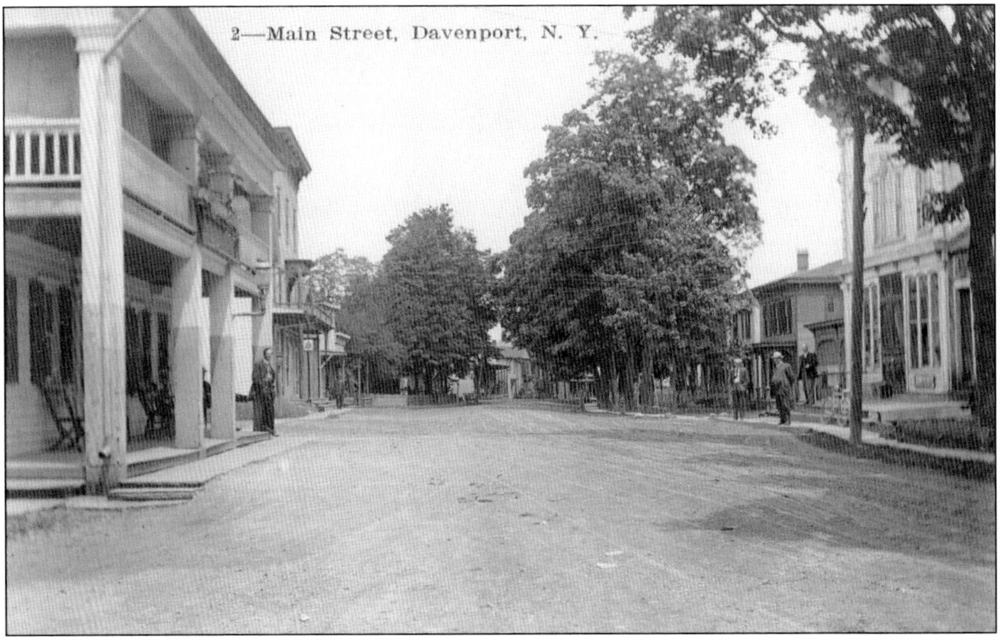

Hotels, stores, residential homes, and some of its leading citizens are all visible in this early-20th-century image of Main Street in Davenport, a town in the northern tier of Delaware County. The mature trees along the roadside add to the air of a mature settlement. And although the road is still unpaved, long gone are the log cabins that once housed most of the area's earlier residents.

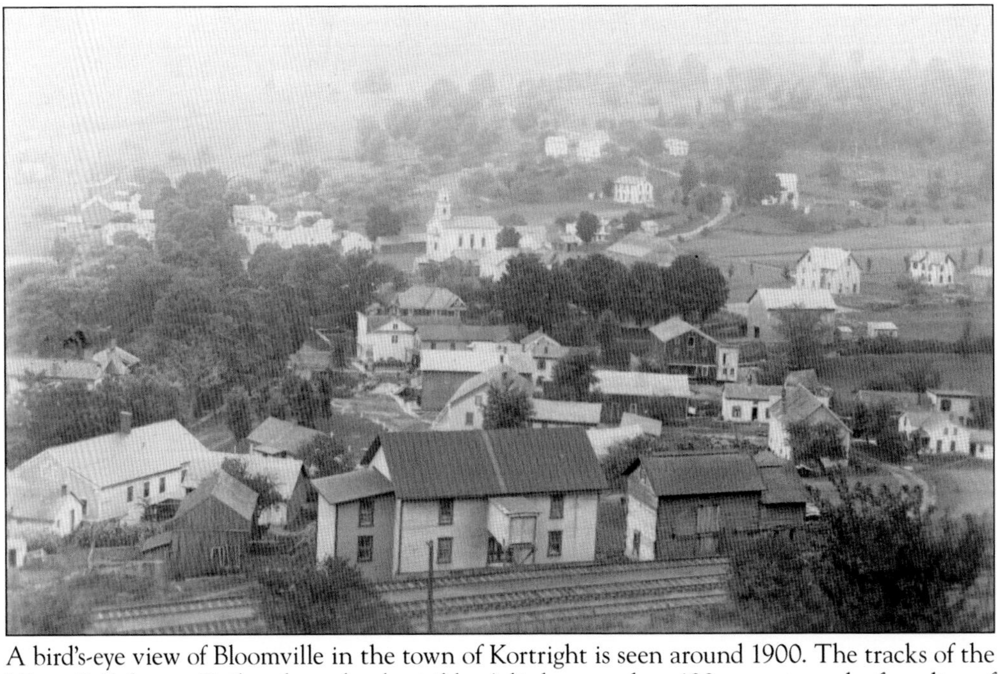

A bird's-eye view of Bloomville in the town of Kortright is seen around 1900. The tracks of the Ulster & Delaware Railroad are clearly visible. A little more than 100 years since the founding of the county, most communities in Delaware County could now boast established commercial centers, residential streets, and communal buildings such as churches. For villages located along, or in close proximity to, rail lines, growth was especially quick in the last quarter of the 19th century.

Two

USING THE LAND

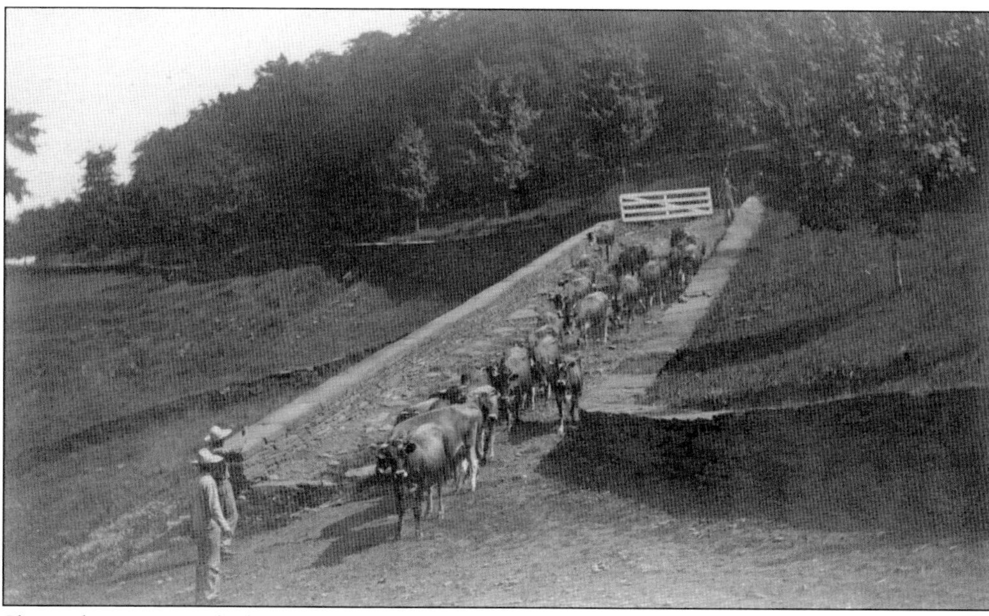

Shown here is an early depiction of a 19th-century upland farm. Here, Jersey dairy cows are being herded from field to field at the well-known Meridale Farms in the town of Meredith. Note the beautiful dry-laid stone walls. Although cattle became the most prominent farm animals on local hillsides after about 1850, it was sheep and the production of wool that had once provided the main source of revenue before that time.

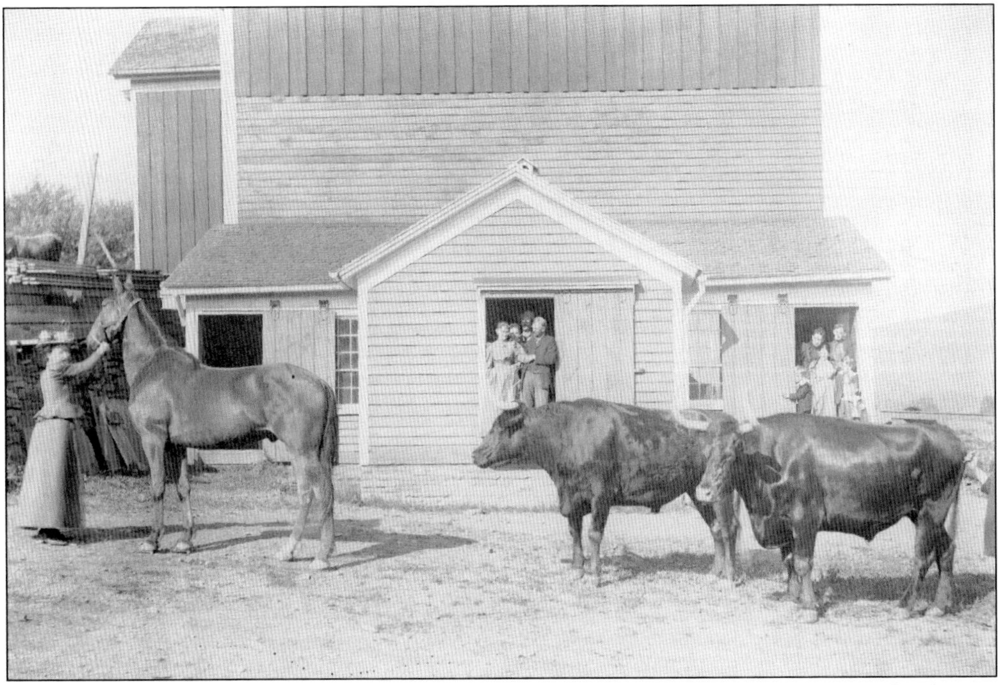

By the end of the 19th century, farming had firmly established itself as the mainstay of Delaware County's economy and as the central facet of its culture. The two images included here show different scenes from a farm located along Montgomery Hollow in the town of Roxbury. Above, the scene depicts what was perhaps the family's prize horse and a couple of fine-looking bulls posing in front of the well-built and well-maintained barn. Below, two members of the family pose with their animals in front of their solid Federal-style farmhouse. Note the prominent stone walls in the foreground.

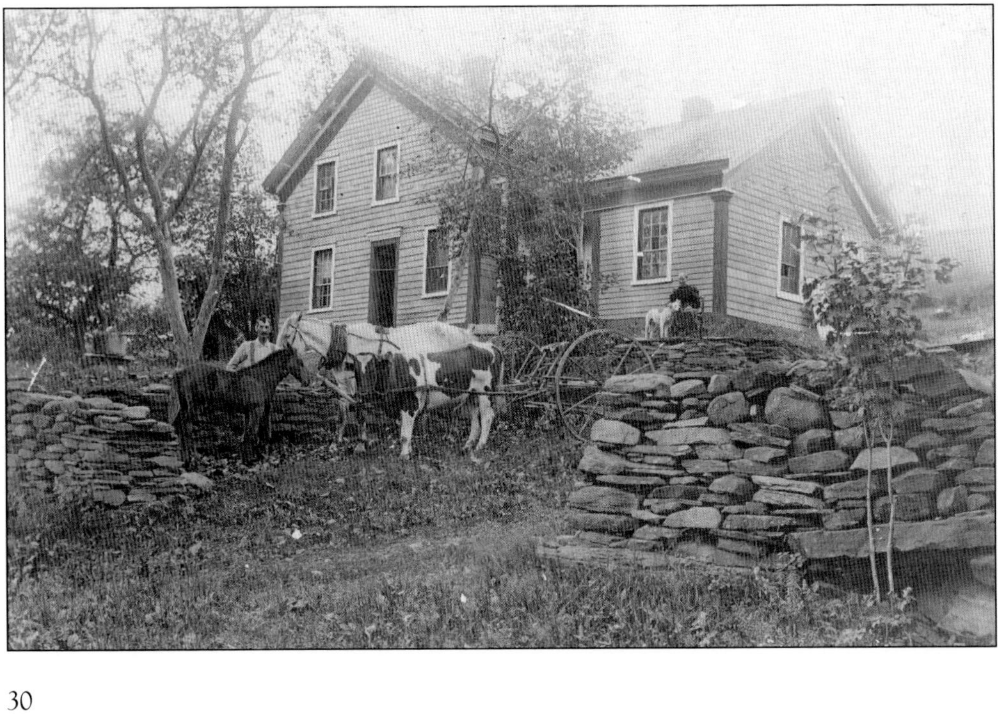

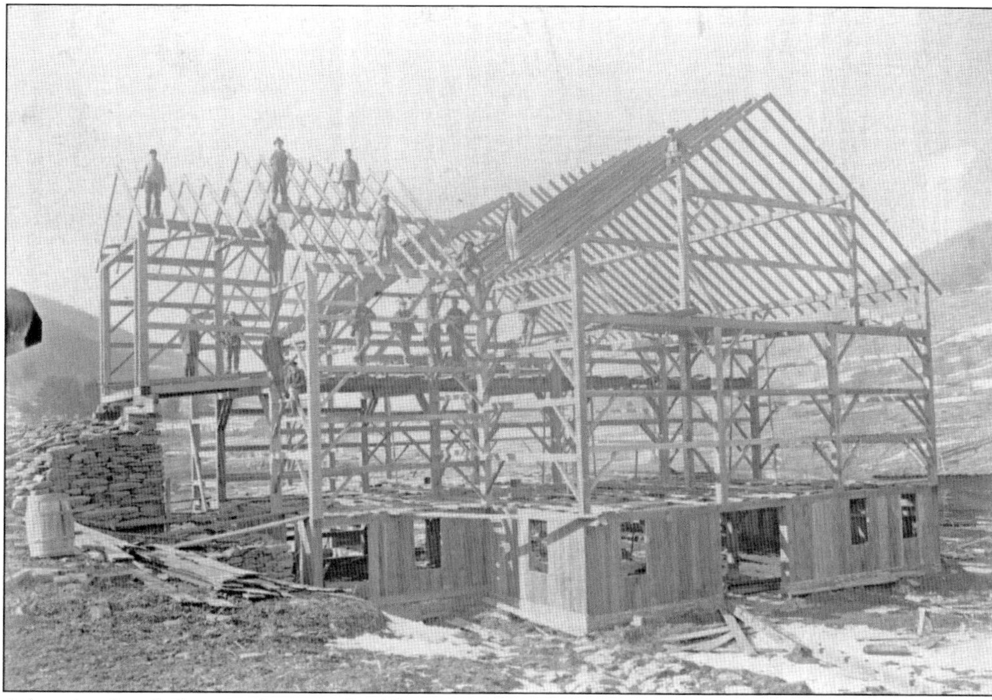

After the family house, the next building appearing on Catskill farms was most often the barn. Farming, although often a solitary life in the hills and hollows of Delaware County, also sometimes involved the larger community as these two images of a barn raising on Terry Clove Road in the town of Hamden clearly depict—a moment when neighbors gathered to help neighbors. Although most of the heavy manual work was performed by the men, women and teenage girls labored long hours to provide food and drink at these occasions. Similar groups of friends, family, and neighbors gathered to share the work during times of harvest in late summer and fall.

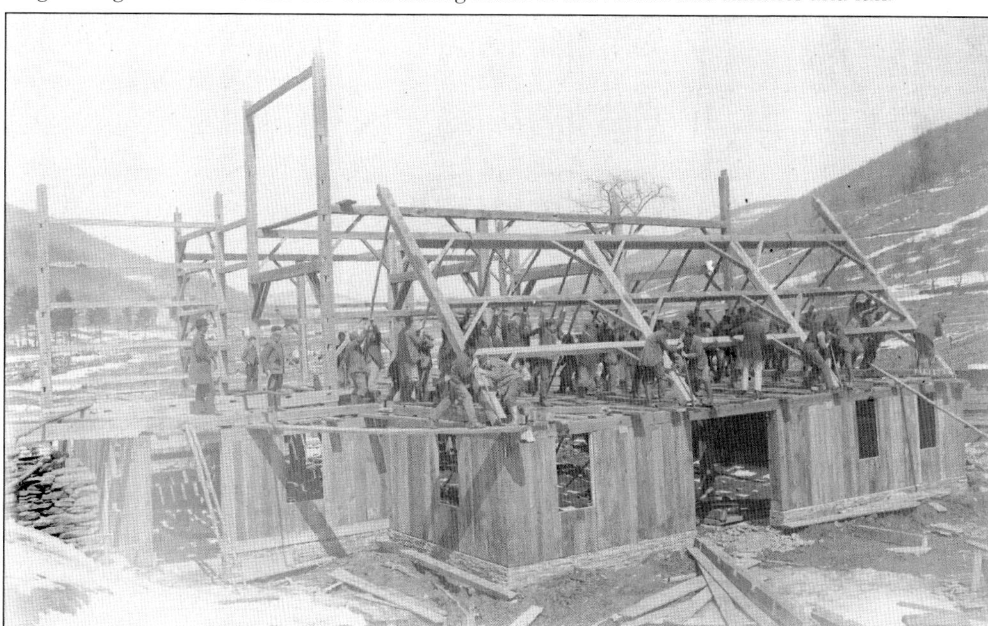

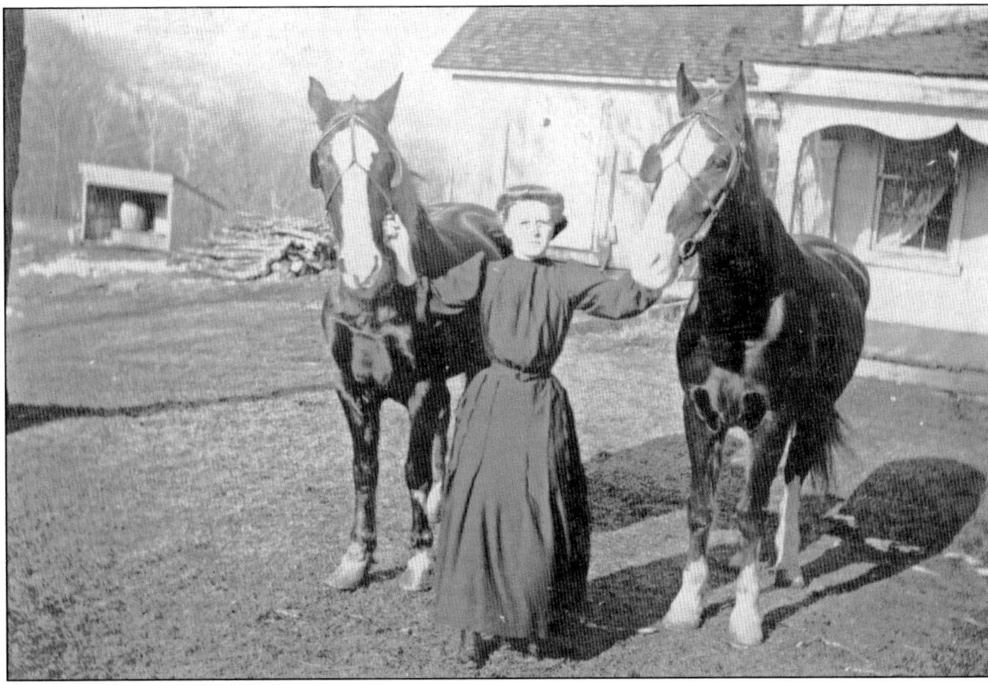

Before the arrival on the farm of internal combustion-driven vehicles after the turn of the 20th century, agriculture depended heavily on those beasts of burden, such as oxen, horses, and, of course, men, women, and children. As these two images show, horses especially were prized not only for their magnificent appearance, but also for their strength and ability to operate on almost all terrains in Delaware County. So too, these photographs depict the strength and tenacity of those hardscrabble farm men and women who cleared and maintained the land of the northwestern Catskills and worked long hours in all seasons.

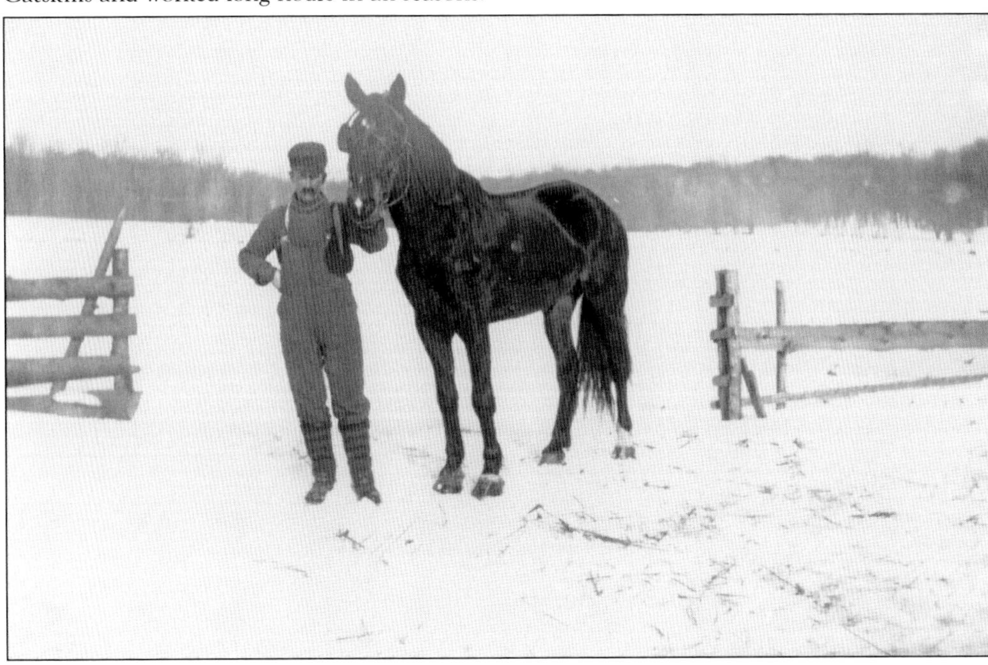

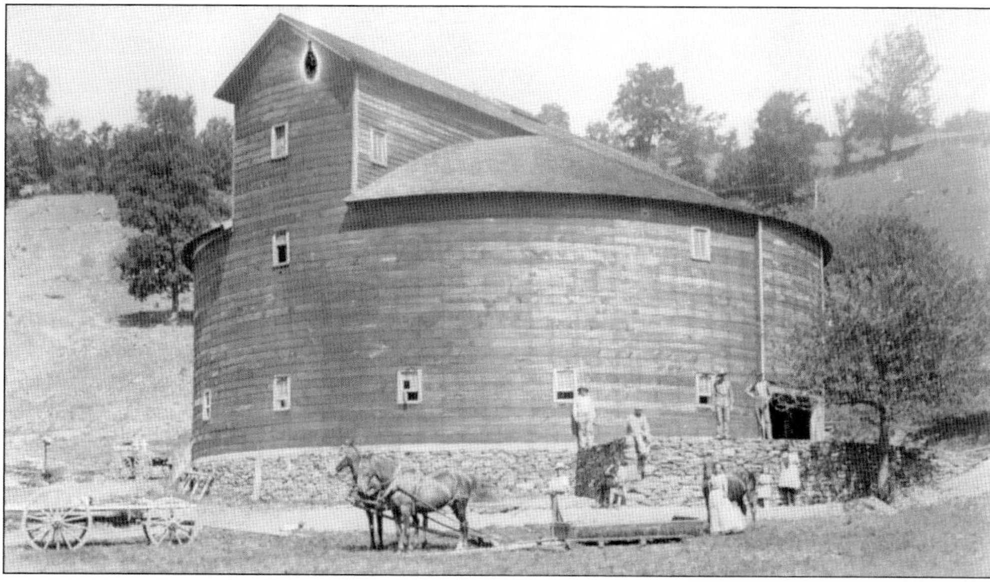

These photographs show the beautiful round barn at Halcottsville in the town of Middletown. The structure's configuration is atypical of Delaware County barns, most of which occupied a square or rectangular footprint and were of post-and-beam construction. The picture below is of a slightly later time frame, and one can clearly see additions to the original round barn. Of note is the activity of the men in the foreground. When not directly involved in the daily chores of a working dairy farm, local men engaged in chores such as this one: cutting and splitting firewood for the following winter. Today, the barn has undergone something of a renaissance and a repurposing in the sense that it is now being utilized as a commercial space and is part of the popular Pakatakan Farmers' Market.

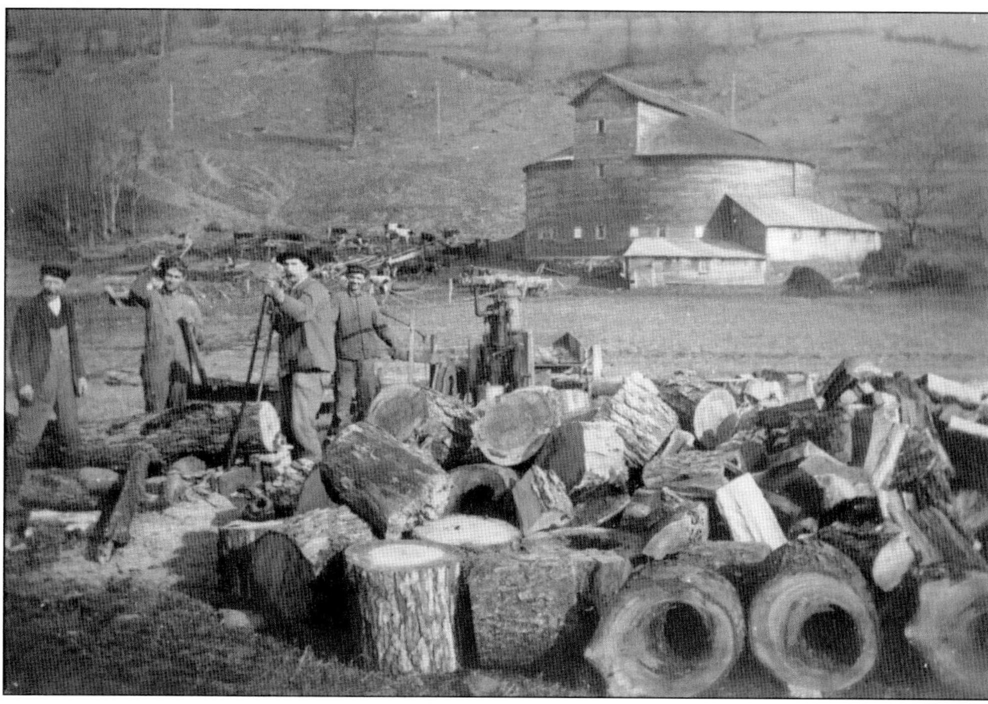

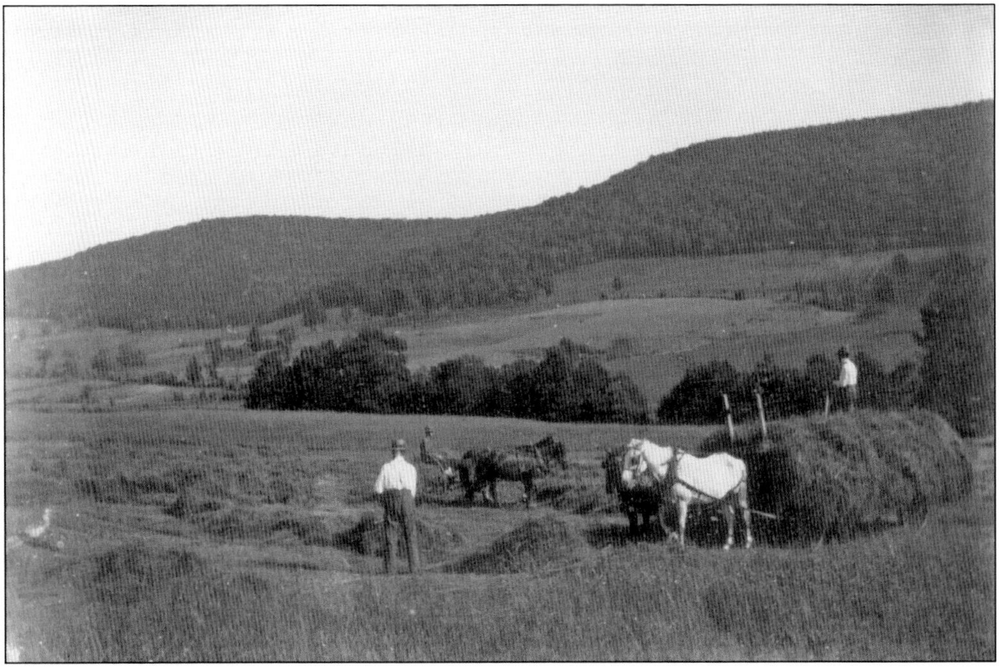

Cutting and safely storing dry hay was an arduous and lengthy job that often involved friends, relatives, and neighbors. Hay was usually cut once in early summer and again, weather conditions permitting, in the late summer or early fall. The dried hay provided life-sustaining nourishment to livestock during the long winter months. Pictured here are hay wagons loaded high with cut, dry hay. All the work leading up to the point captured in the photographs had been done by hand and by horse and, perhaps, rudimentary horse-powered mowing machinery.

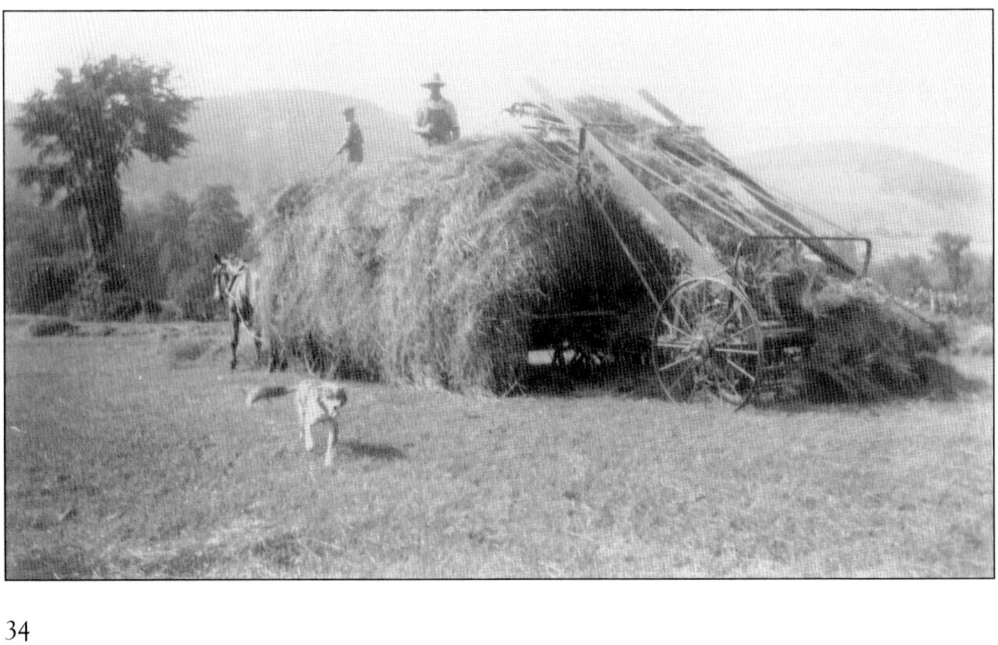

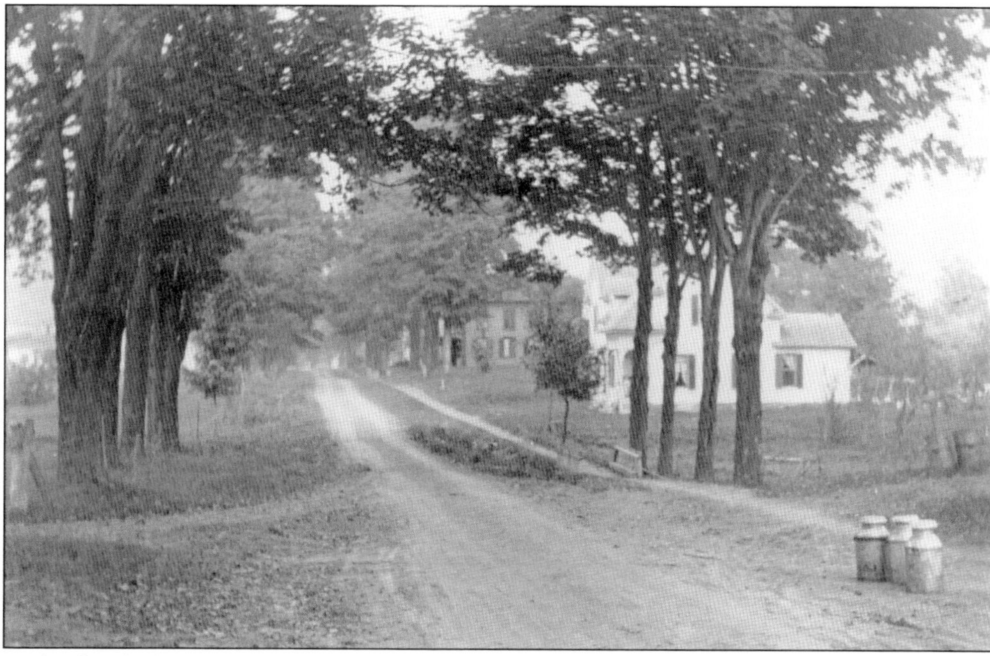

In the days before gas-powered trucks, local farmers would leave their milk in cans alongside the road, as shown in the photograph above. The cans would be picked up each day by horse-drawn wagons and taken to nearby creameries, or by the 1870s, perhaps, to railroad depots and thence by train to urban areas outside the Catskills. The image below shows a milk wagon in the winter, transporting cans of milk. The picture was taken near Treadwell in the town of Meredith. By the 1920s, better roads, large milk trucks, and then electricity on farms meant that farmers could produce and store larger and larger quantities of milk in bulk milk tanks on their own farms, obviating the need for small-scale pickup operations of this type.

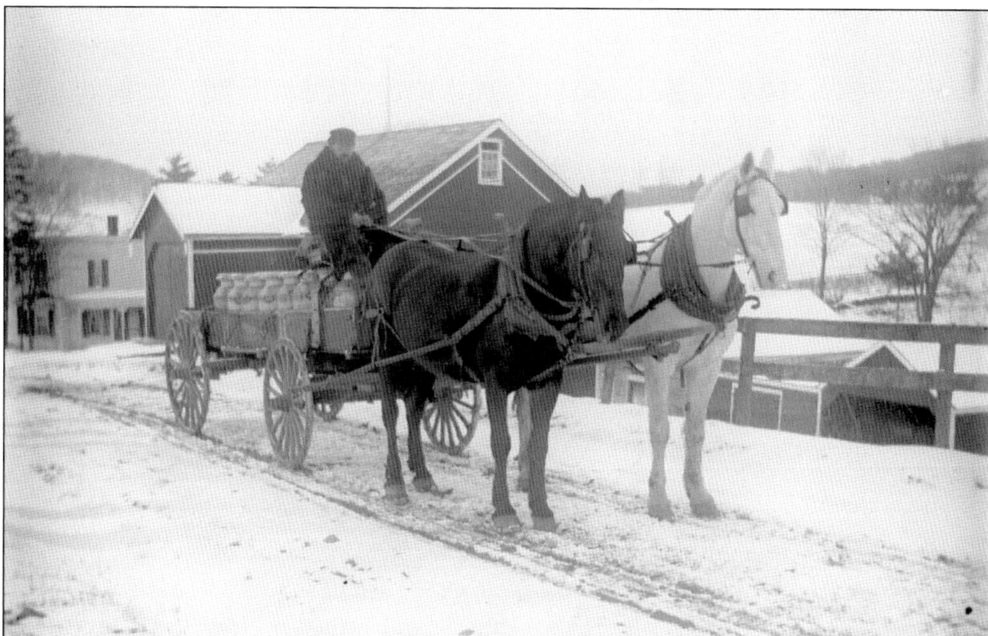

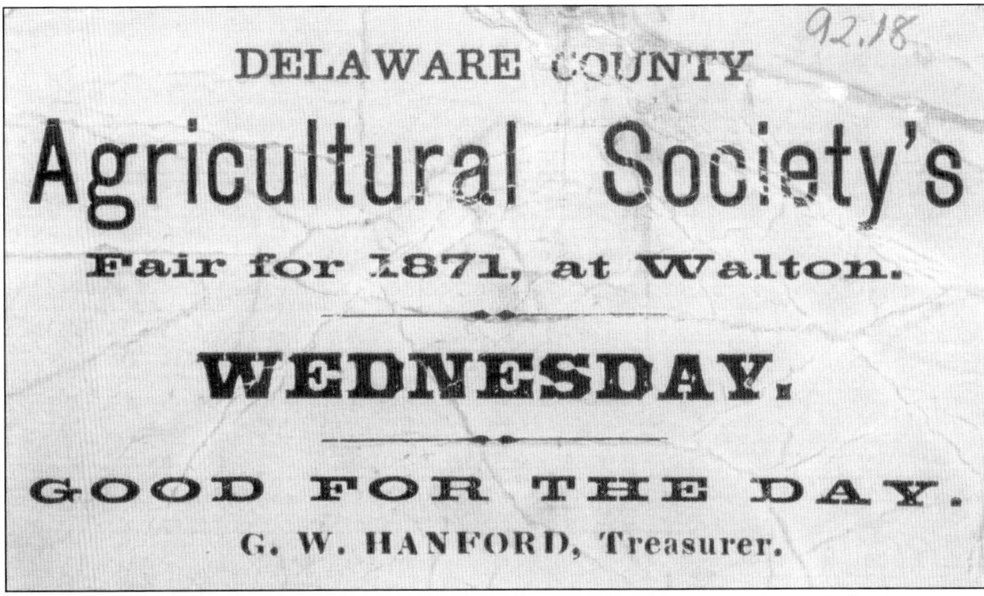
DELAWARE COUNTY

Agricultural Society's

Fair for 1871, at Walton.

WEDNESDAY.

GOOD FOR THE DAY.

G. W. HANFORD, Treasurer.

A ticket for the Delaware County Agricultural Society's 1871 fair is seen here. Held that year in Walton, the fair included not only rides, games, and other fun activities for all the family, but so too animal shows and competitions. Agricultural fairs of this type had been held in various locations throughout the county since 1841 and were often considered the high point of the social calendar for local farm families. Other communities that hosted fairs until the 1920s included Hobart Andes, Franklin, and Bloomville. Since 1926, the Delaware County Fair has been a permanent fixture in Walton.

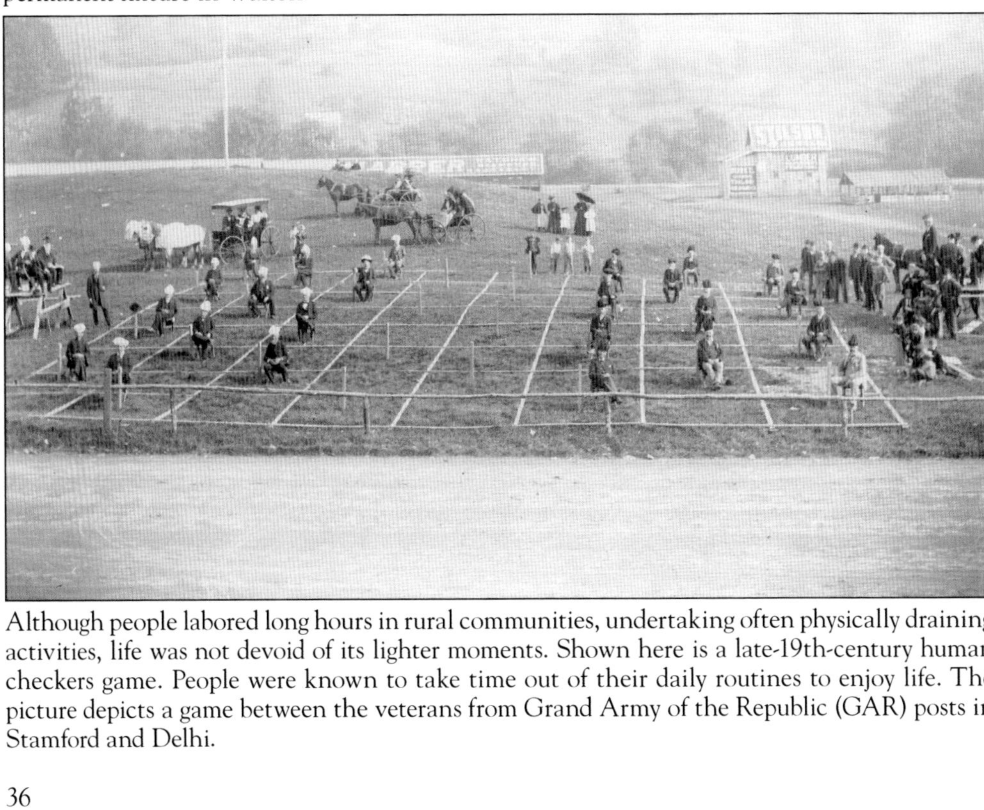

Although people labored long hours in rural communities, undertaking often physically draining activities, life was not devoid of its lighter moments. Shown here is a late-19th-century human checkers game. People were known to take time out of their daily routines to enjoy life. The picture depicts a game between the veterans from Grand Army of the Republic (GAR) posts in Stamford and Delhi.

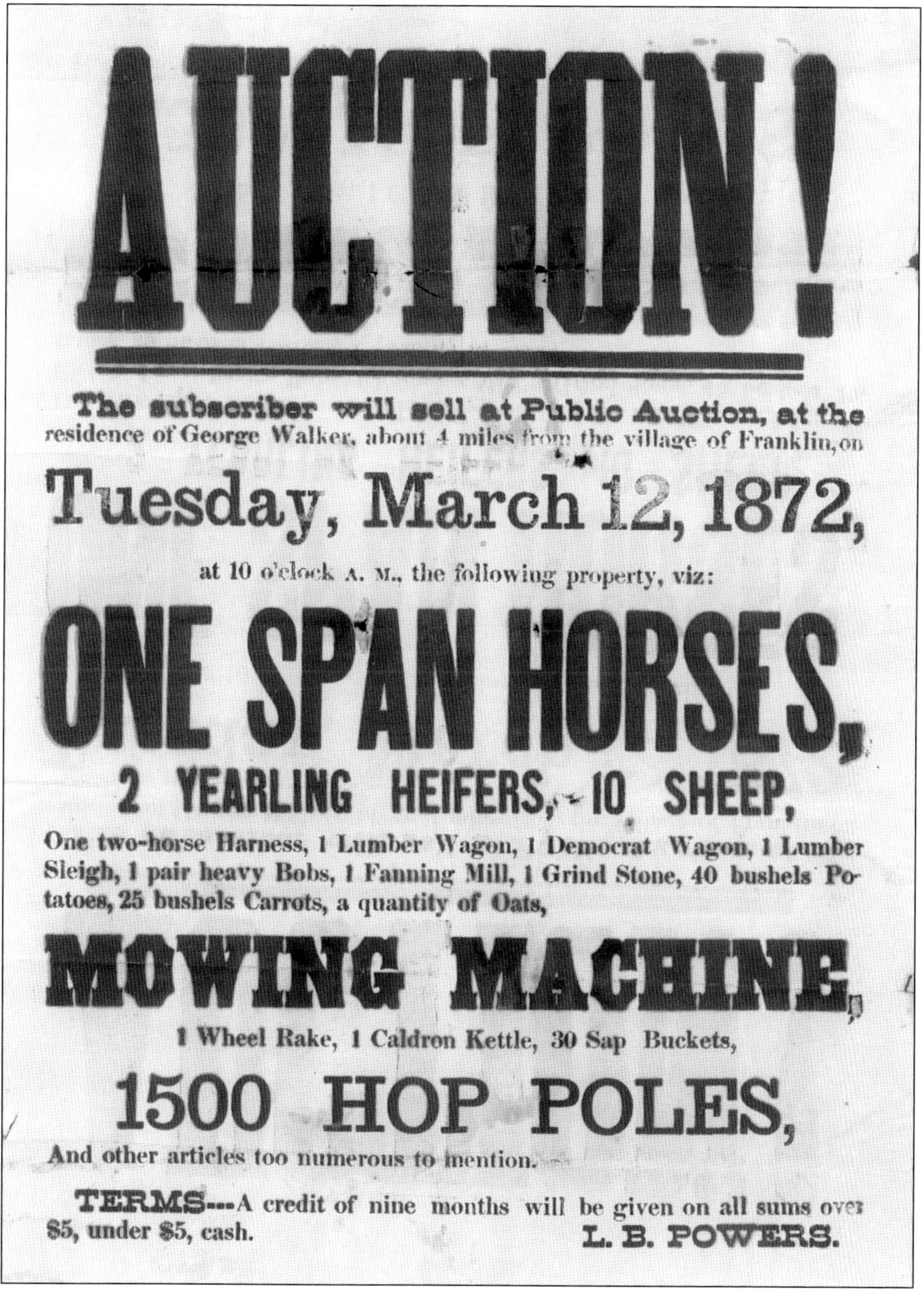

Here is a poster advertising an 1872 auction of agricultural implements and animals. The completion of railroads through central Delaware County in the early 1870s provided a significant impetus to the area's farmers, allowing them to expand and diversify. This poster advertising an 1872 sale in the town of Franklin gives some indication of the growing diversity of agriculture, which then, in addition to sheep and dairy, included hop cultivation.

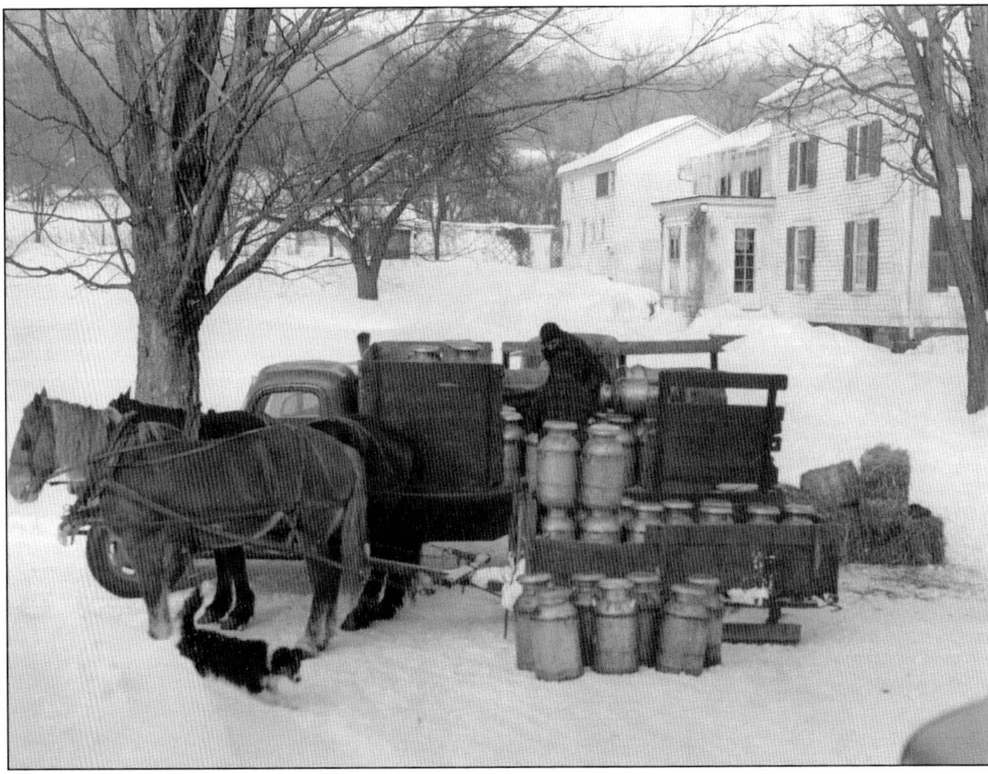

Pictured above is a midwinter pickup of milk from the MacDonald Farm on Elk Creek Road in the town of Meredith. Note the different modes of transportation in use. The MacDonald Farm was renowned far and wide for its innovative use of technology. In the 19th century, it was one of the first upstate dairy farms to generate its own hydropowered electricity, and in the 20th century, sisters Amelia and Elizabeth MacDonald were at the forefront of efforts to establish an agricultural college in nearby Delhi (now State University of New York at Delhi). Below is a photograph showing a rather typical scene of the hubbub of activity surrounding a 19th-century creamery; this creamery is at Bartlett Hollow in the town of Franklin.

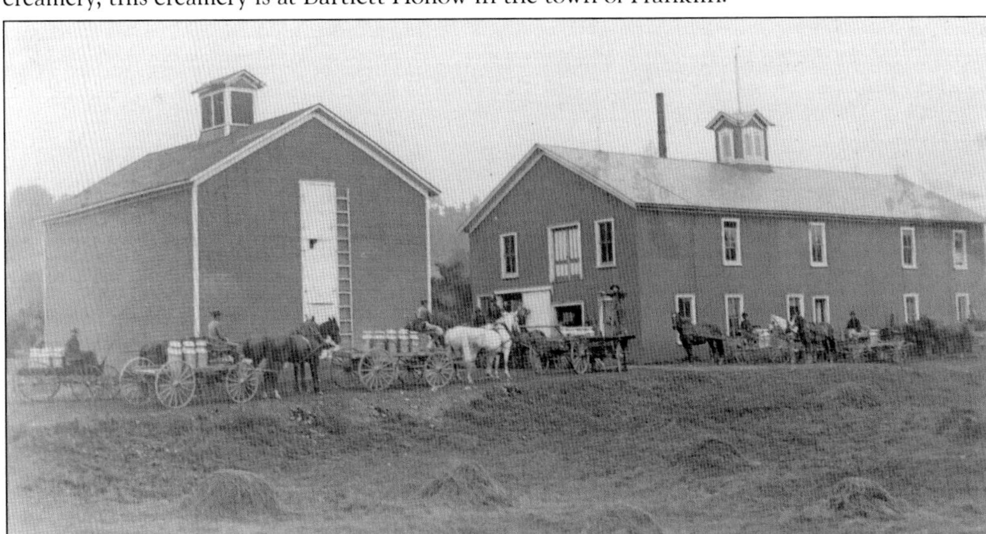

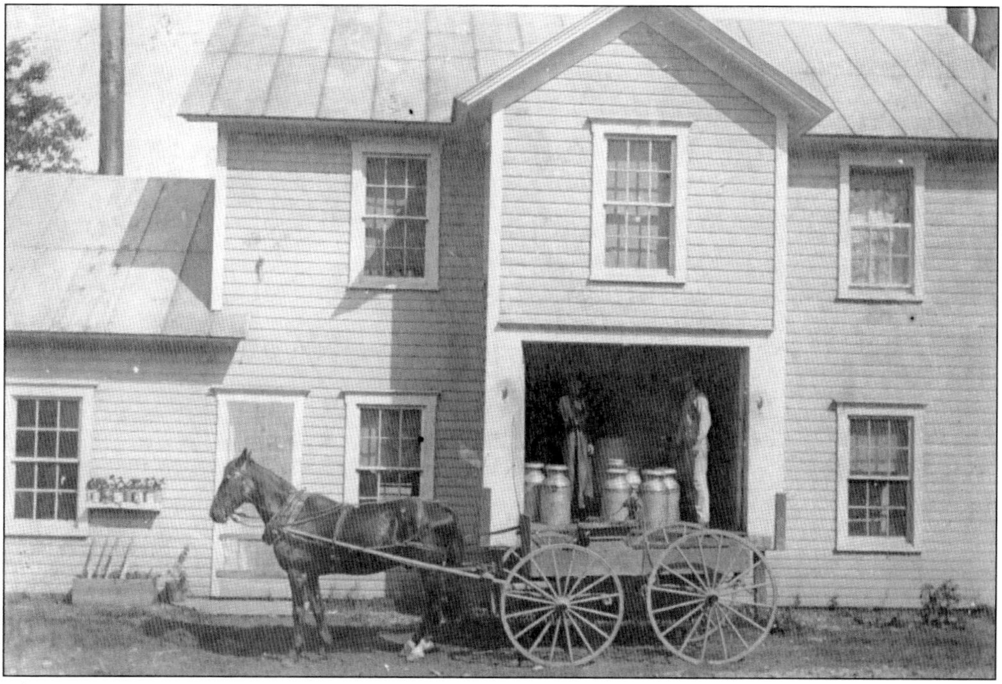

The Pine Creamery, located near Treadwell in the town of Meredith, is seen sometime around the turn of the 20th century. The creamery was not located adjacent to a railroad line, hence the "old-fashioned" mode of transportation in view.

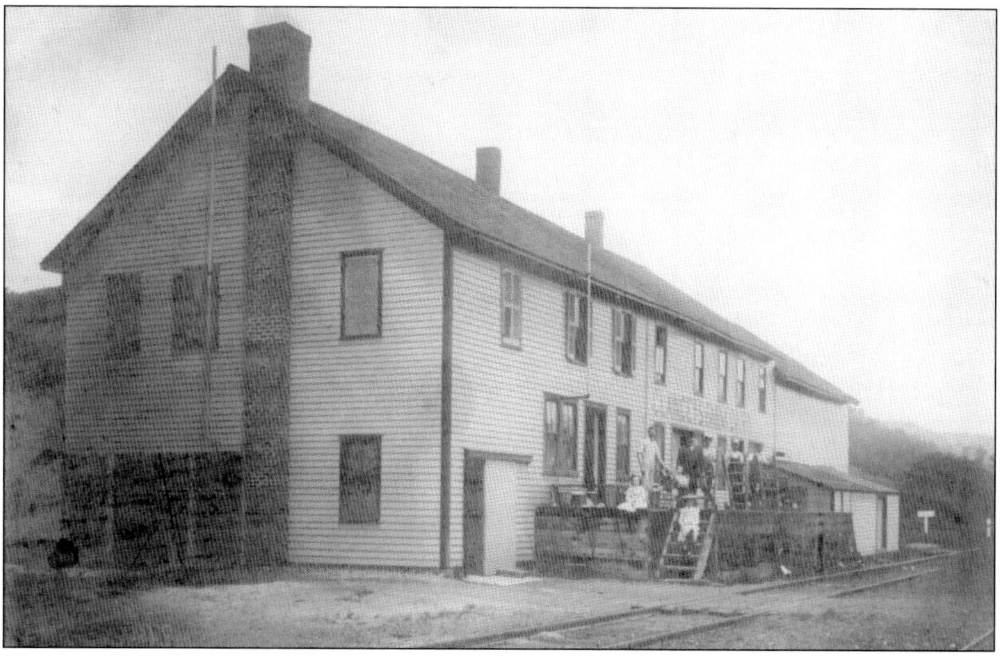

Clancey's Farm Dairy in Delhi is seen during the early years of the 20th century. Once railroads reached central parts of Delaware County in the 1870s, farmers were able to begin shipping their produce via creameries, such as this, to urban markets. The Clancey Farm Dairy was located south of the village of Delhi, alongside the tracks of the Ontario & Western Railway.

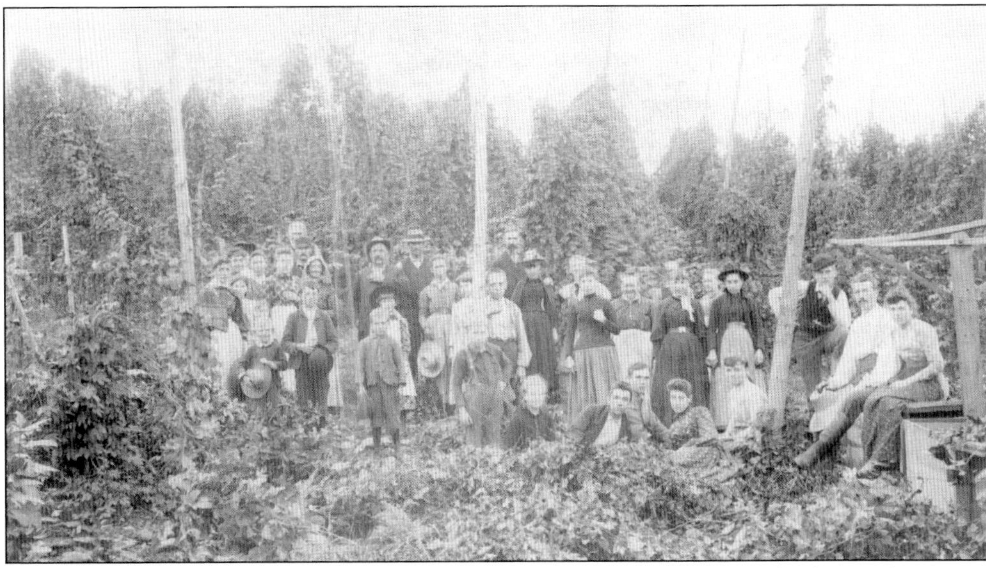

These two images show workers harvesting hops in Delaware County in the late 19th century. The northern tier of the county (along with neighboring Otsego County) was once a major hop producer—one of the main regions in the country for hop growing. During the month of September, hundreds of urban workers were transported by rail to area hop farms to labor in the fields. Most workers who came were young and of both sexes, and work for a few weeks in the late-summer countryside was considered almost like a holiday and was a paid one at that. In the evenings these young urbanites often held dances and enjoyed other forms of entertainment, a rare opportunity for young men and women to mingle in mixed company without the stern eyes of older relatives looking on. These evenings came to be known as a "hop."

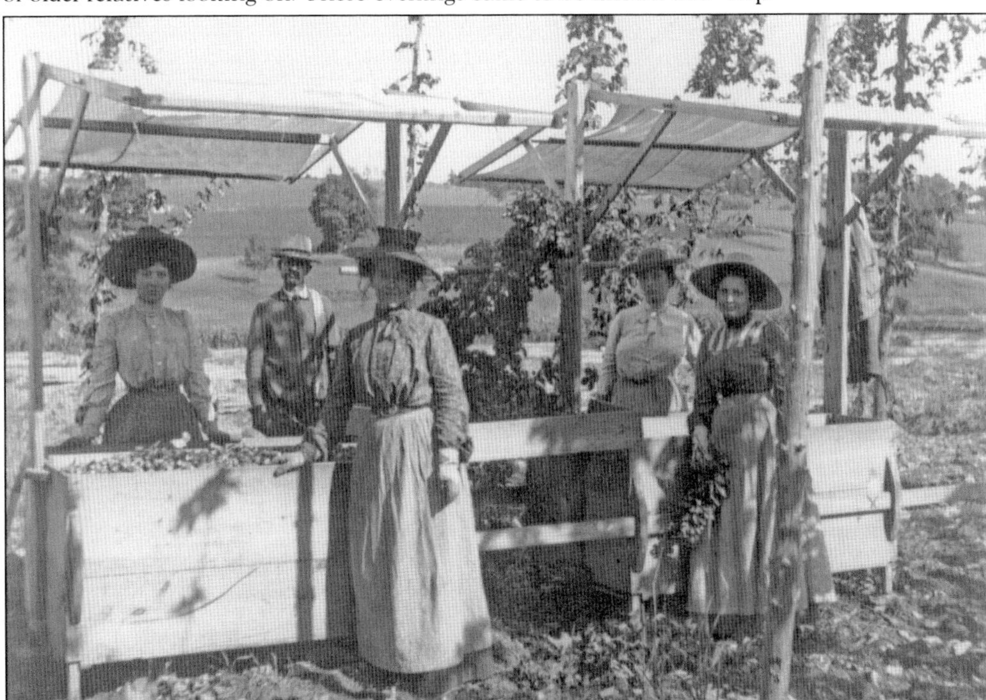

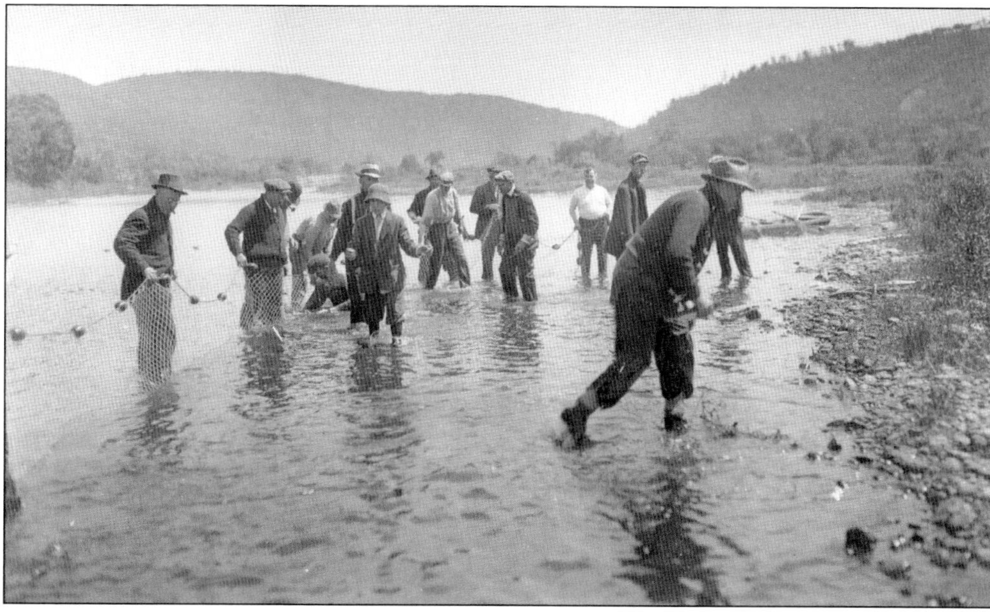

Catskill residents often earned their yearly income from a variety of sources, or simply added to their household's food intake. Depending on the time of year, locals may have engaged in logging, cutting ice from area ponds, and, in spring and summer, fishing in the region's bountiful rivers. The two scenes shown here were recorded by Julian Campbell about 1910. Both pictures depict local men fishing for shad in the Delaware River in the town of Hancock. The two branches of the Delaware River come together in Hancock to form the main, much wider branch. Fishing, once vital in sustaining human life before the 19th century when the Catskills formed part of the nation's sparsely populated frontier, is now more of a leisure pursuit. As such, the pastime draws visitors to the region and plays an integral role in Delaware County's tourist industry.

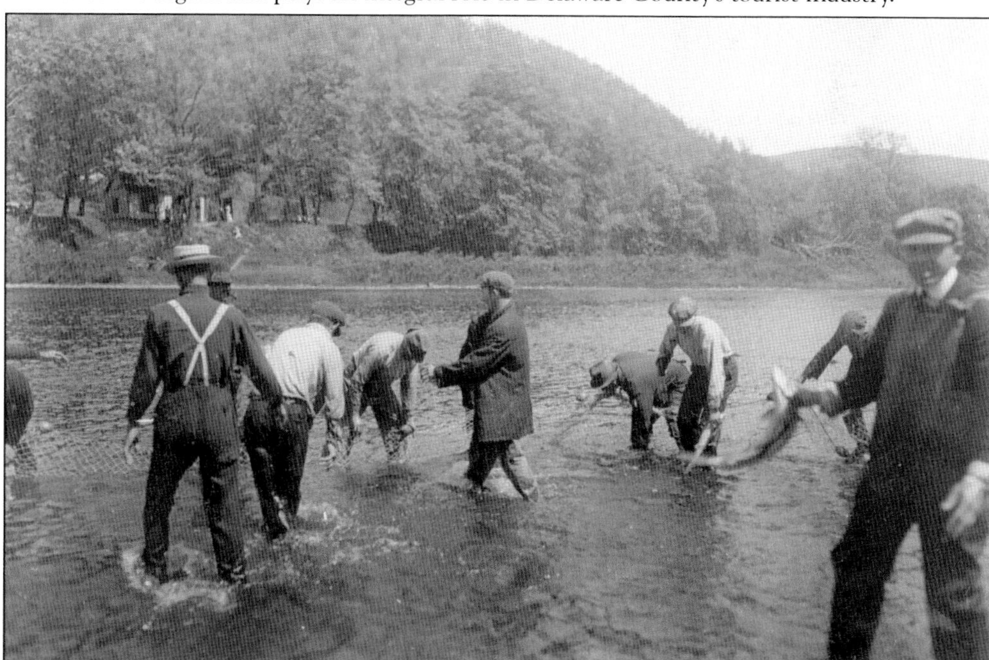

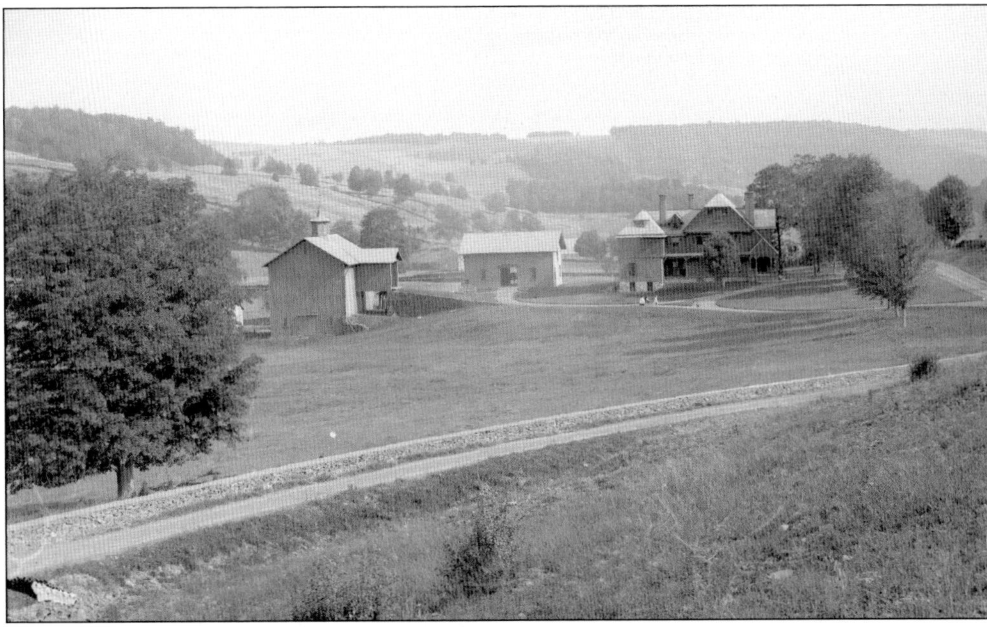

Greenleaf Farm, located on Elk Creek Road in the town of Meredith, is seen between 1900 and 1910. Greenleaf was something of a "show farm" in the county, owned by wealthy city folk from outside the area. By the 1920s and 1930s, Delaware County was one of the foremost counties in the east in terms of milk production. In 1933, only St. Lawrence County in New York produced more milk than Delaware County in the eastern half of the United States.

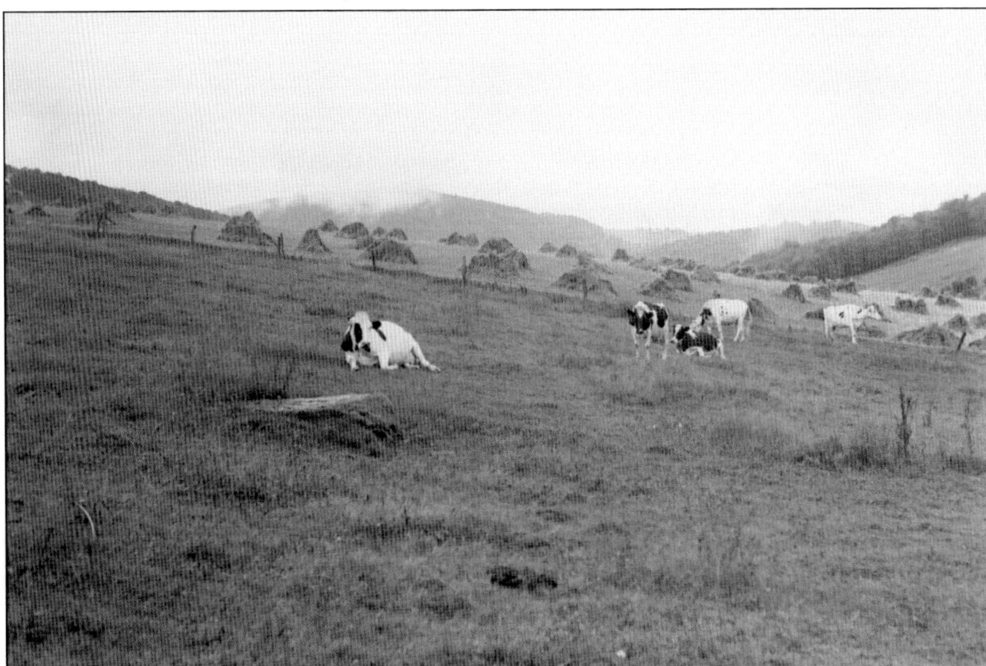

By the middle of the 20th century, Holstein cows had become a common sight throughout Delaware County. Shown here is a scene from Pink Street in the town of Bovina in 1955. Note the haystacks in the background. (Photograph by Bob Wyer.)

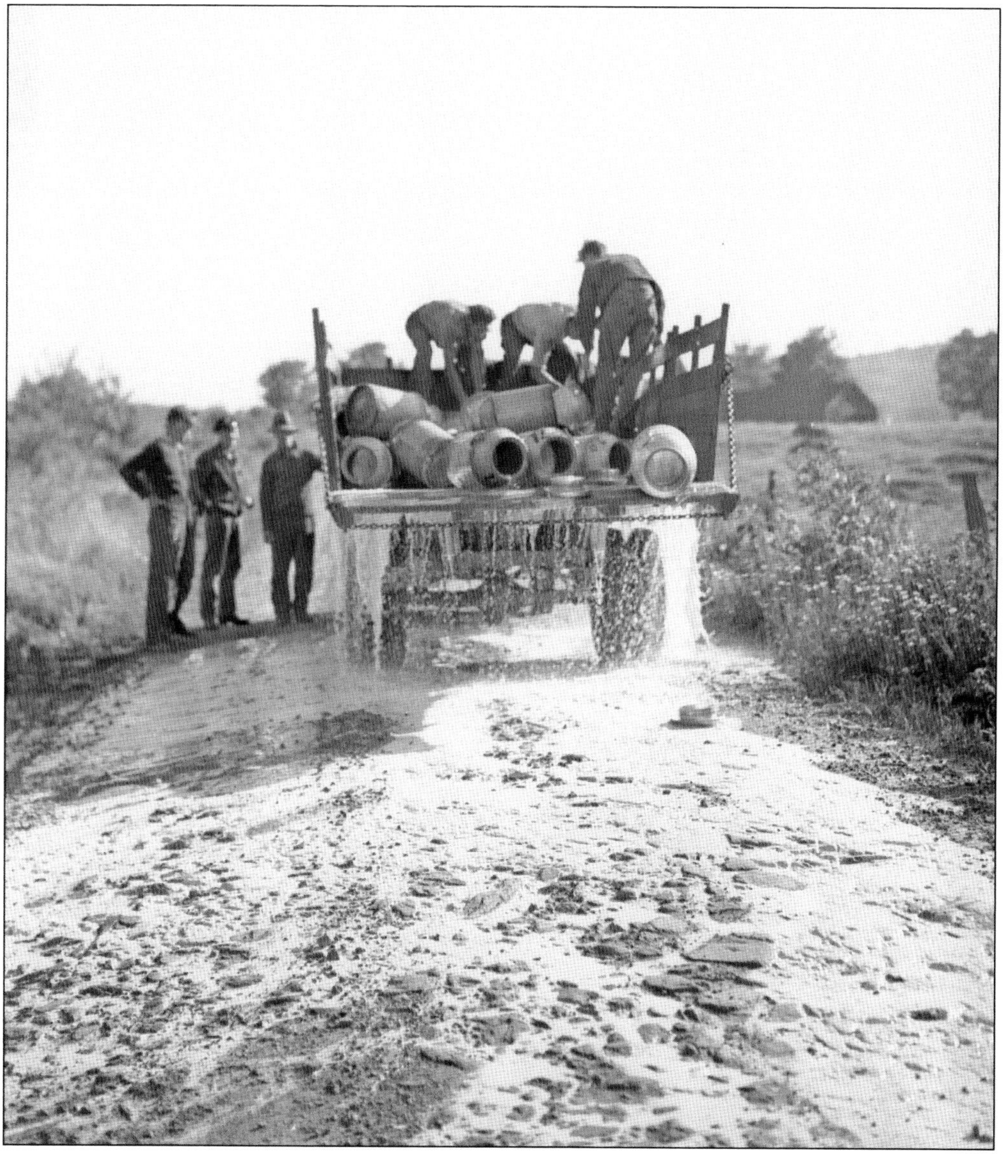

Despite its prominence in the dairy industry, Delaware County was not immune to the disruptions in production caused by serious labor strife during the 1930s and early 1940s. The so-called "milk strikes" of that period pitted farmer against farmer and neighbor against neighbor in a bitter struggle to earn more money for milk. As shown here, striking farmers took to stopping the milk trucks of those who continued to produce and sell their milk, dumping their liquid cargoes on the roads. (Photograph by Bob Wyer.)

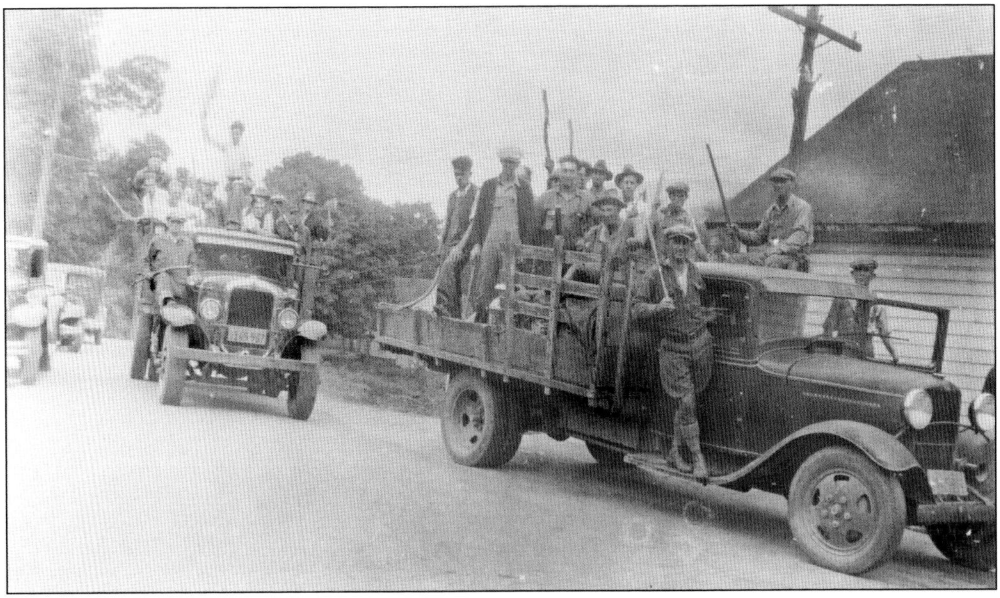

Tensions reached their boiling point in the county during the milk strikes in the summer of 1939 with numerous acts of violence carried out by farmers and their supporters on both sides of the issue. Shown above, striking farmers armed with sticks and other weapons aimed to shut down the production of milk in Delaware County. Shown below, convoys of milk trucks guarded by police became a common sight in Delaware County and throughout upstate New York in the mid-1930s. (Below, photograph by Bob Wyer.)

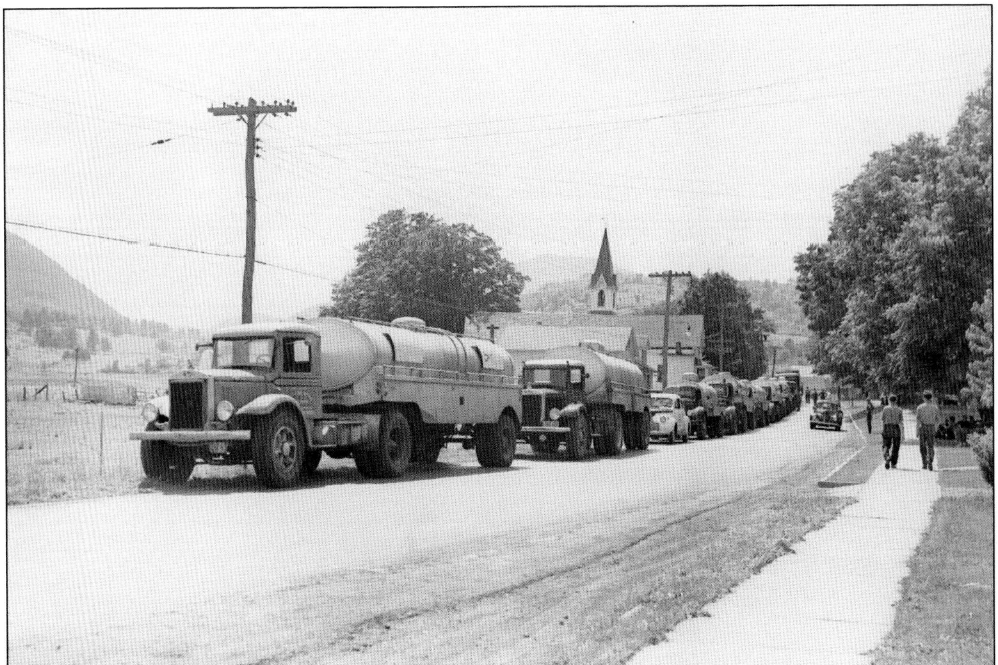

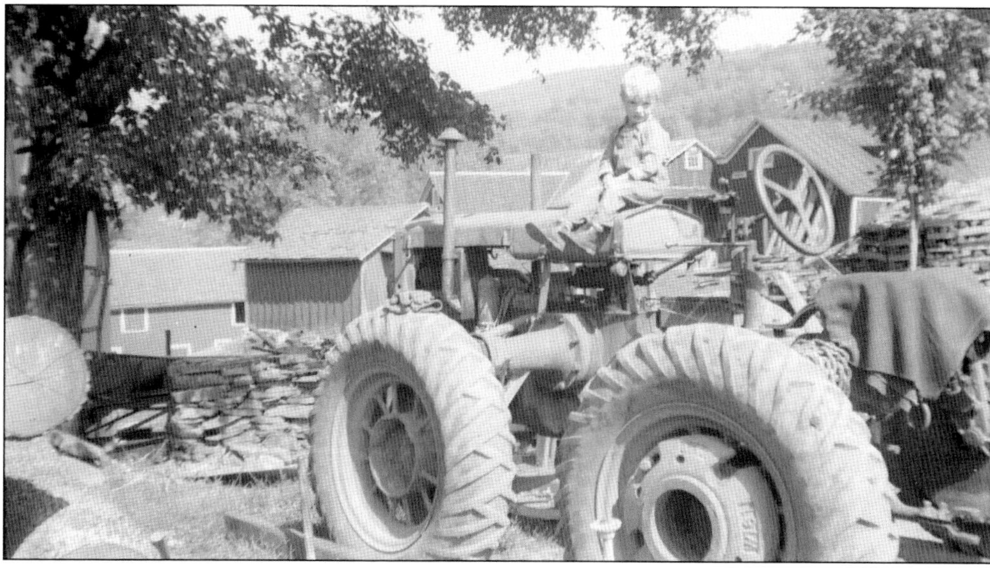

These images from the 1930s or 1940s show farm life on the Hubbell farm in the town of Middletown. Above, children on the farm quickly learned how to operate tractors and other machinery. Below, harvesting corn is taking place in late summer. By World War II, Delaware County farms had become increasingly mechanized. Tractors and trucks had replaced horses and wagons, and electricity had transformed life for men, women, and children on isolated farmsteads.

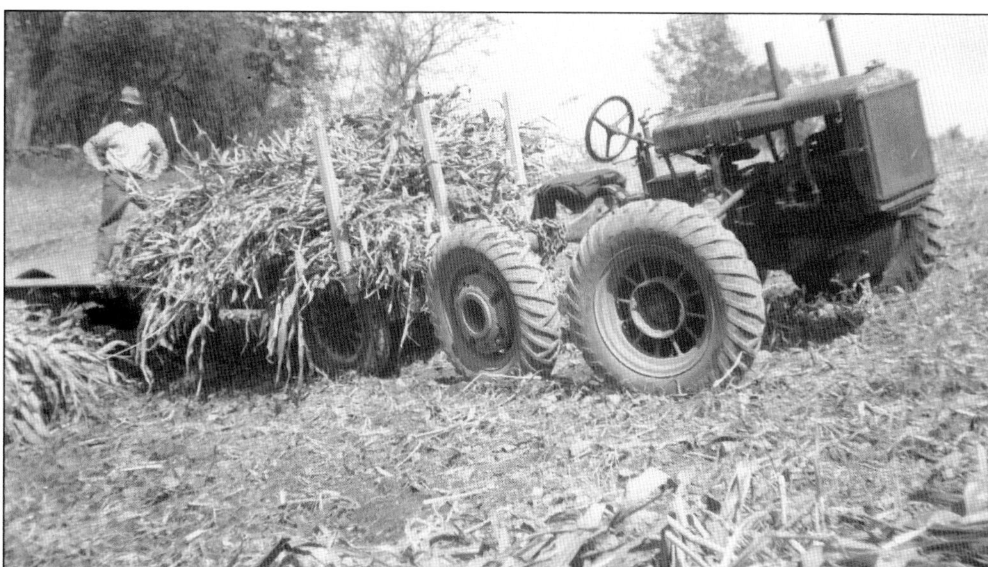

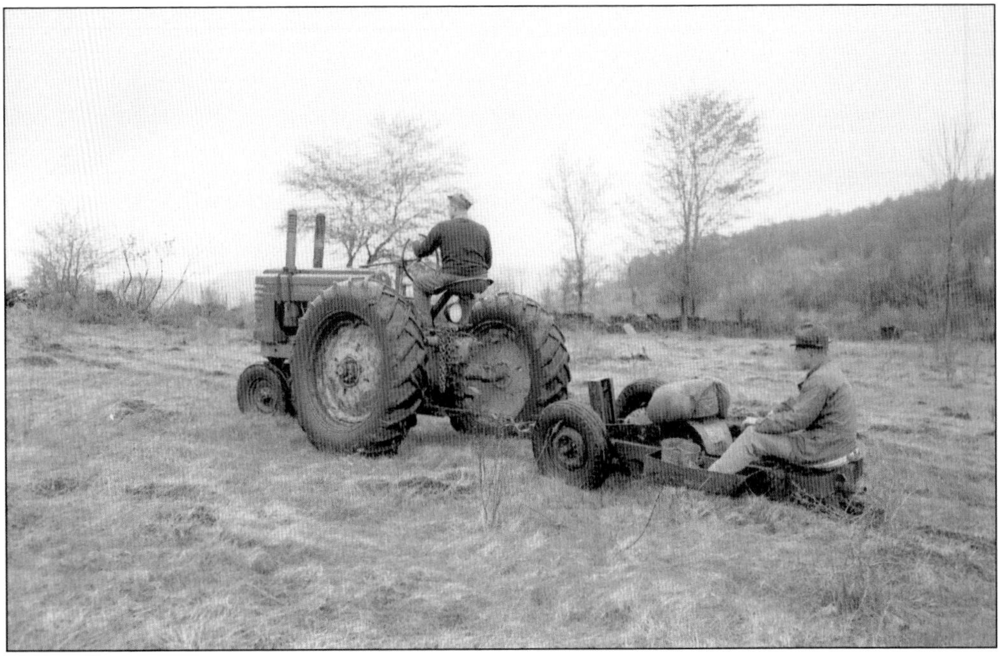

This c. 1940 picture shows men planting seed on farmland in the town of Delhi. Planting took place in springtime once the snows had receded from the fields. This image would not be too dissimilar from a picture showing the same field and the same chore 100 years earlier, except, of course, that the motive force at work is provided by a tractor, not a team of horses.

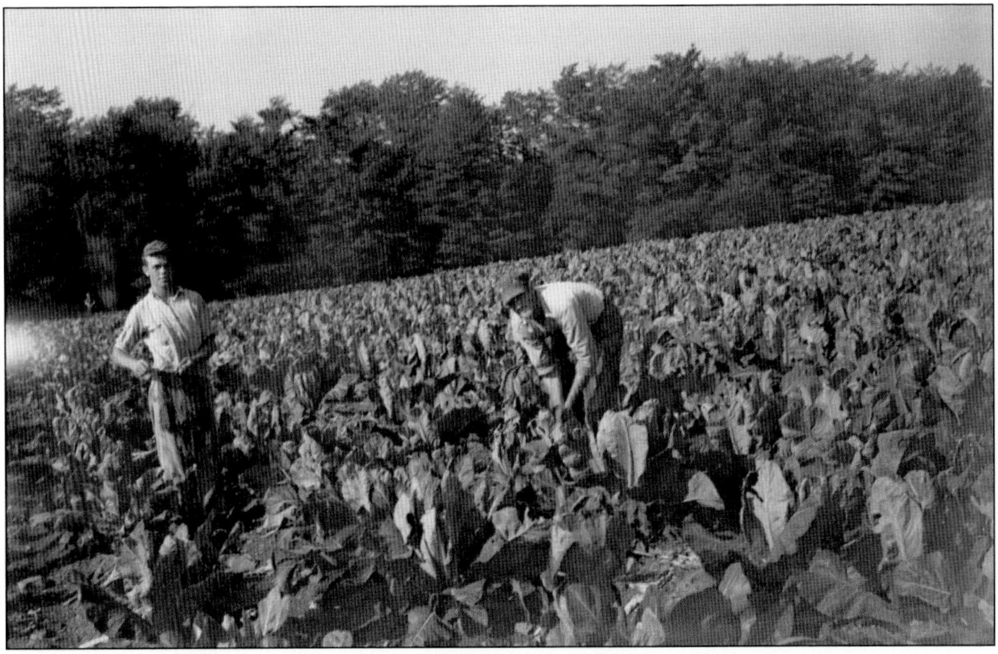

Here, people are picking cauliflower in the late summer of 1938 on the Joe Rosa farm in the town of Delhi. Even though tractors and other machines had alleviated some of the hard physical work associated with agriculture, some chores, as shown here, were still performed by hand. (Photograph by Bob Wyer.)

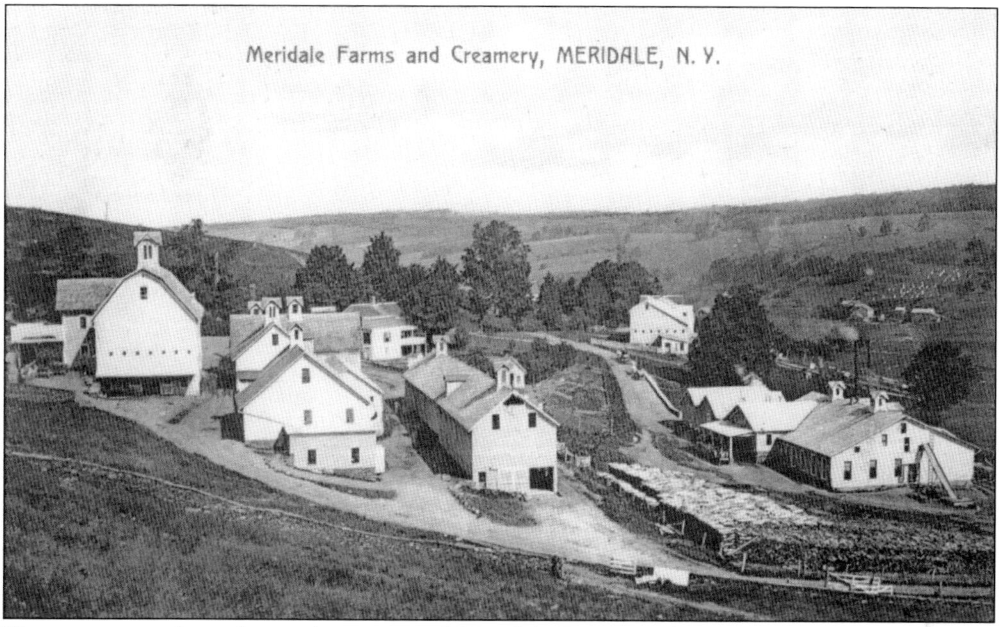

The two images here depict the renowned Meridale Farms in the town of Meredith. Meridale Farms was established in 1888 by two partners, F.W. Ayer and H.N. McKinney, in a profitable Camden-Philadelphia advertising agency. At one time in the early to mid-1900s, Meridale Farms enjoyed a reputation as the foremost Jersey breeding operation in the Northeast and probably the entire country. Indeed, Ayer and McKinney's cattle breeding business grew to become the second-largest Jersey farm in the world, and its scope of operations eventually spread over thousands of acres, spanning the hamlets of Meredith Square, Meridale, and beyond. Another component of the business was the production of high-quality butter, most of which was eventually shipped by rail to urban consumers in New York and Philadelphia.

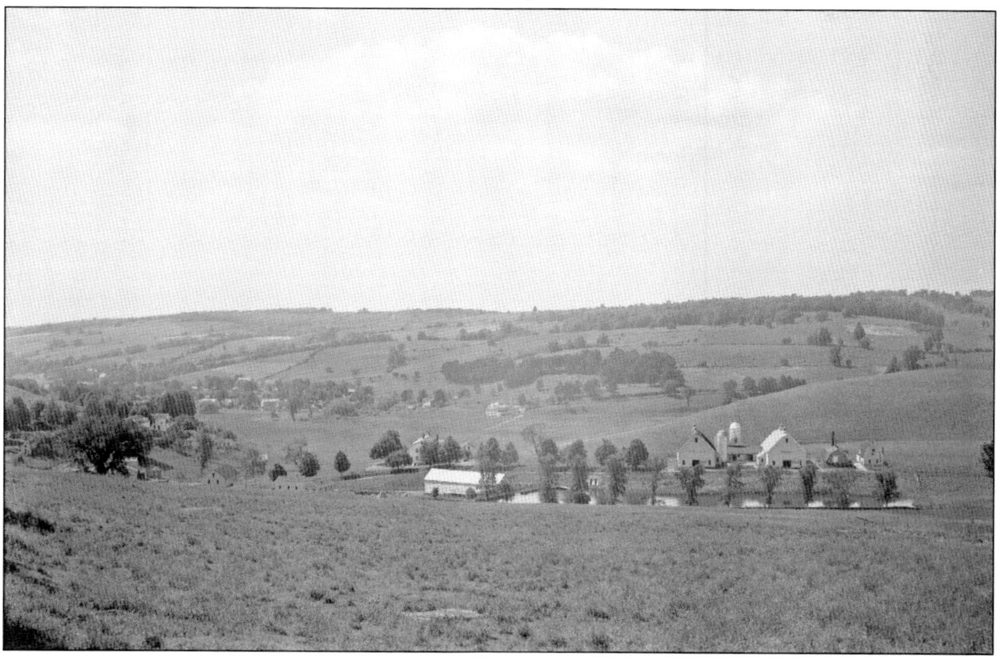

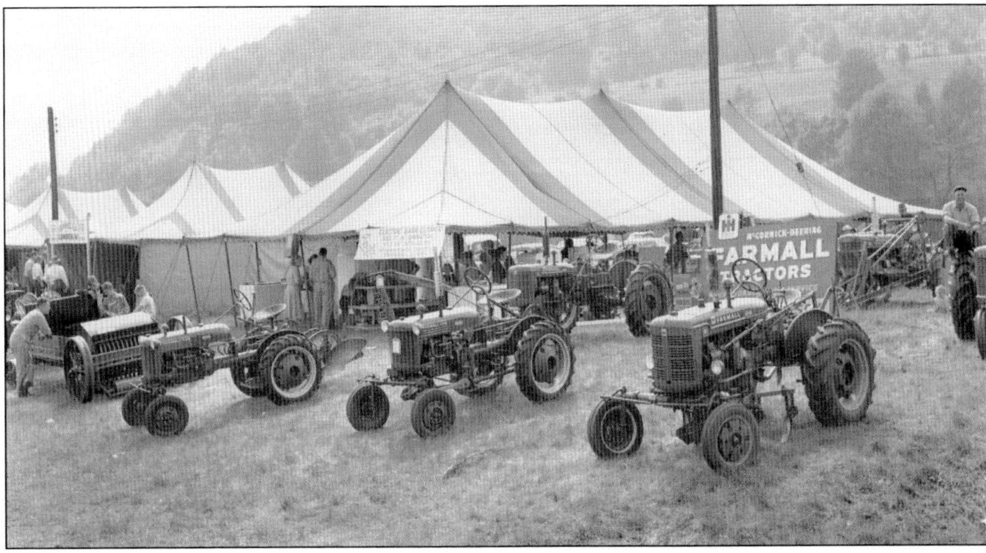

Pictured above is the c. 1950 Delaware County Fair in Walton. The increased mechanization of agriculture can clearly be seen in this view of tractors and other machinery at the fair. This view is not dissimilar to views of the county fair in the 21st century. The Delaware County Fair has remained the focal point for farm families in each calendar year, offering an opportunity to showcase their livestock and agricultural products. In the same way, numerous organizations, such as the Grange, 4-H, and Future Farmers of America, held shows and competitions—all so as to highlight farm production in Delaware County. Pictured below is the Delhi Horticultural Society's Harvest Show in 1949.

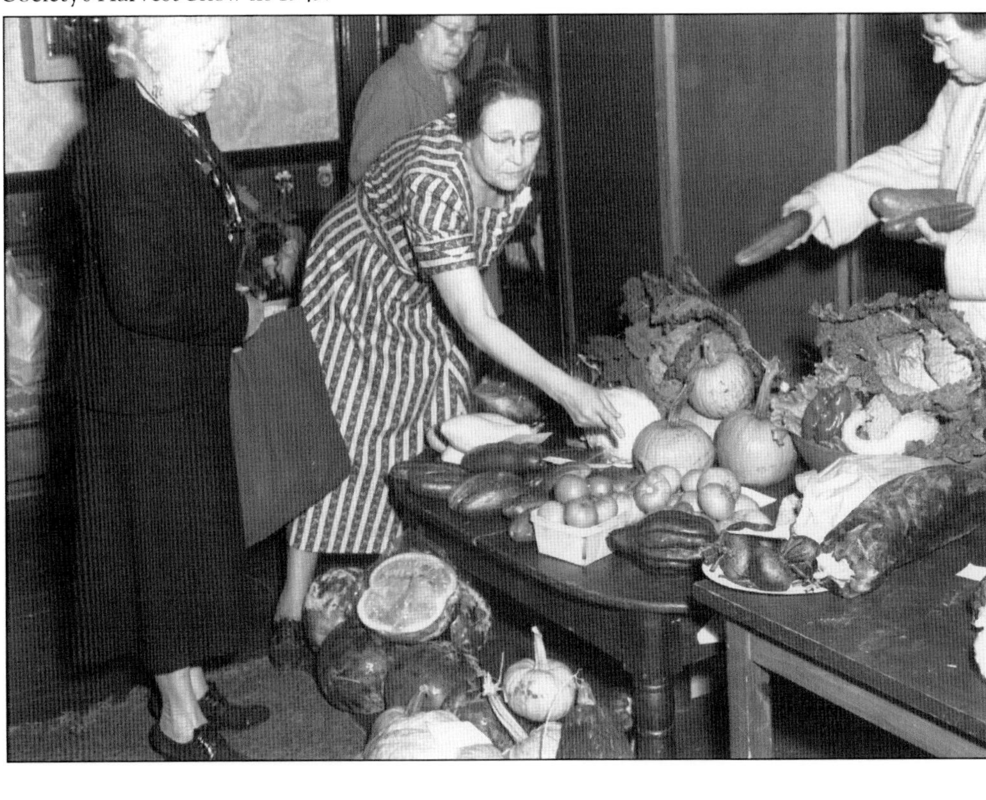

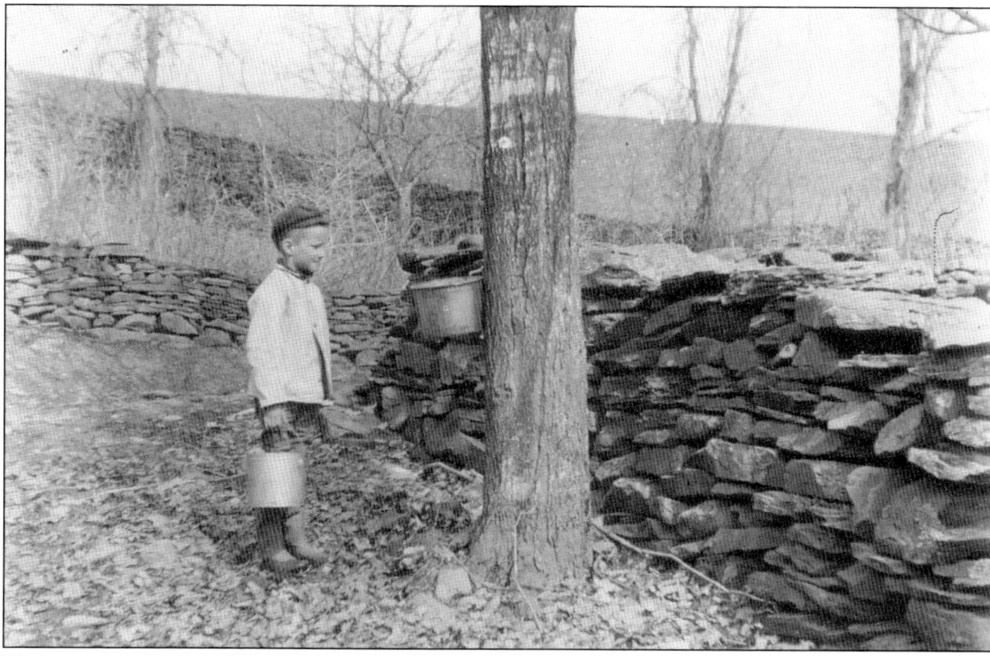

The region's farmers have always turned to other pursuits when possible to supplement their income from agriculture. In late winter and early spring, when the nights are still below freezing, but the day temperatures climb above 32 degrees, the sap from sugar maple trees begins flowing. Traditionally, this has been the time to tap the trees to collect the sap. Above, a boy is making his rounds collecting sap from buckets on the Hubbell Farm in the town of Middletown. Pictured below between 1908 and 1910 is a group boiling sap outdoors on Roses Brook in the town of Hobart. Those identified are, from left to right, William P. Lyon (left, small boy), Fred M. Lyon (center, with pail), Anna Carroll (standing at right, back of chair).

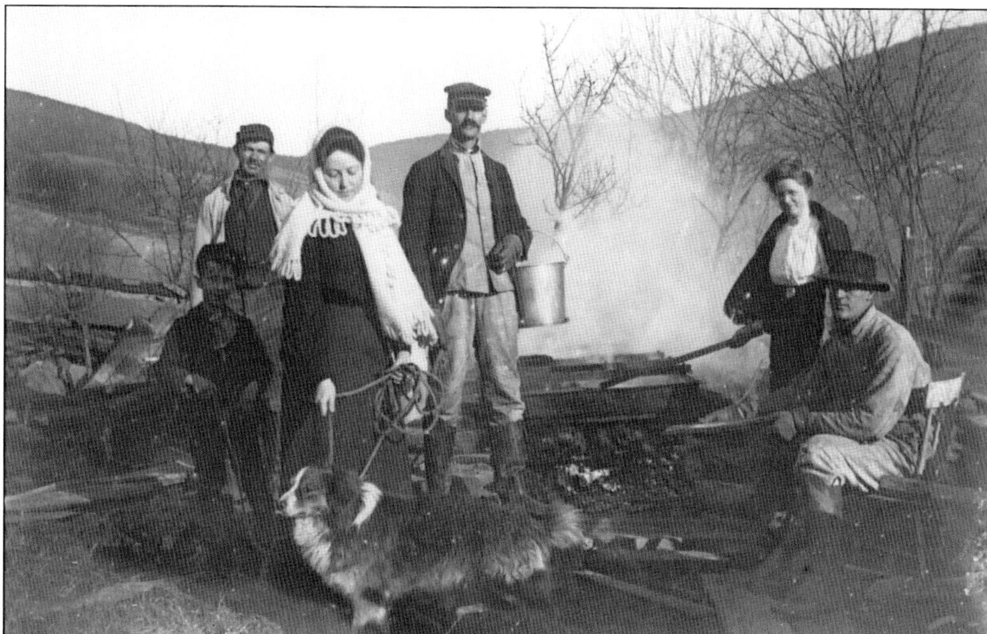

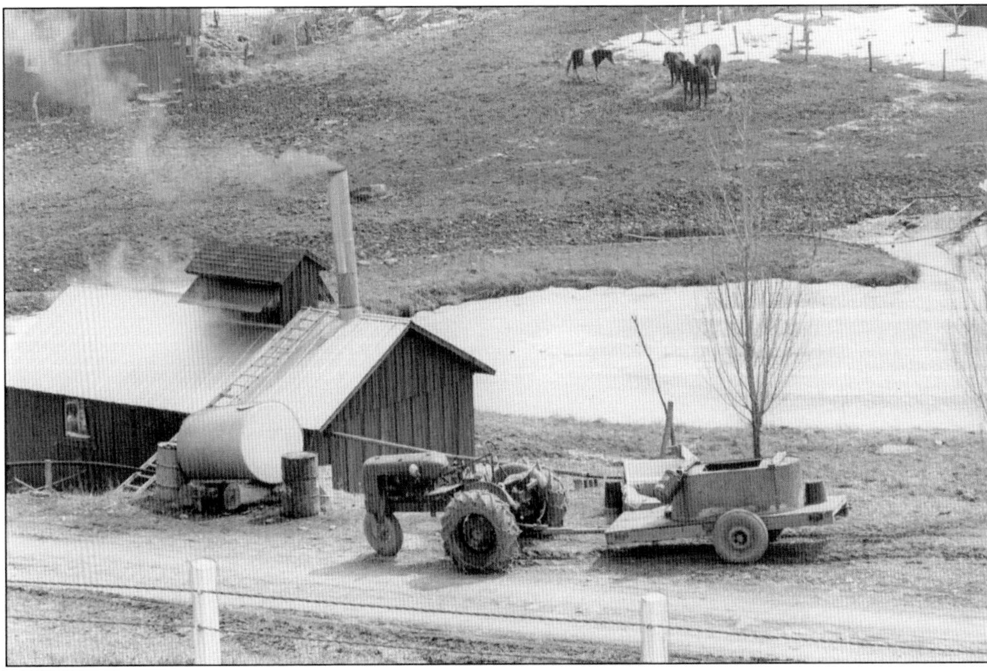

Nowadays few people boil down sap outside. Indeed, some maple syrup operations have become fairly large-scale affairs and increasingly sophisticated. The images here depict one such operation in the town of Masonville. Above is the sap house on the Harold Fisher Farm on East Masonville Pond, April 10, 1967. Note the smoke pouring from the smokestack. Below, the same photographer captures a Mrs. Fisher inside the sap house. Here, she is seen at the modern controls boiling down sap.

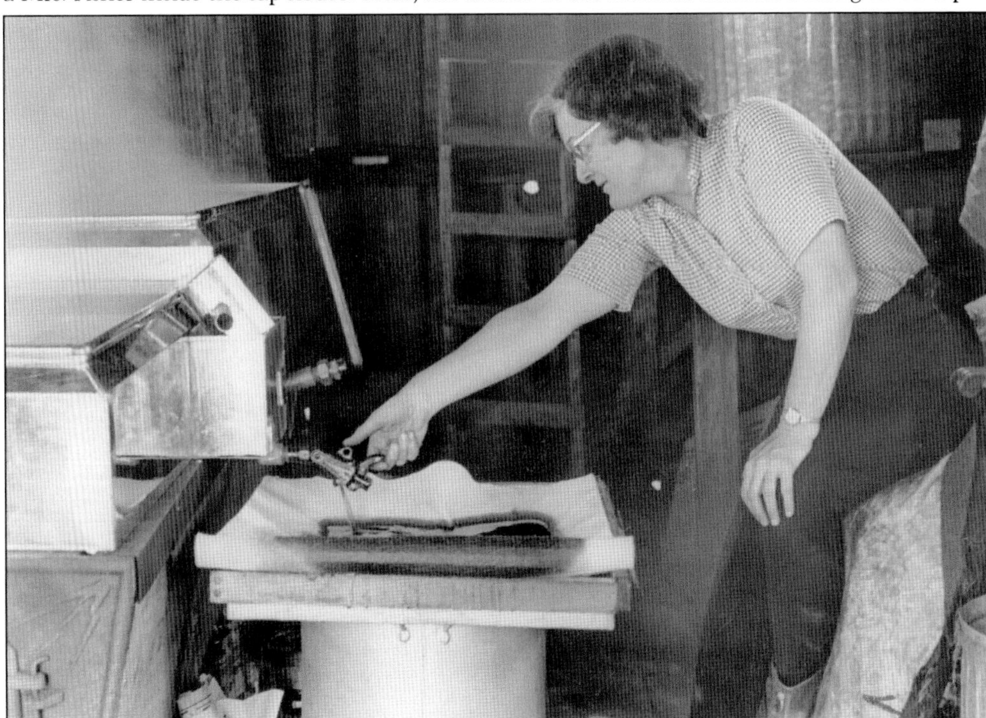

Three

GETTING AROUND

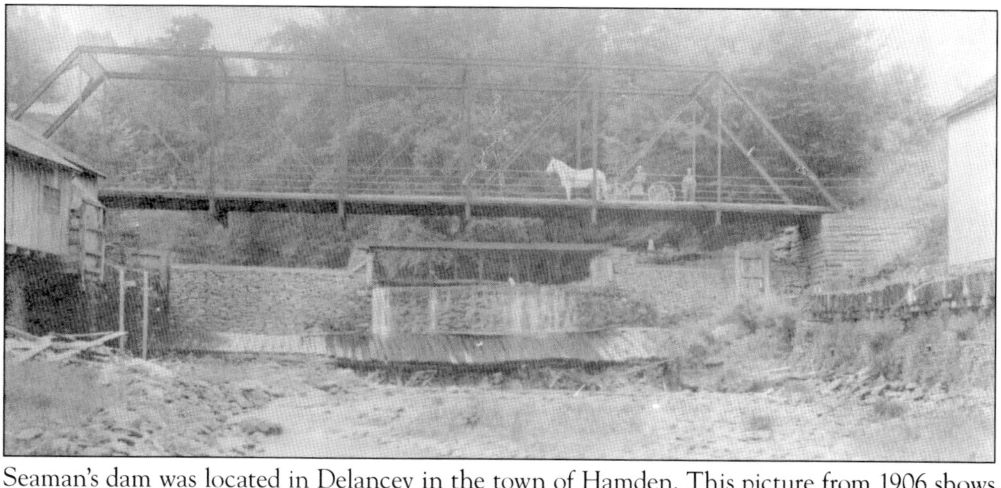

Seaman's dam was located in Delancey in the town of Hamden. This picture from 1906 shows the bridge over the dam with a horse and buggy and riders posing for the camera.

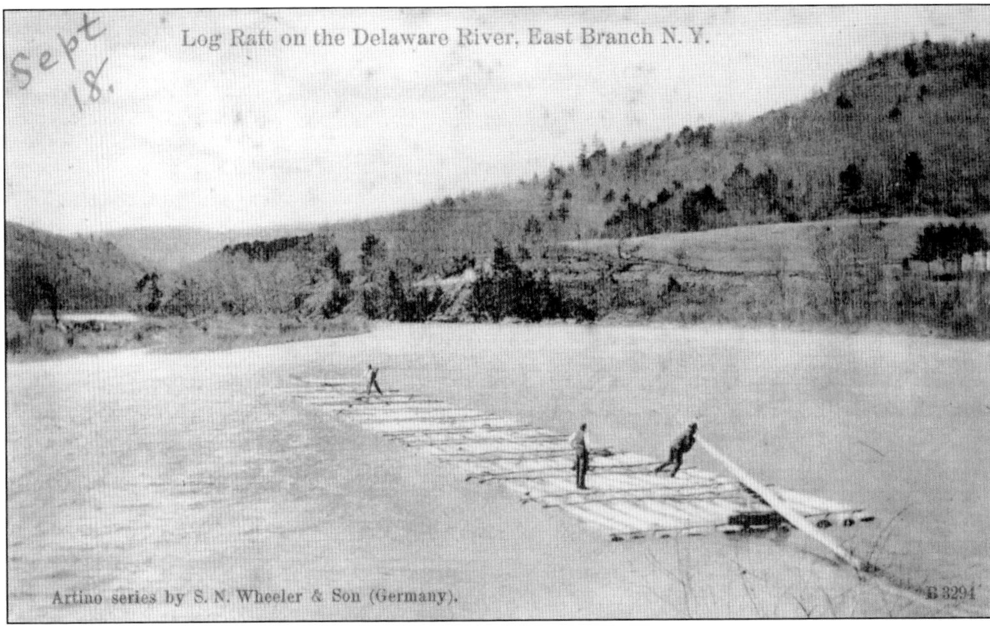

Delaware County was considered part of the nation's Western Frontier until after the American Revolution in the late 18th century. In the absence of good roads, rafts provided the mode of transit for many an early and intrepid adventurer into and out of the Catskill Mountains. Rafts, made from tall trees lashed together, carried cargoes of lumber, foodstuffs, bluestone, potash, wool, and even whiskey. The cargo and the lumber that made up the rafts was sold in urban markets as far down the Delaware River as Philadelphia. Above is a view of a raft in midstream with a "crew" on board. Below is another view of rafts along the East Branch of the Delaware River at the small hamlet of East Branch.

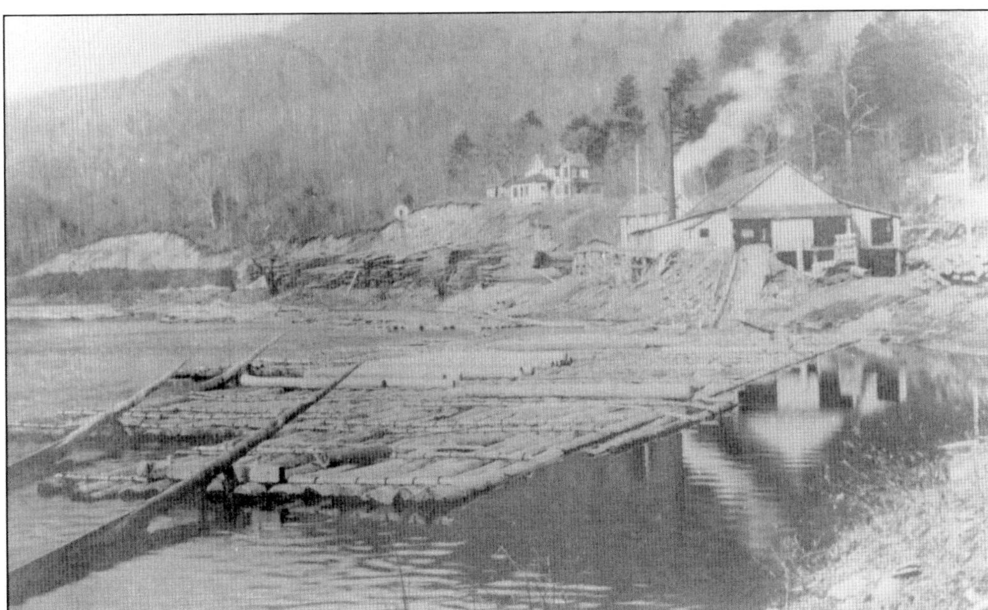

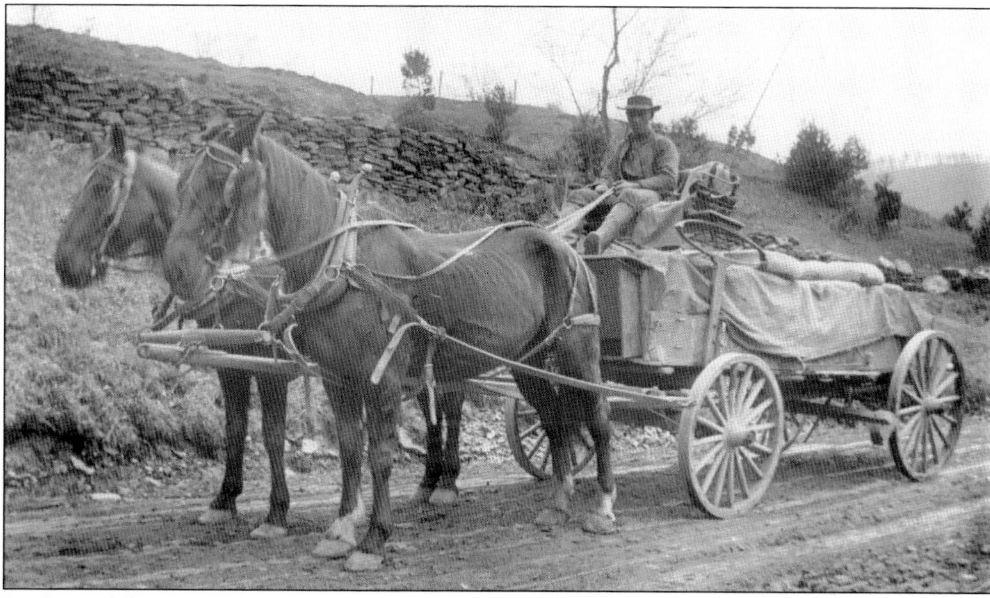

By the middle of the 19th century, roads had been improved to the extent that they provided the main methods of transit in and through the mountains of Delaware County. Still, as this image attests, the region's roads remained very poor, especially in the spring and fall when rains and melting snow made quick quagmires of their surfaces. Above, a man attempts to navigate just such a road with his horses and a heavily laden wagon. Although it was obviously a cold undertaking, travel in winter was considered by locals to be far easier than at other times of the year. As this image of a horse and sled in late-19th-century Hobart shows, snow- and ice-covered surfaces offered much quicker and smoother travel here in the Catskills. A winter traveler may have arrived at his or her destination thoroughly chilled and weary, but usually did so without the bumps and bruises caused by the state of the county's dirt roads at other times of the year.

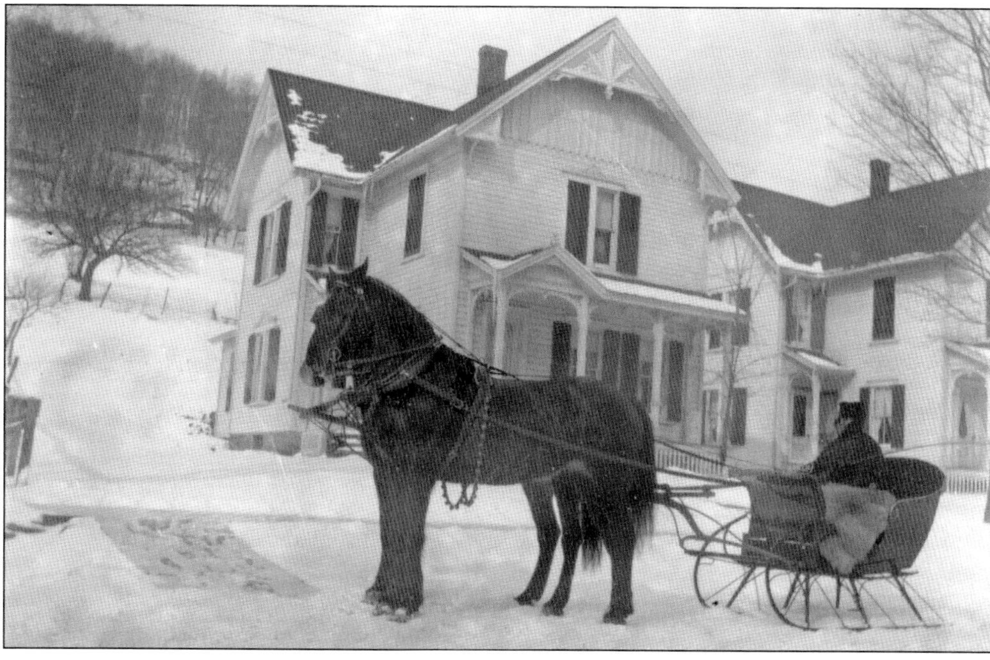

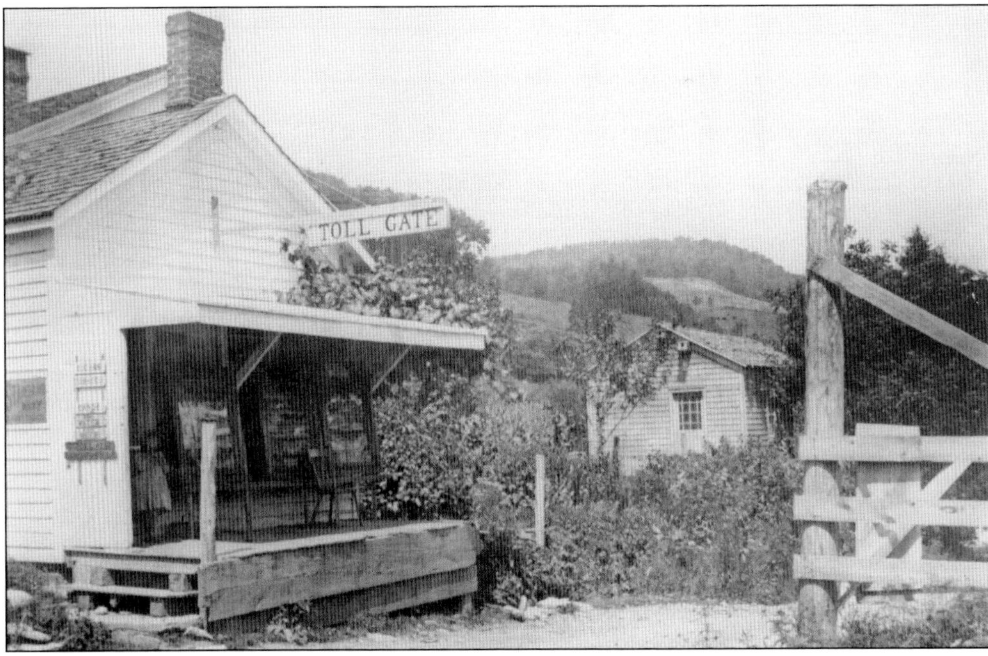

A number of turnpikes—improved roads whereby travelers paid to use them—were in operation in Delaware County by the mid-19th century. The best known of these was the Susquehanna, or Catskill, Turnpike, completed in 1806, which connected the Hudson River at Catskill, New York, to the Susquehanna River at Unadilla. Tollgates, as pictured here, were situated at regular intervals along these roadways, giving rise to unofficial roads, which were deliberately created by regular travelers to avoid paying the tolls. These roads were known as "shunpikes," and their remains can still be found in the county. The image above shows a typical tollgate that was located in the town of Delhi along the Little Delaware River. The image below depicts the tollgate that once stood along the Catskill Turnpike a little to the east of the village of Stamford. This building was painstakingly removed from its original site in the 1970s and now sits on the grounds of the Delaware County Historical Association in Delhi.

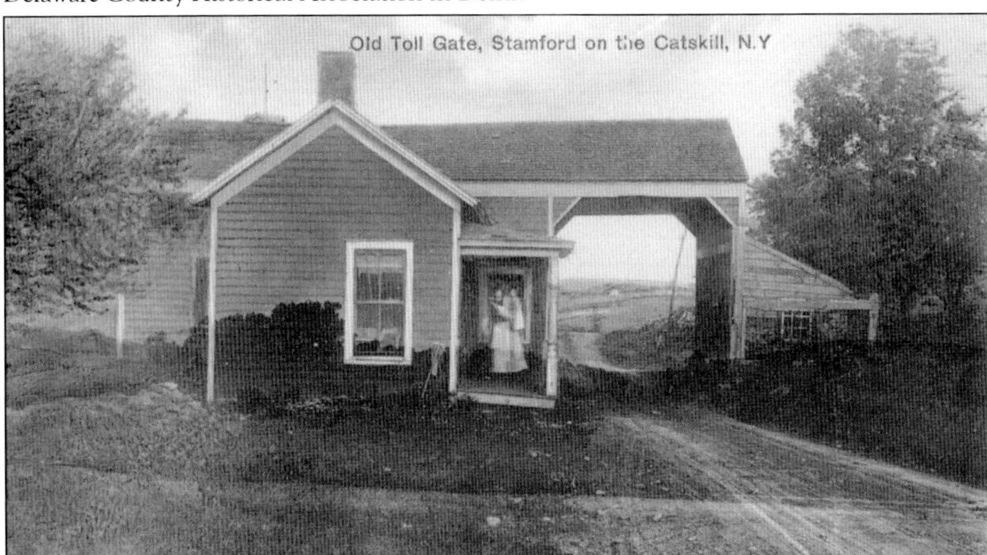

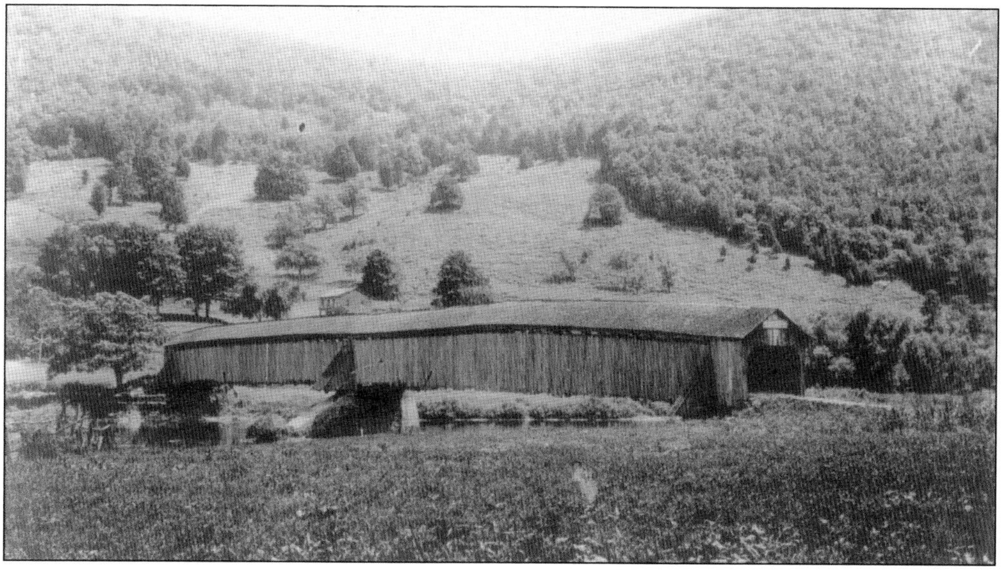

The Downsville Covered Bridge is shown in the image above. Delaware County once boasted a number of these now iconic structures. Today, just six remain, including the refurbished bridge seen in this photograph. Numerous theories exist as to why these wooden bridges were covered in the first place. One has it that a roof helped entice horses to cross without panic. However, the real reason was simply that the roof cover prolonged the life of the wooden bridge underneath. Pictured below is the steel truss bridge spanning the Charlotte River in Davenport. The era of wooden bridges had come to an end with the engineering and technological developments of the late 19th century. Iron and steel allowed for the construction of bridges, such as the one shown below.

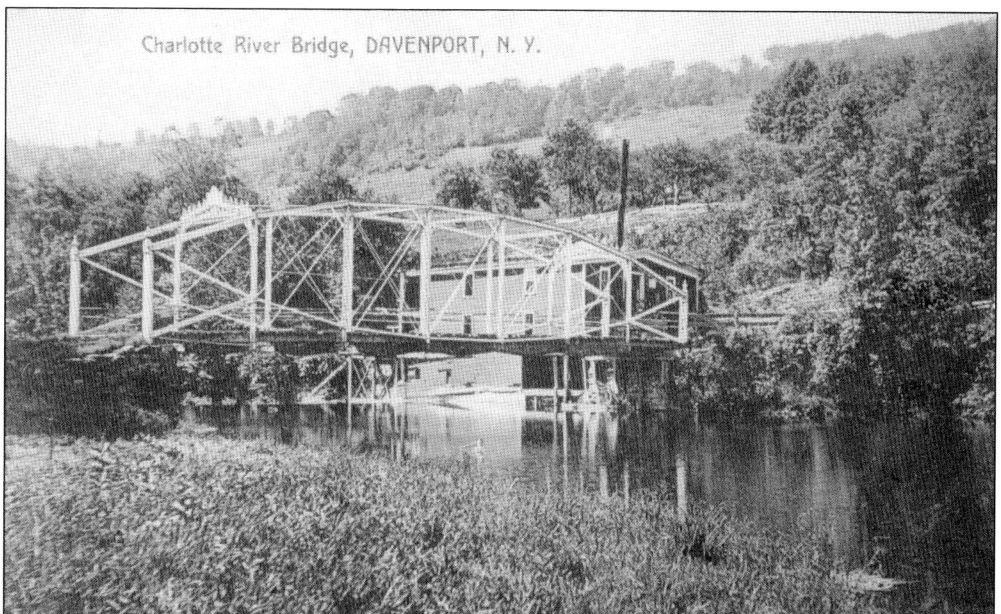

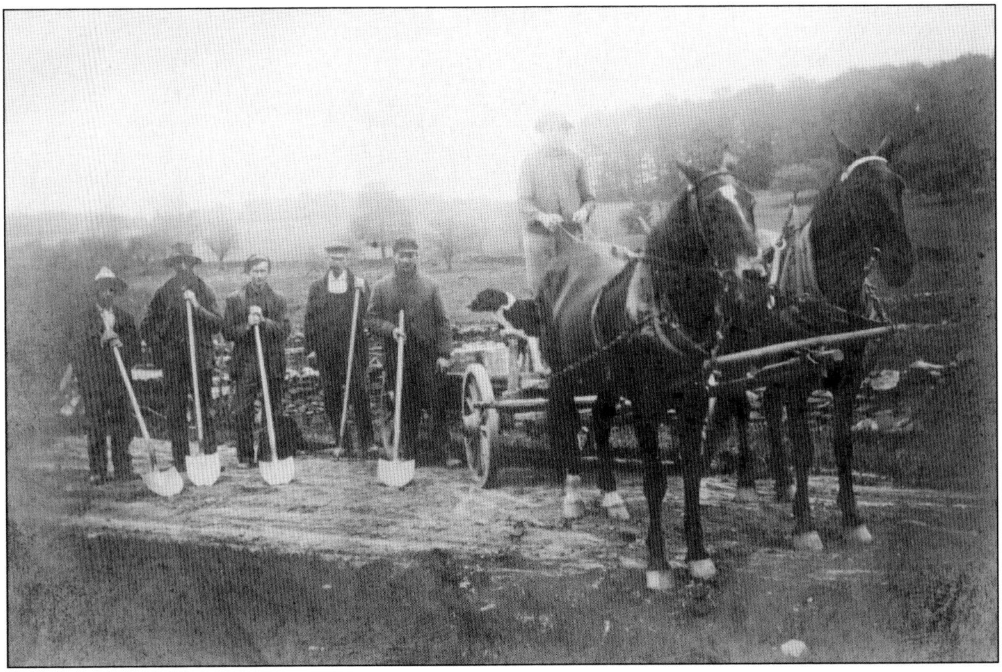

Before the dawn of the automobile era in the first decade of the 20th century, the maintenance of local roads remained for the most part under the control of local towns and villages. Instead of paying taxes to fund road upkeep, able-bodied local men were required to spend a set time every year working on their local roads. The image above shows a crew of locals performing just such a task. Still, as the image below, taken in the town of Middletown, clearly shows, the state of many a mountain road remained in very poor condition until well into the 20th century.

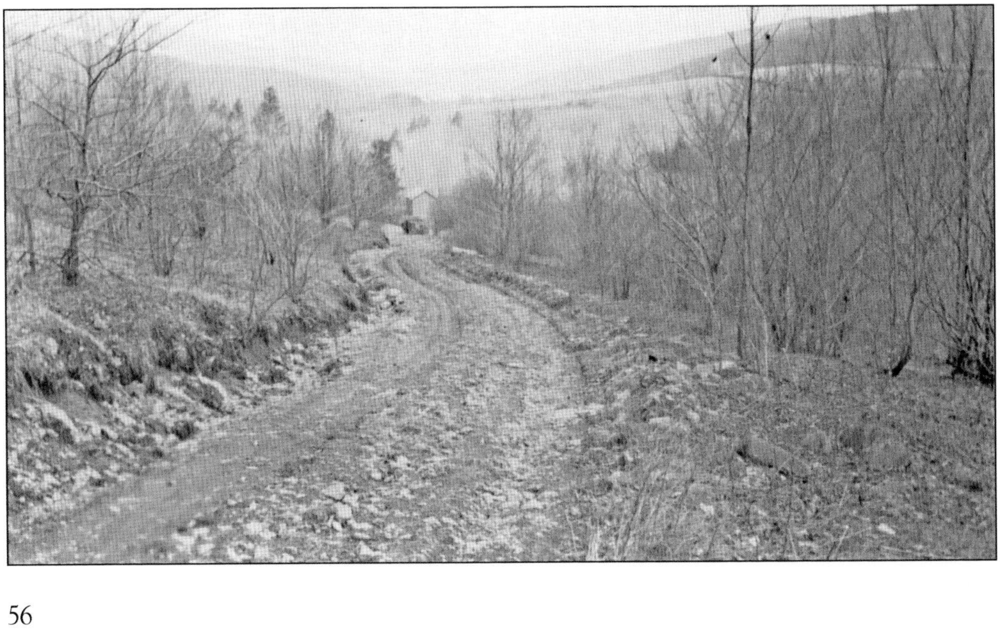

Although in a remote location in upstate New York, Delaware County was not immune to cultural trends occurring elsewhere. As the two images included here show, by the late 19th century, the national craze for bicycling had swept through the Catskills. Young people took to pedaling with gusto along county byways. The c. 1900 photograph at right depicts Vestina Taylor posing with her "machine" in front of the covered bridge at Davenport. Pictured below in the 1890s is a group of young men with their bicycles along Delhi's Main Street.

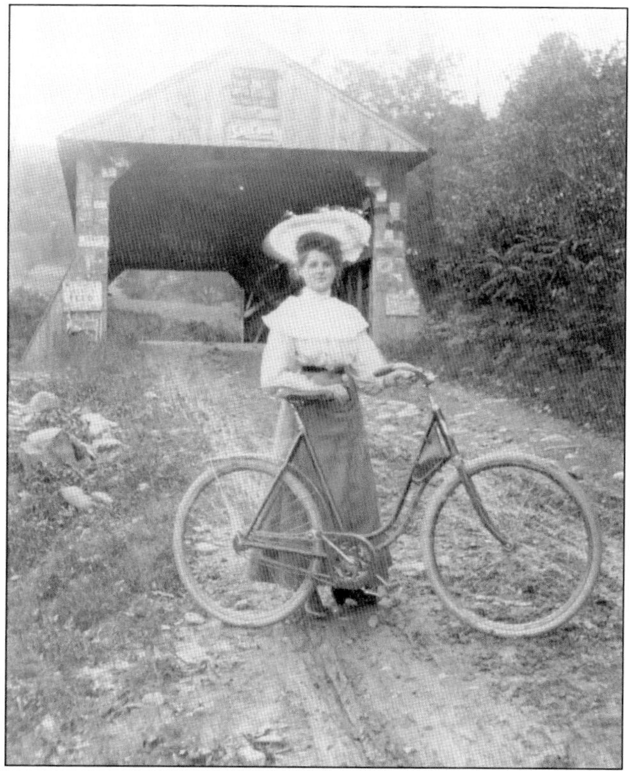

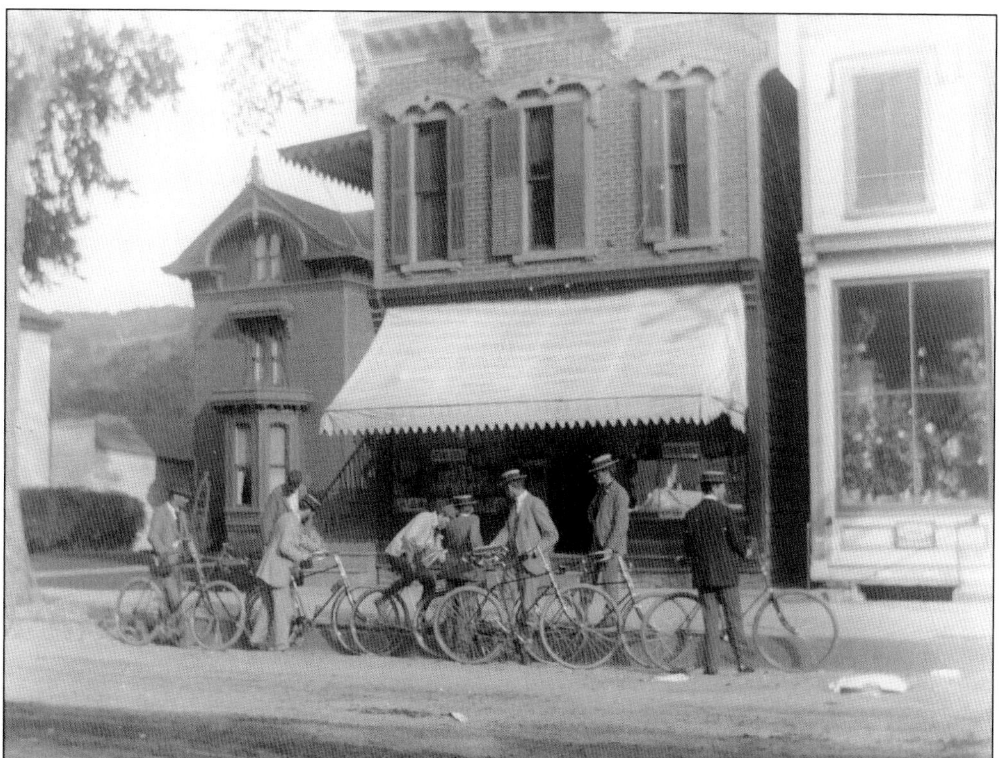

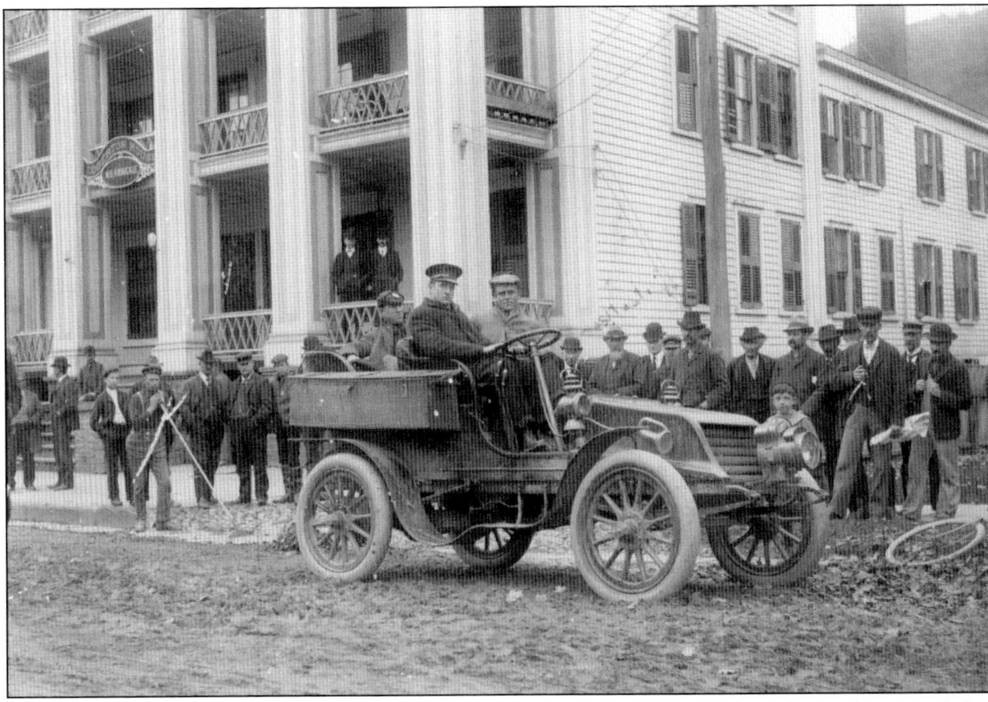

During the first two decades of the 20th century, with the advent of trucks and automobiles, the improvement of roads came to be viewed as having national and statewide importance. One way in which automobile enthusiasts aimed to stir up attention to the state of the roads was via long-distance endurance races. In October 1903, one of America's very first races passed through Delaware County en route from Weehawken, New Jersey, to Buffalo and beyond. In a driving rain on terrible, muddy roads, 26 automobiles made it as far as Delhi. Shown above is a vehicle in front of Delhi's Edgerton Hotel. Meanwhile, most early automobile owners enjoyed more leisurely pursuits. Below is an early-20th-century excursion in an open-topped automobile in the countryside around 1918 or 1919.

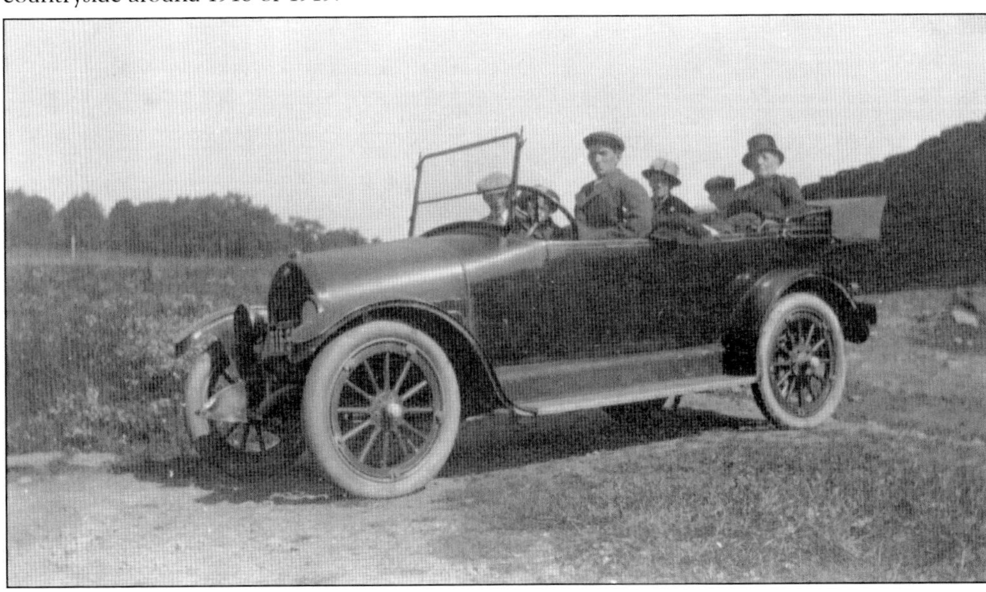

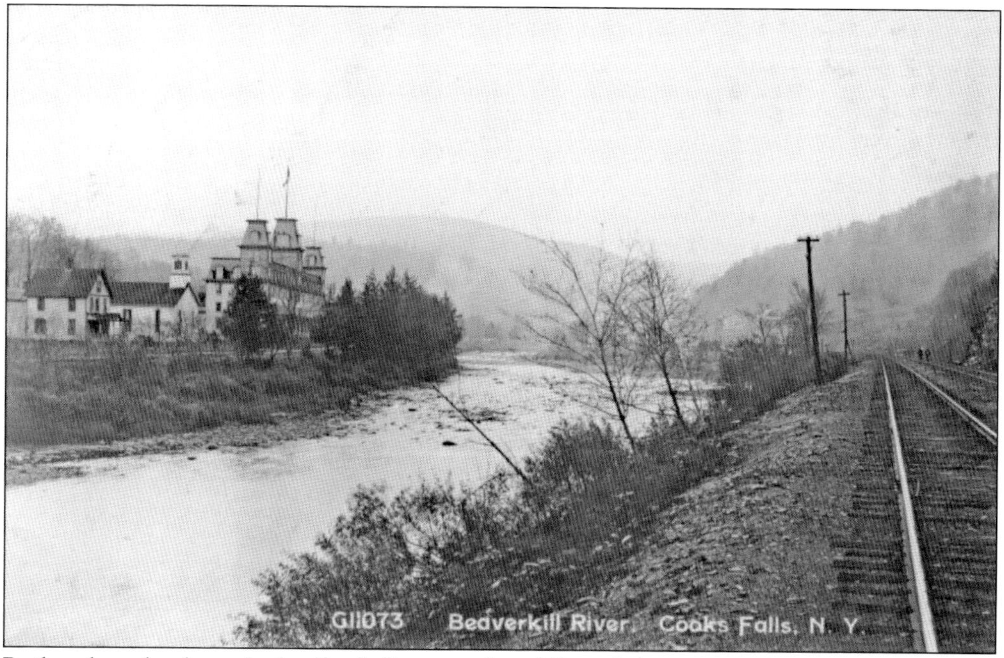

Railroad tracks through the Catskills very often followed the course of rivers, weaving their course in between higher mountains. Pictured above are those tracks of the Ontario & Western Railway hard alongside the Beaverkill River at Cooks Falls, in the town of Colchester. The arrival in Delaware County of both the O&W Railway and the Ulster & Delaware Railroad during the 1870s gave rise to a veritable tourist boom. Note the large hotel on the opposite bank of the river. Below, roads, rivers, and rails are all evident in this image of East Branch, New York. After 1906, the tiny community of East Branch became a transportation hub when the Delaware & Northern (D&N) Railroad was completed. The D&N ran from Arkville along the East Branch of the Delaware River and connected to the O&W at East Branch.

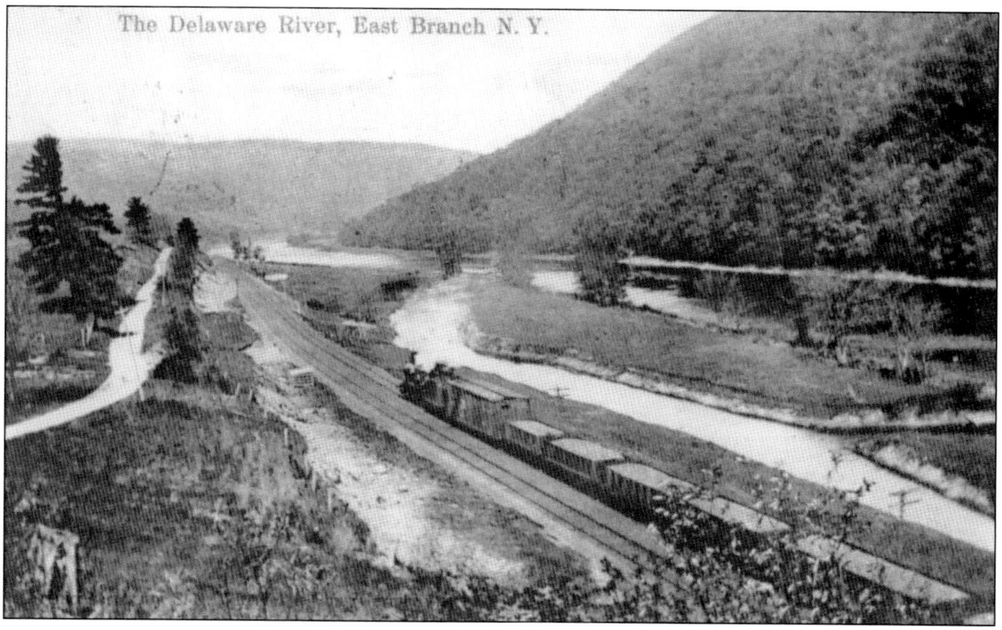

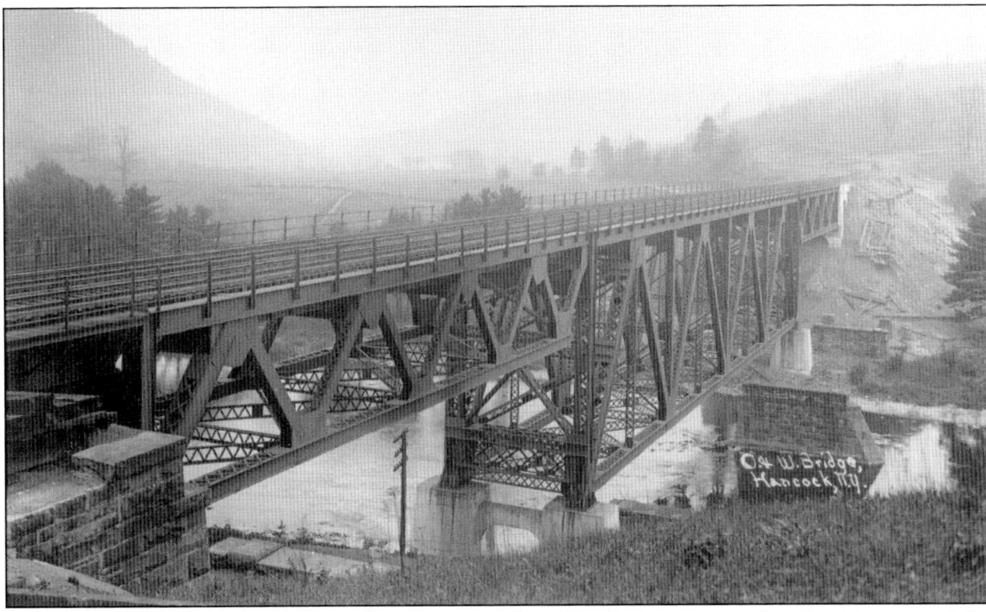

The c. 1910 image above depicts the O&W Railway Bridge spanning the East Branch of the Delaware River at Cadosia near Hancock. Meanwhile, East Front Street in the center of the thriving village of Hancock is shown in the c. 1910 photograph below. During the 19th century, Hancock also became a railroad hub. Where the tracks of the O&W and the New York & Erie (NY&E) passed in close proximity to one another, hotels, stores, and other commercial businesses sprang up. The NY&E was the nation's first long-distance line and the first to enter Delaware County in 1848. The entire line, when finished, ran from Weehawken, New Jersey, to Dunkirk on Lake Erie.

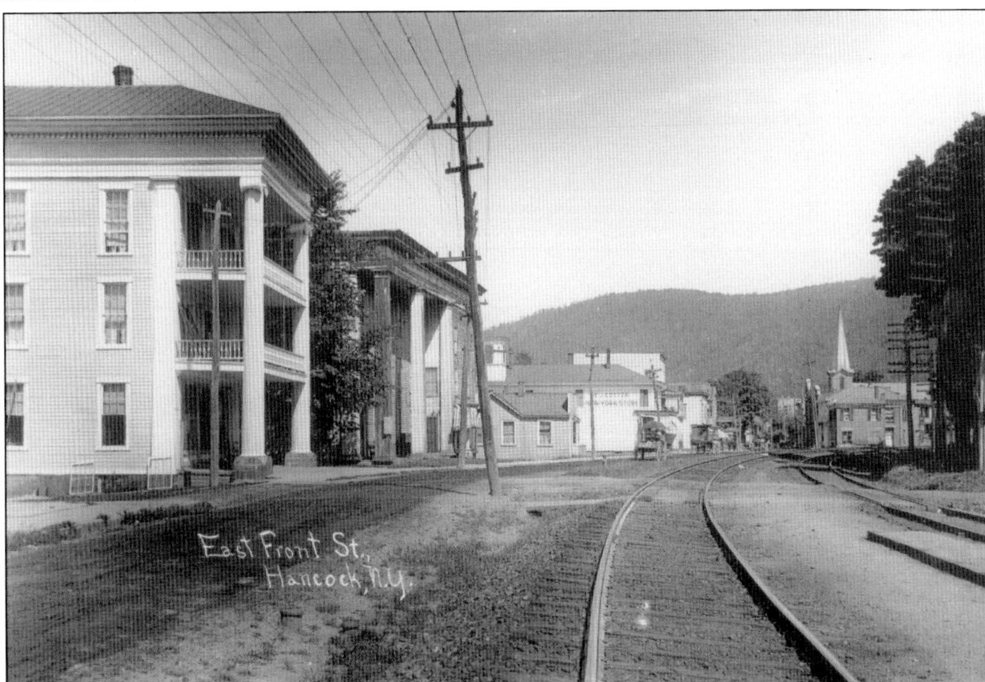

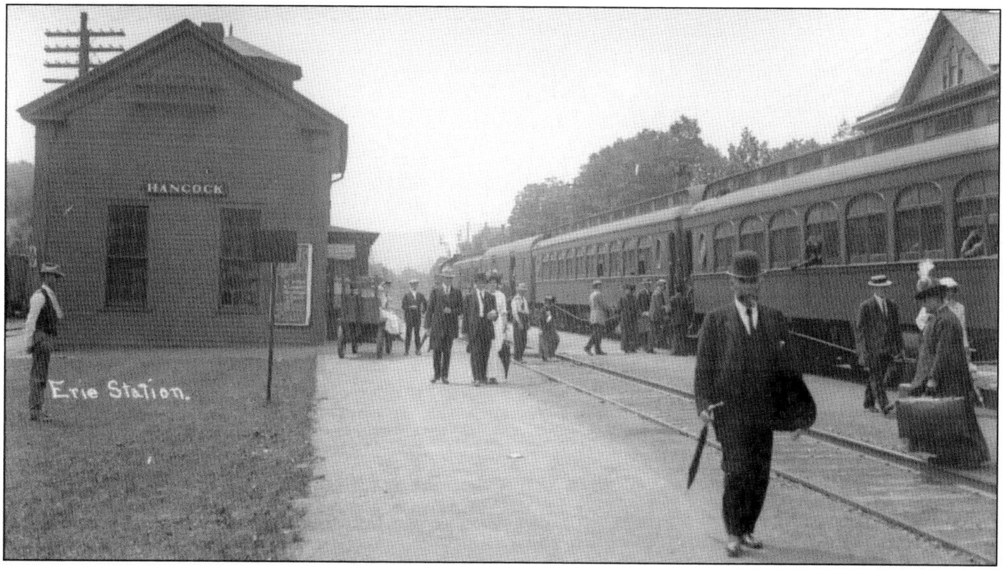

The view above is of the New York & Erie Railroad station around 1910. Train travel provided the region with a major tourism boost during the late 19th and early 20th centuries. Now only a few hours from New York City, as opposed to a few days, urban families could easily come to the mountains to spend several days or an entire summer. Special "Husband Trains" were provided on Fridays and again on Sundays and Mondays for the men to return to their weekly labors in the city.

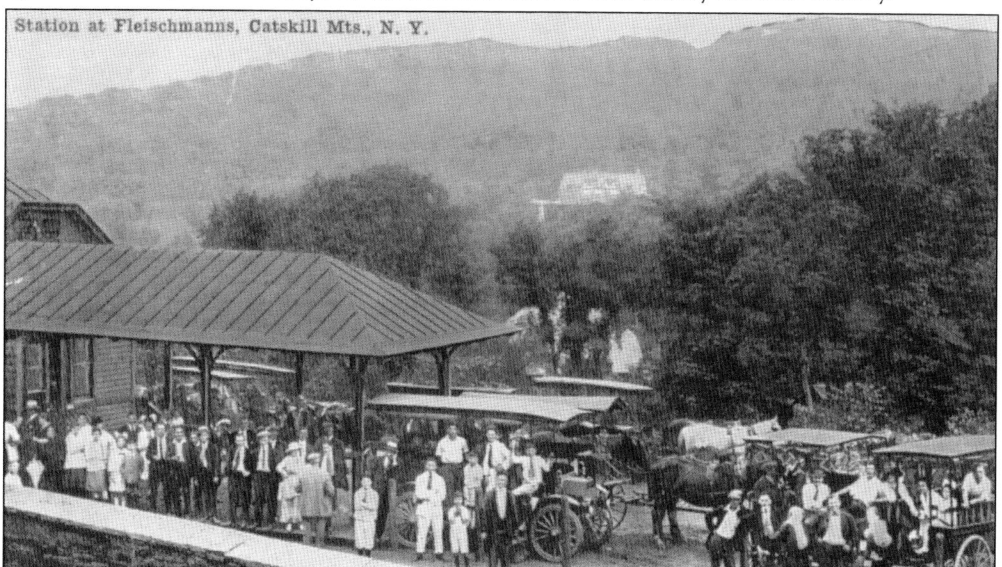

The Ulster & Delaware (U&D) Railroad first entered Delaware County at Griffin Corners (later Fleischmanns) in 1871. Because of the mountainous terrain it traversed, the U&D was swiftly nicknamed the "Up & Down." This is a view of the U&D station at Fleischmanns around 1910. Horse-drawn wagons and motorized vehicles can be seen awaiting the arrival of the train at this popular vacationing spot. Fleischmanns was one of several villages in Delaware County that saw a major boost in tourism after the completion of railroad lines in the 1870s. Hotels and boardinghouses sprang up here and in villages with easy rail connections. Visible in the background is one such hotel.

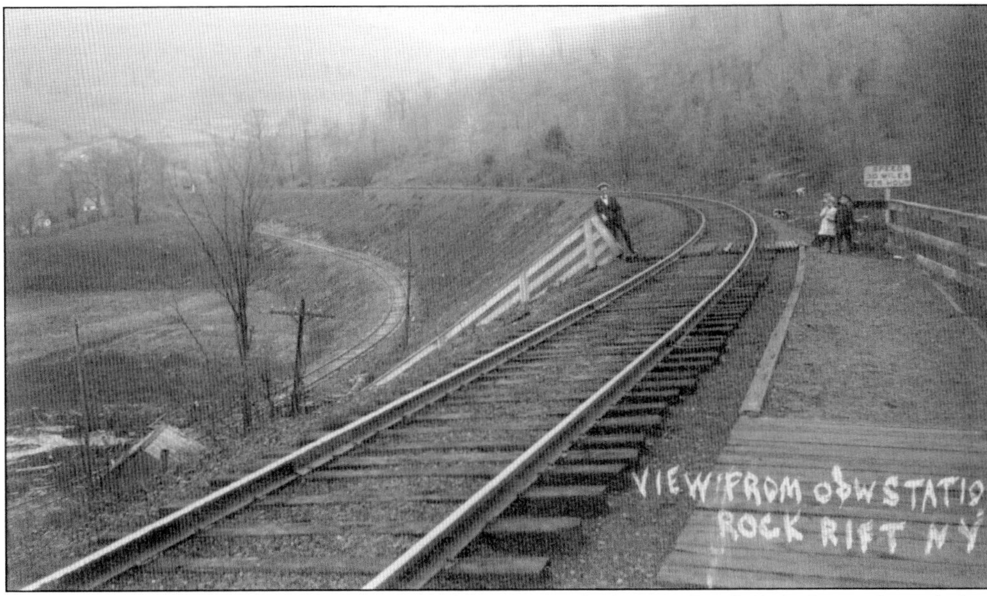

Above is a view of the O&W tracks from the station platform at Rock Rift, located just below Walton. In the mid-20th century, Rock Rift became one of Delaware County's drowned towns, when the community was submerged by the rising waters of New York City's Cannonsville Reservoir. Before the reservoir was completed in 1965, the O&W Railway had ceased to exist. North of Rock Rift and Walton along a spur line of the O&W Railway was the county seat at Delhi. Delhi, in fact, was the northern terminus of the spur, and its depot is pictured below. In the foreground at left, a railroad worker loads cargo from his freight wagon onto the wagon of a local delivery service. Behind them a coach from Delhi's Central House Hotel awaits its passengers.

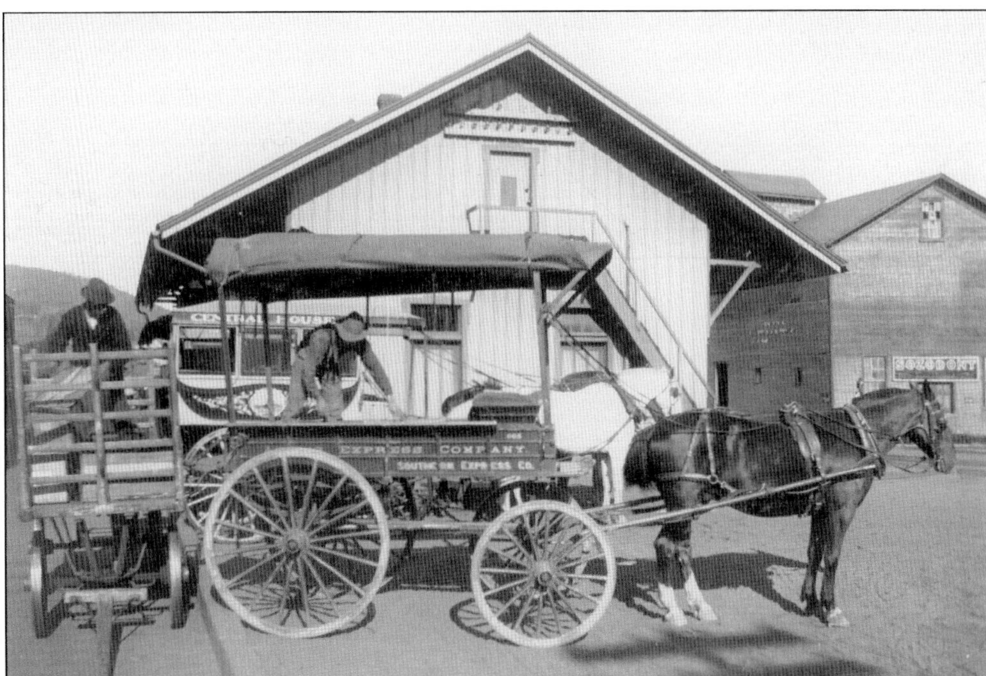

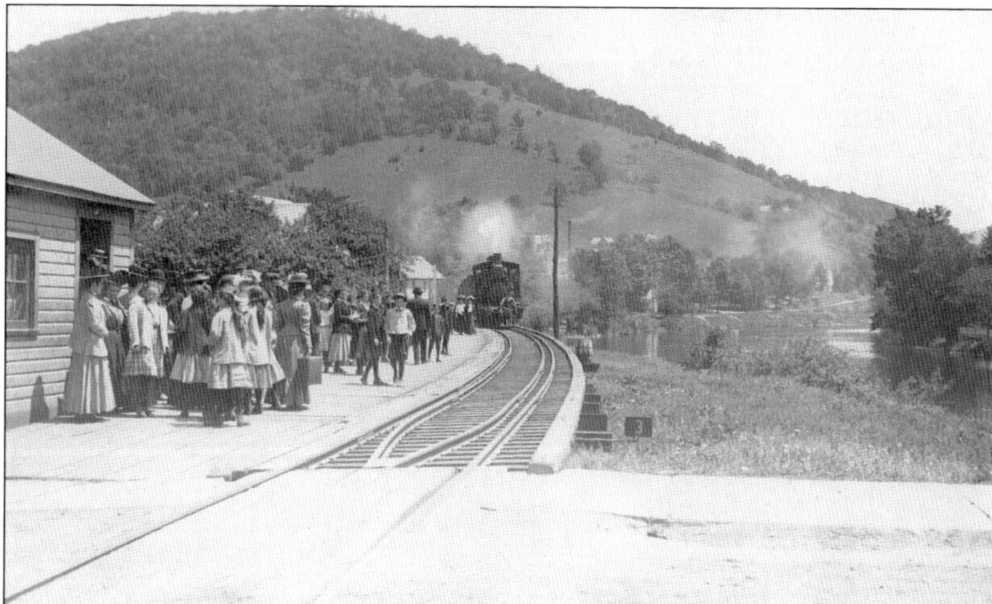
29—The O. & W. Platform Station, Walton, N. Y.

Pictured above, on a fine summer day, a southbound O&W locomotive is seen pulling into Walton station from Delhi around 1890. At right is the West Branch of the Delaware River. The spur line of the O&W split from the main branch in Walton and led northward along the river to Delhi, passing through Hamden. The c. 1910 photograph below is of the locally renowned *Utica Flyer.* As the name implies, the *Utica Flyer* sped passengers and freight on the O&W through Walton, Sidney, and Norwich and farther north toward the industrial city in the Mohawk Valley. The *Flyer* would typically depart Delhi at 7:00 a.m., arriving at Utica at 11:59 a.m. The return trip would begin from Utica at 4:35 p.m. and arrive back at the Delaware County seat at 9:25 p.m.

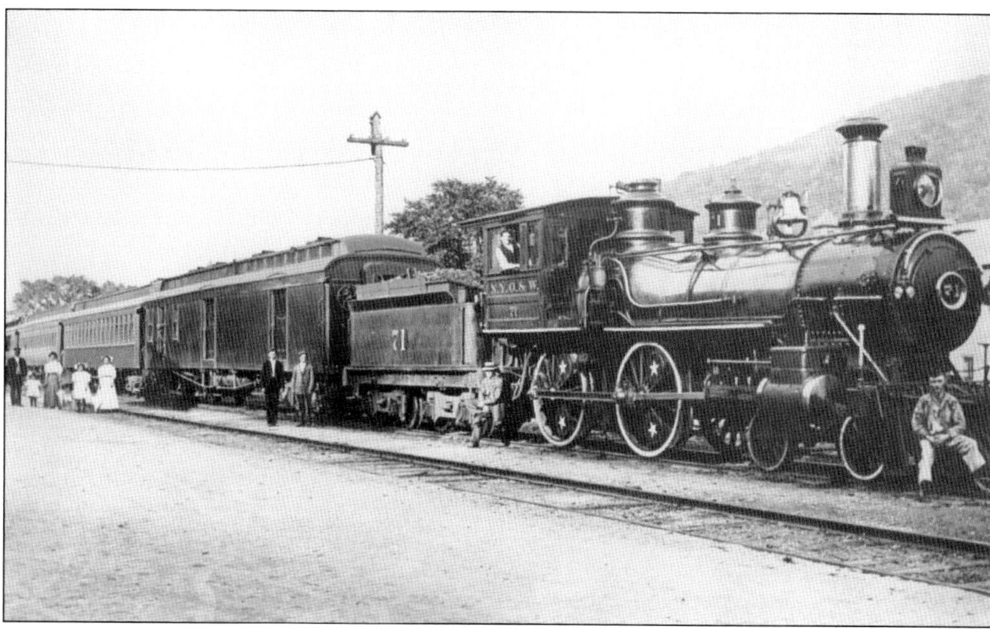

Roughly halfway between Walton and Delhi on the O&W spur line lay the rail depot at Hamden. The image above shows a passenger and freight train stopped at the Hamden station, probably sometime during the 1890s. Note the Borden's Creamery building at left. Below is an early-20th-century view of workers at the Borden's Creamery at Pepacton, town of Colchester. The tracks visible in this image belonged to the short-lived Delaware & Northern Railroad. Not only did the railroads give rise to a tourist industry, but so too, after the 1870s, to a huge increase in the region's dairy production. Creameries such as these popped up alongside tracks throughout the Catskills. Early morning "milk trains" sped milk loaded at such creameries to thirsty urbanites.

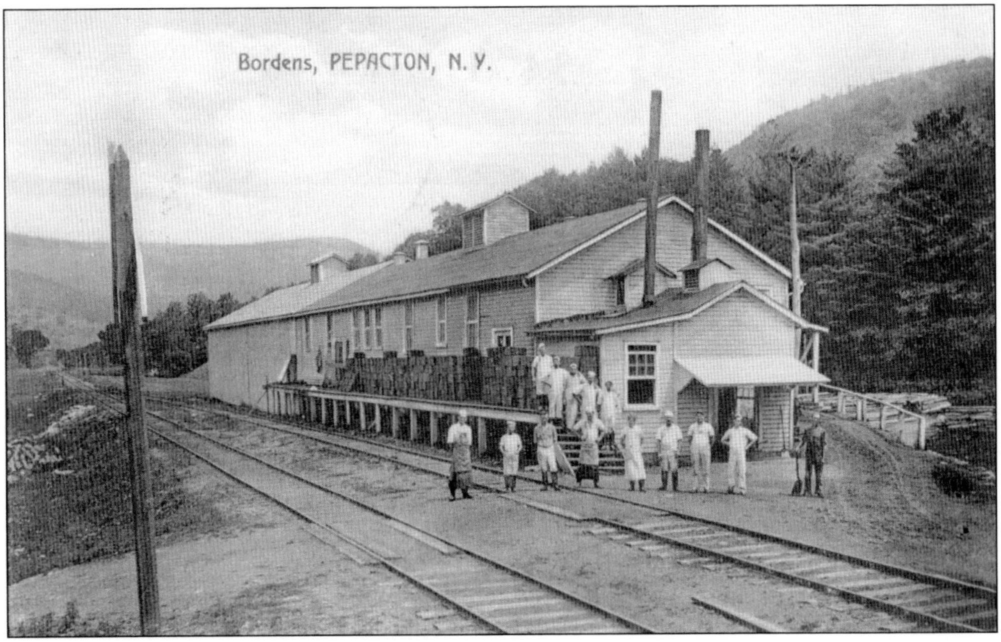

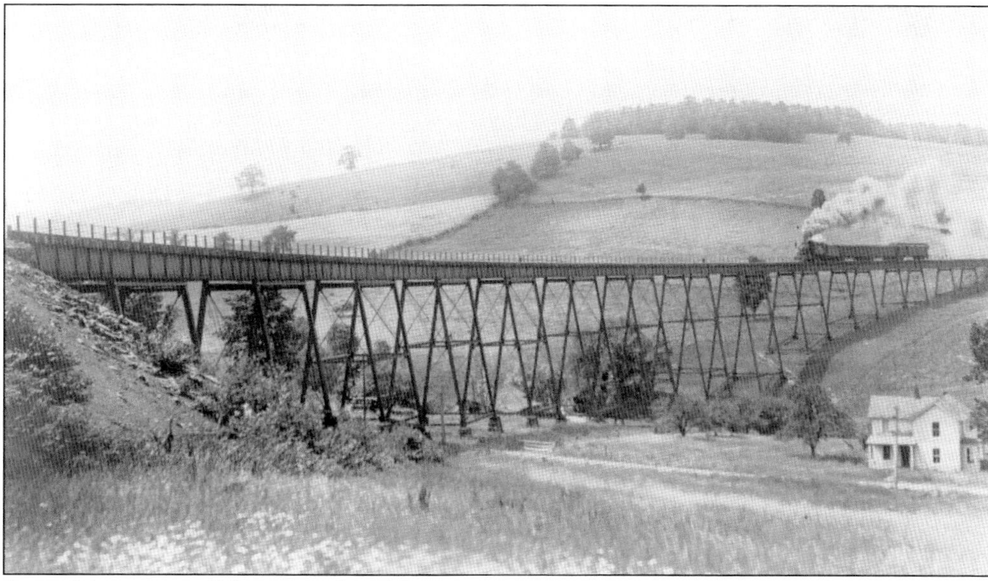

One of the more well-known railroad features in Delaware County, the trestle at Sidney Center (Maywood) in the town of Sidney was actually two trestles that spanned the valley and skirted the hamlet below. Located along the main O&W line, the trestles were originally built in 1871 entirely of wood. In 1898, they were replaced with spans made of iron. During World War I, to prevent an enemy attack, the trestles were guarded by soldiers. The trestles are now gone, demolished in 1961, but the Maywood Train Depot Museum remains at the site.

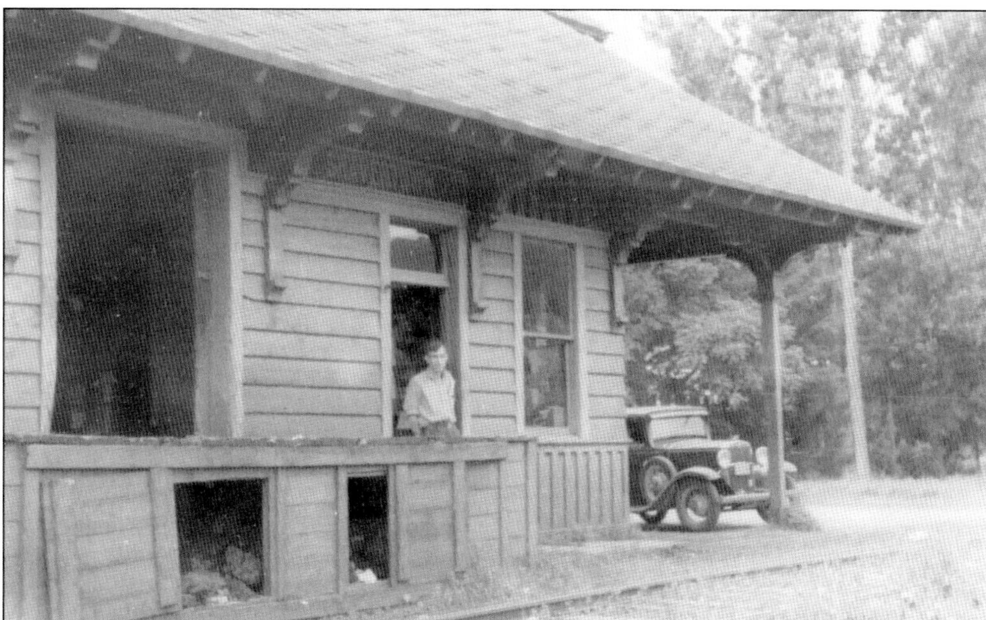

This is a 1930s view of the Delaware & Northern train station at Shavertown in the town of Andes. This site, alas, has also since vanished. The depot, along with the entire community of Shavertown, was submerged by the rising waters of the Pepacton Reservoir in the 1950s.

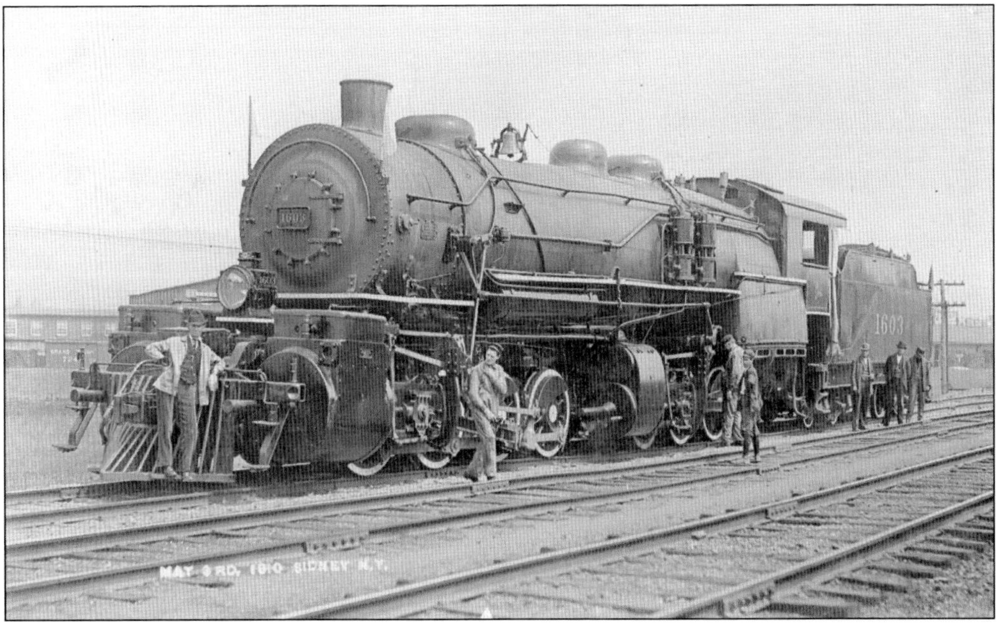

Above, a locomotive is seen on the tracks in Sidney, New York, in May 1910. The village of Sidney has for some time been the largest and most industrial community in Delaware County. Much of the growth of the village had to do with the construction of two rail lines that once crossed here. In 1866, the Albany & Susquehanna began service to the village, connecting Sidney to Albany in the east and Binghamton to the west. This line eventually came to be known as the Delaware & Hudson. In 1873, the Ontario & Western was completed, and Sidney became a railroad hub, attracting businesses because of its proximity to the tracks. Below is the new passenger depot at Sidney in 1913.

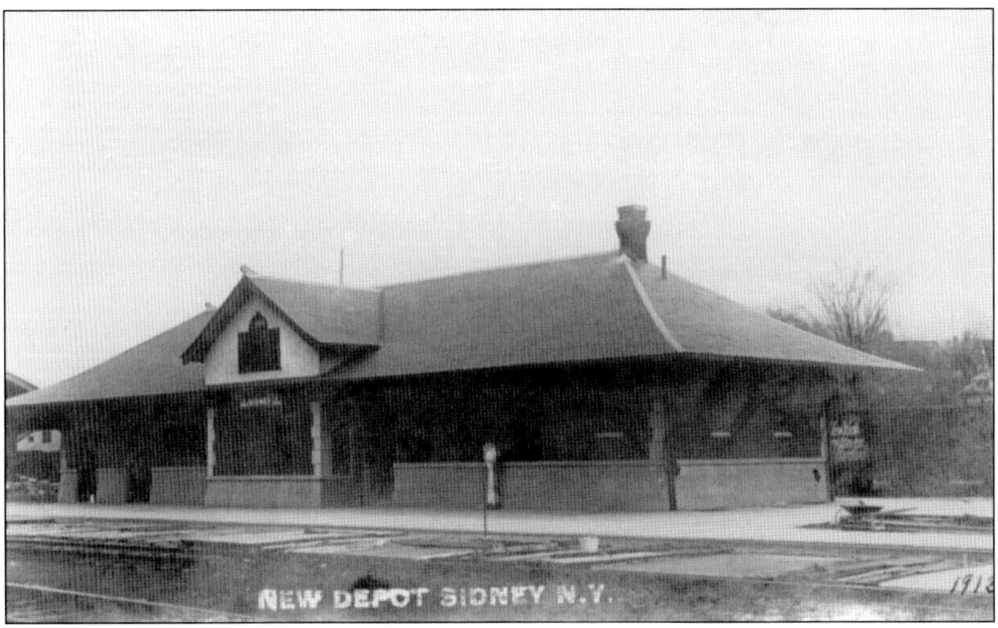

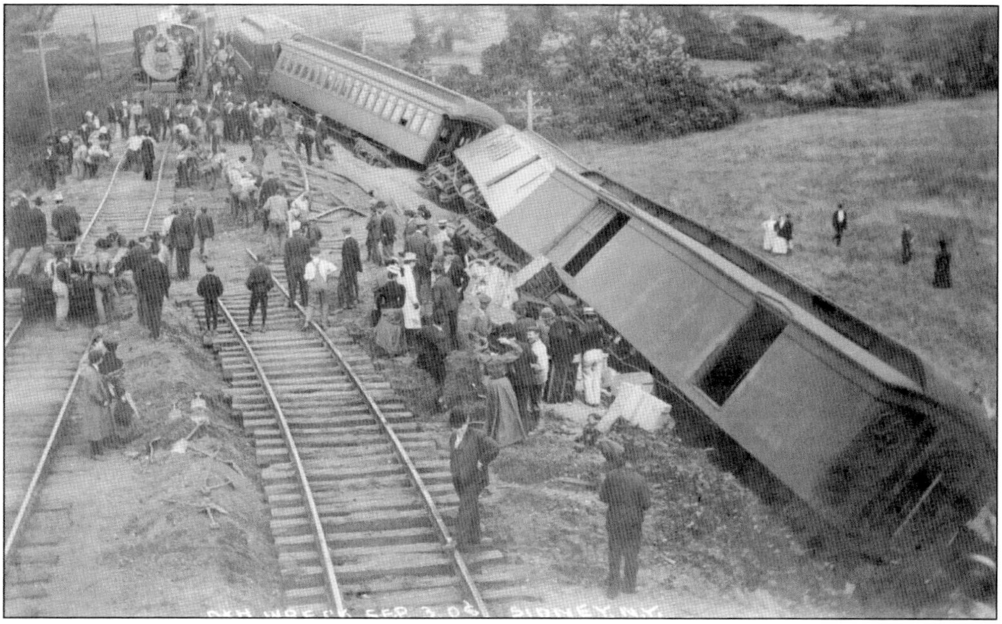

Trains provided an enormous boost to Delaware County's economy during the second half of the 19th century and into the early years of the 20th century. In addition to those industrial concerns popping up in communities such as Sidney, railroads allowed people easier access to the fresh air and water of the countryside, prompting a veritable boom in tourism. Additionally, regular and swift transport to towns and cities enabled farmers to ship their milk directly to urban consumers. However, not all was so rosy. As these two images highlight, things sometimes went horribly wrong on the county's railroad tracks. Above, a serious train wreck along the Delaware & Hudson Railroad in Sidney occurred on September 3, 1908. Below, another serious incident is depicted; this time, it was a head-on collision on the D&H in Sidney on October 18, 1922.

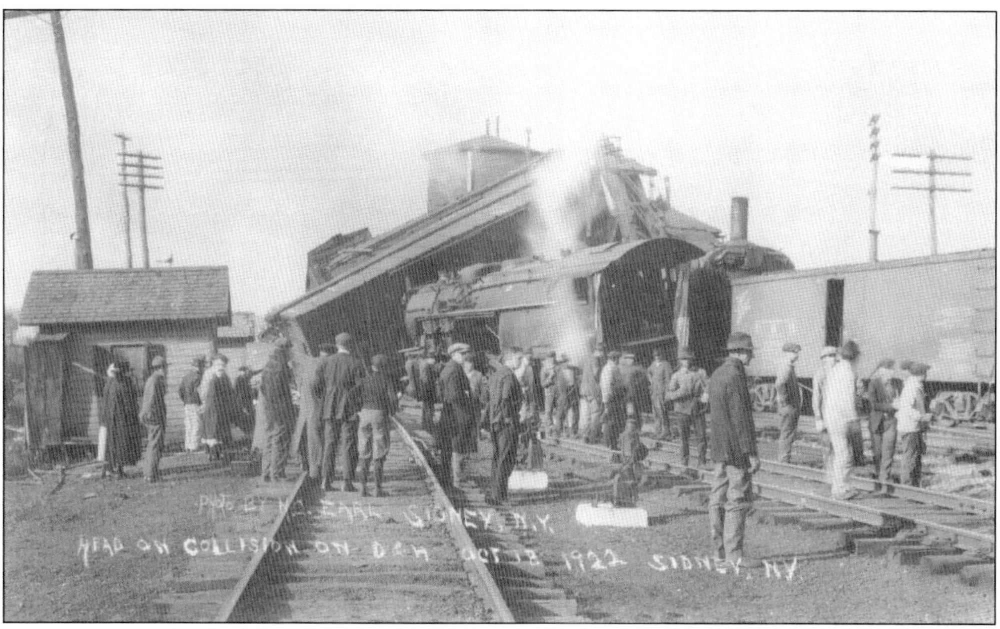

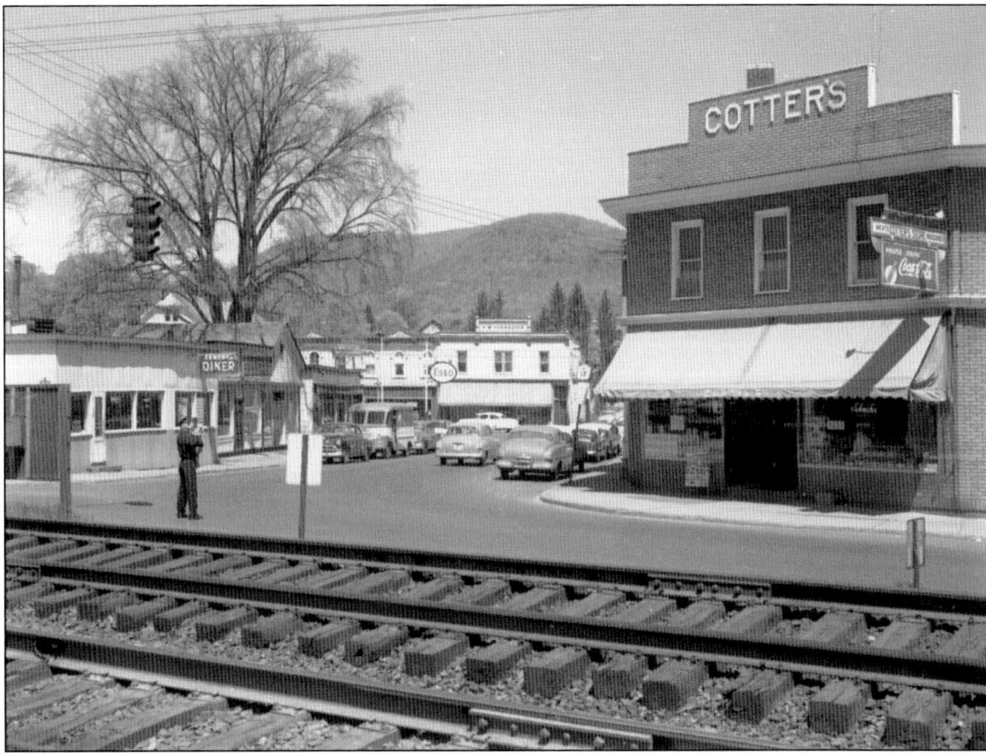

Above, the tracks of the NY&E are passing directly through downtown Hancock in the 1950s. After World War II the region's railroading days would prove numbered. A brief reprieve was earned by the O&W, the U&D, and other rail lines due to an increase in wartime orders from the federal government, but when peacetime returned, the railroads quickly fell into disuse, victims of the gasoline-powered cars and trucks and better roads of the era. Below, an earlier scene depicts an automobile pulled up in snowy weather at the O&W depot in Delhi. Railroads were still king when this photograph was taken in 1917 but would not remain so for long.

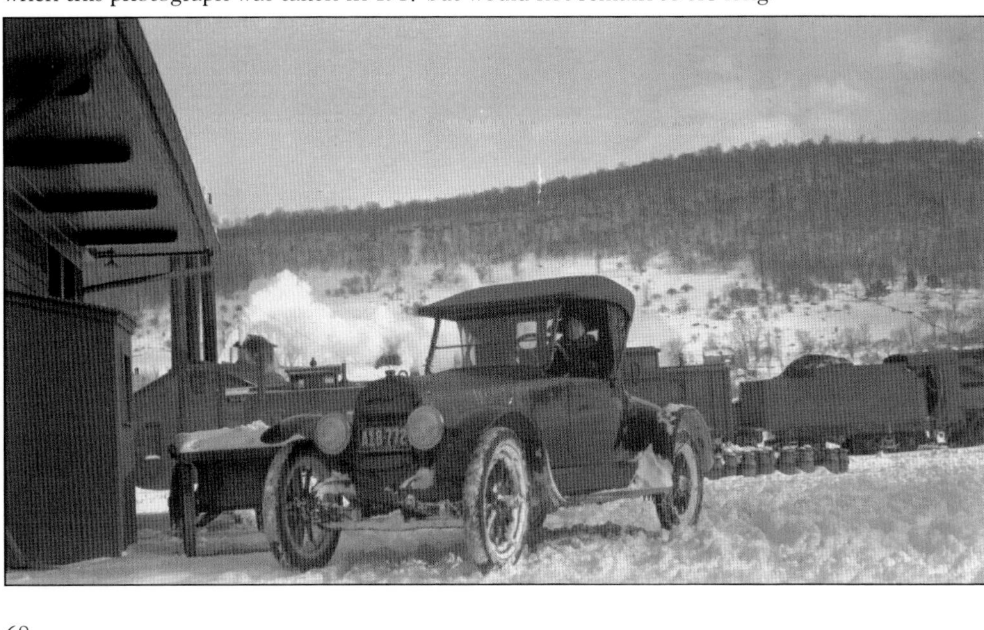

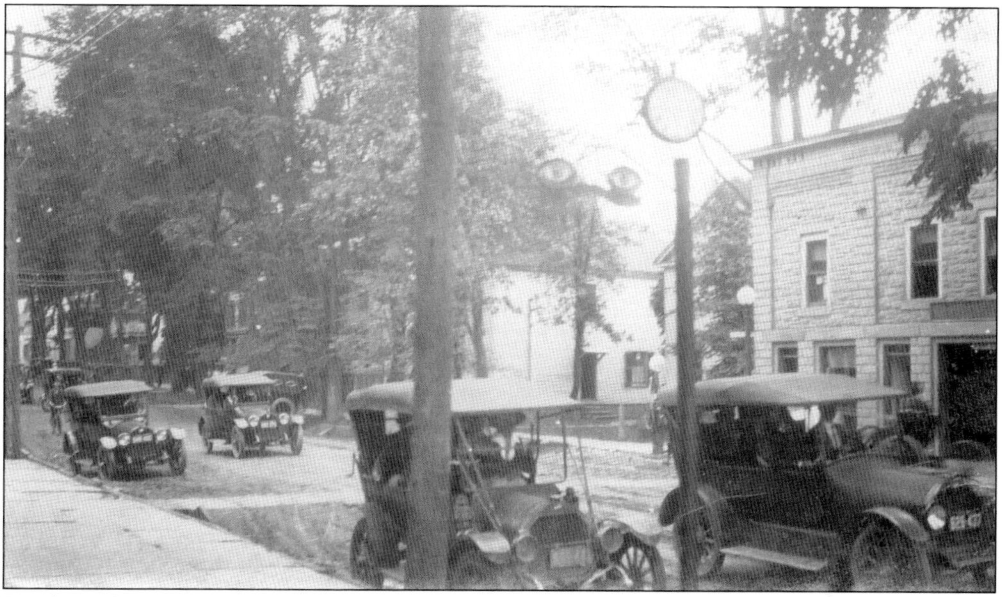

Roads in the county remained, for the most part, in terrible condition until well into the 20th century as the two photographs here, both depicting Delhi's Main Street, clearly show. Not until the end of the 1910s would Main Street become a hard-topped road. Above, early automobiles are seen on Main Street in Delhi around 1918. Note the single gas pump in rear on the far side of street. Below, an early version of a pickup truck with a load of pipes is pictured in 1915. The building in the background is clearly recognizable as the current home of the Delhi Telephone Company.

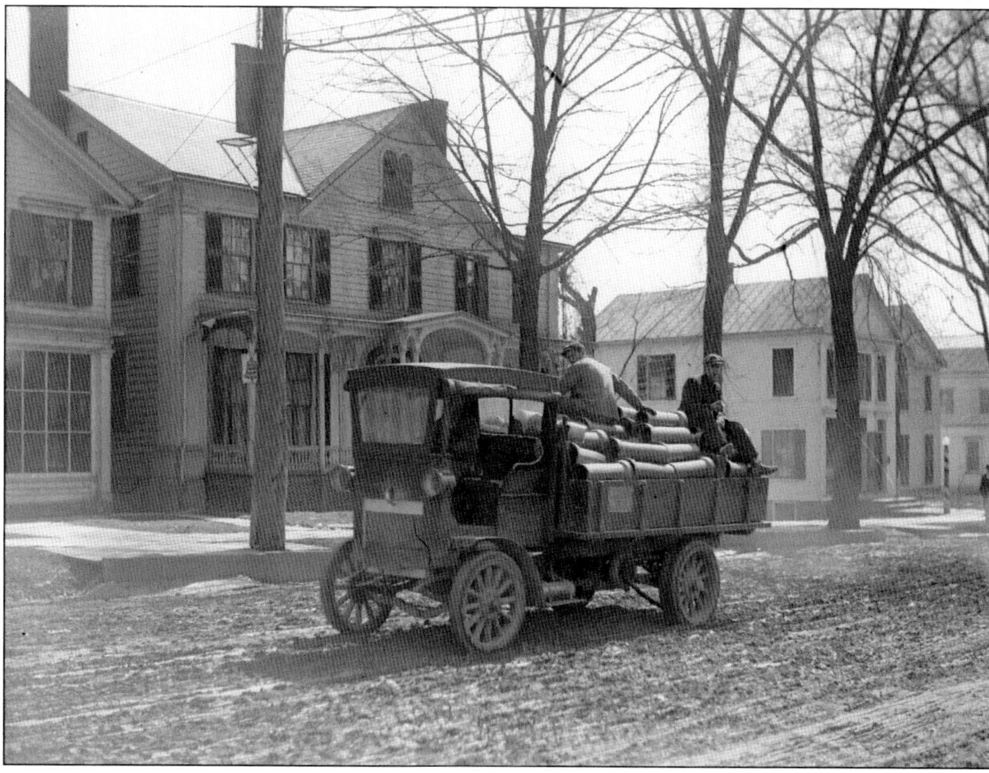

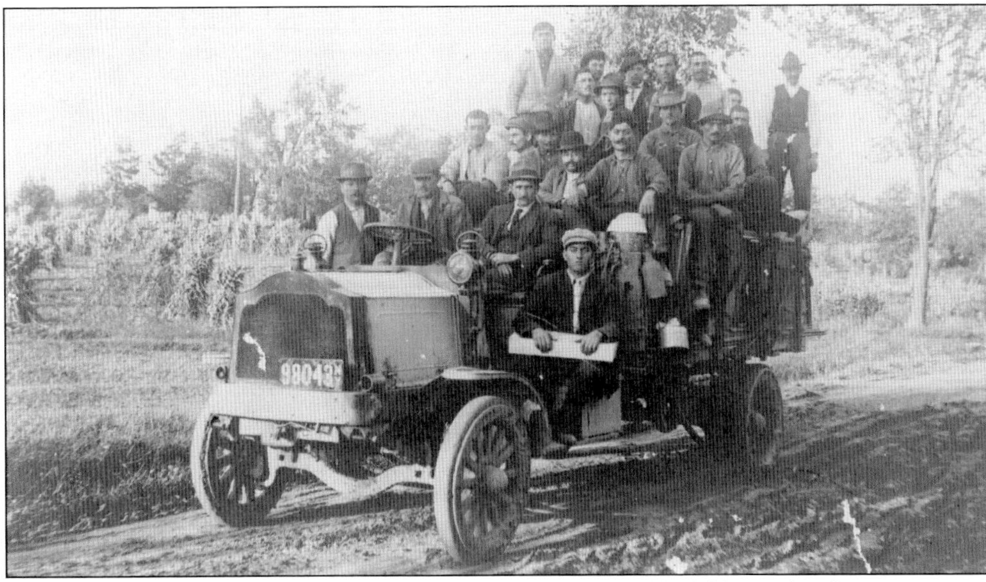

The advent of the automobile as a viable and increasingly affordable mode of conveyance in the first decade of the 20th century, coupled with the needs of the rural postal delivery service, spurred a major effort to improve the region's roads. After 1907, with help from both state and federal sources, the Delaware County Board of Supervisors voted consistently to allot money to improve the roads. Pictured above is a 1912 "concrete gang" setting out for a day's work. Road workers, many of them Italians, were employed by the state and local governments to improve roads throughout upstate New York, including here in Delaware County. Numerous newspaper accounts reported on feelings of distrust and tension between the Italians and Delaware County's native population of predominantly northern European extraction and Protestant faith. Below is a "roller gang" sometime between 1905 and 1915.

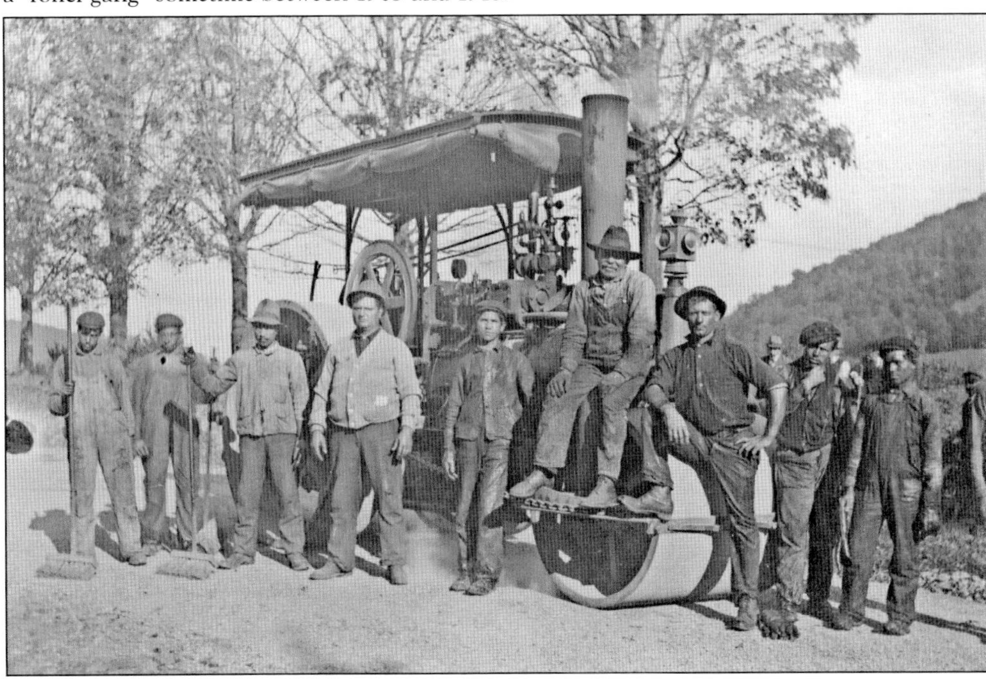

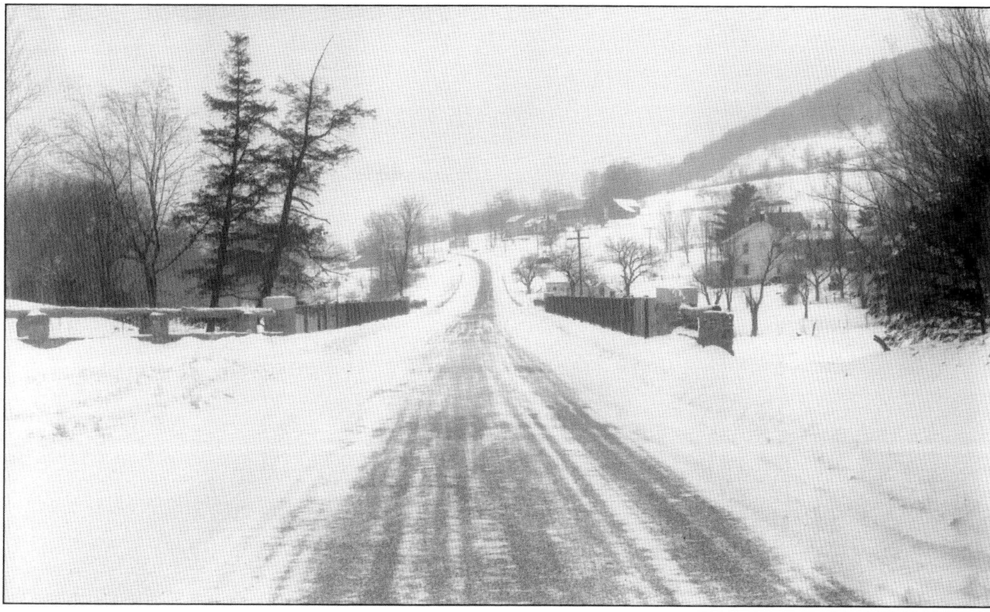

As a result of those efforts in the 1900s and 1910s and the importation of workers from outside the region, by the 1920s and 1930s, Delaware County had a vastly expanded network of good roads, even passable in midwinter, as the photograph above shows. In 1922, a concrete road was completed between Andes and Margaretville, and by the summer of 1923, work had been completed on a new hard-topped road between Delhi and Walton. By 1928, Delaware County boasted 229 miles of state road and 2,120 miles of total roads. Despite these improvements, in very snowy weather it was still difficult to move around in the Catskill Mountains. The scene below depicts a truck fitted with a snow plow in 1917. Note the horse and wagons in rear.

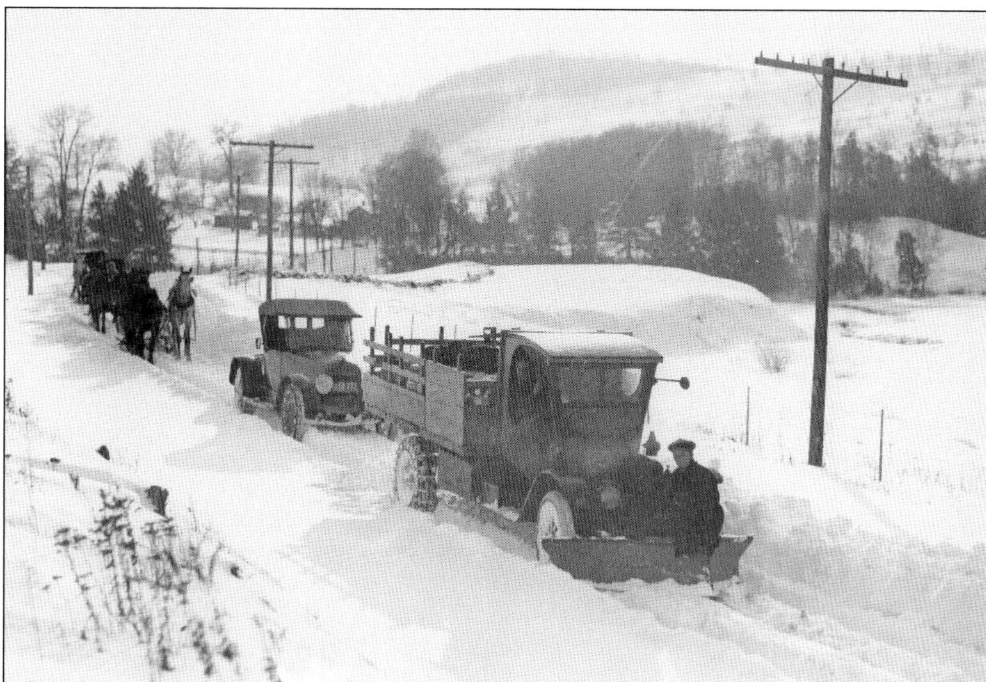

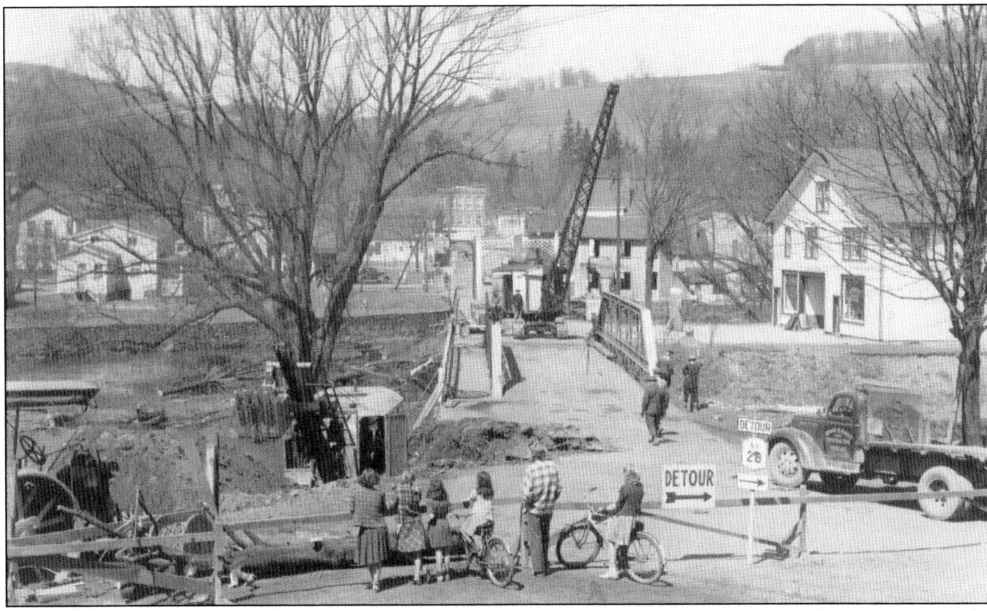

Above, Kingston Street Bridge is seen under construction in Delhi on November 19, 1940. The bridge carrying State Highway 28 over the West Branch of the Delaware River was demolished and then replaced between 1940 and 1941. Because of its upland terrain, over the course of most of its history Delaware County has remained a relatively difficult place to get in and out of. Difficulty of travel was ameliorated somewhat in the first two or three decades of the 20th century with the completion of state roads such as Route 28, Route 10, and others. More recently still, in the 1960s travel became even more convenient with completion of Route 17 ("the Quickway") through the extreme southern section of the county. A portion of the new highway can be seen in the photograph below. In the late 1970s and early 1980s, in the far northwest of the county, Interstate 88 was completed through the town of Sidney. Interstate 88 allows for rapid car and truck travel between Albany and Binghamton. (Below, photograph by Bob Wyer.)

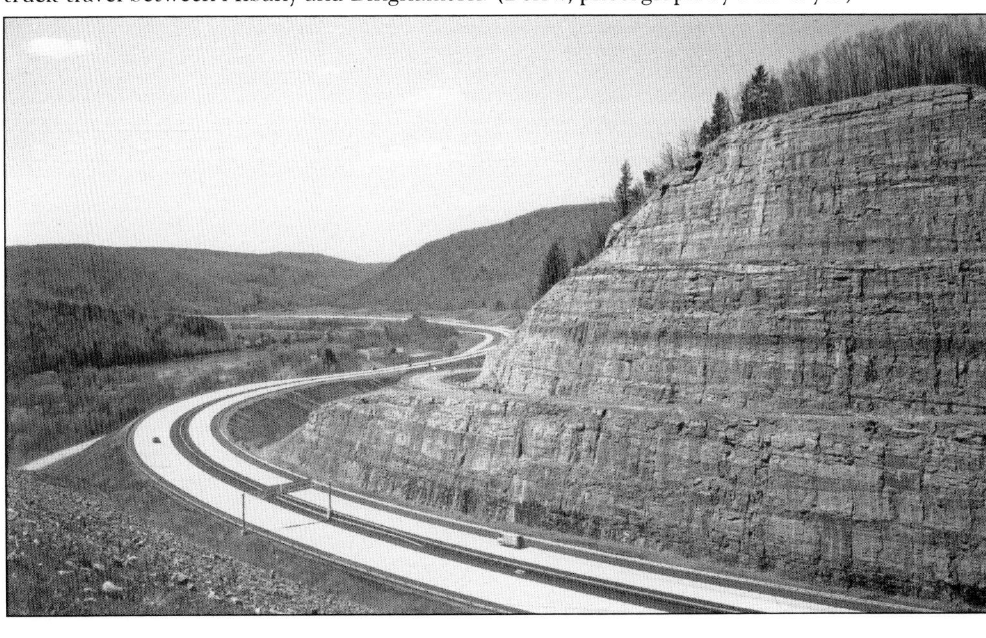

Four

Business and Industry

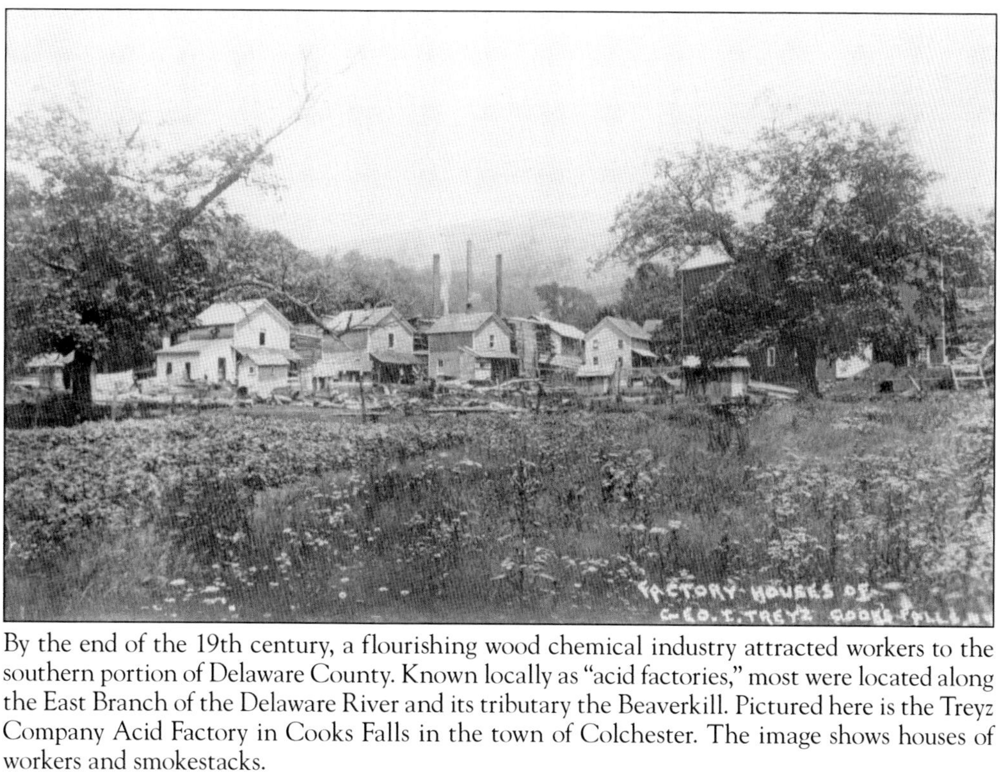

By the end of the 19th century, a flourishing wood chemical industry attracted workers to the southern portion of Delaware County. Known locally as "acid factories," most were located along the East Branch of the Delaware River and its tributary the Beaverkill. Pictured here is the Treyz Company Acid Factory in Cooks Falls in the town of Colchester. The image shows houses of workers and smokestacks.

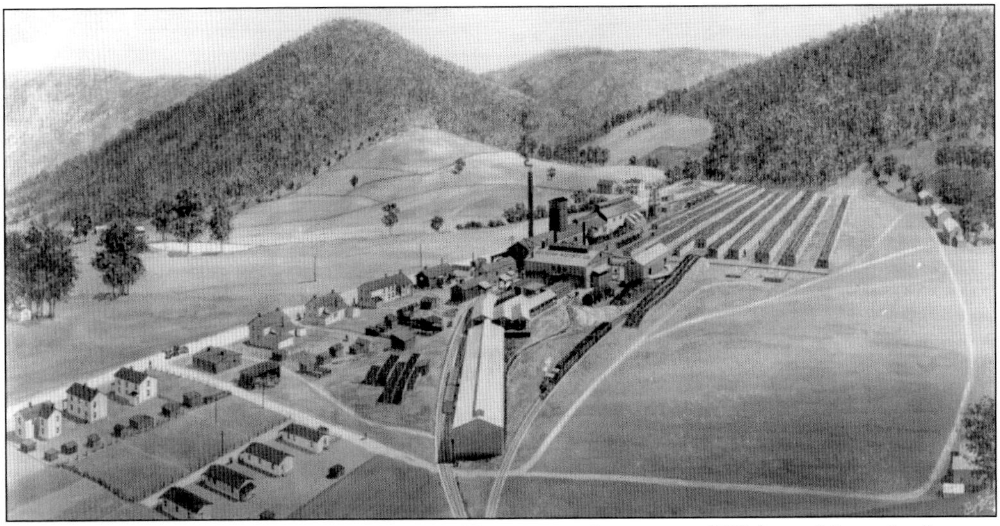

A print shows the busy Beerston Acetate Factory in the town of Walton. Note the houses provided for the plant's workers at lower left and the cords of wood at upper right. The factory was located below the village of Walton close to the West Branch of the Delaware River and along the Ontario & Western rail line.

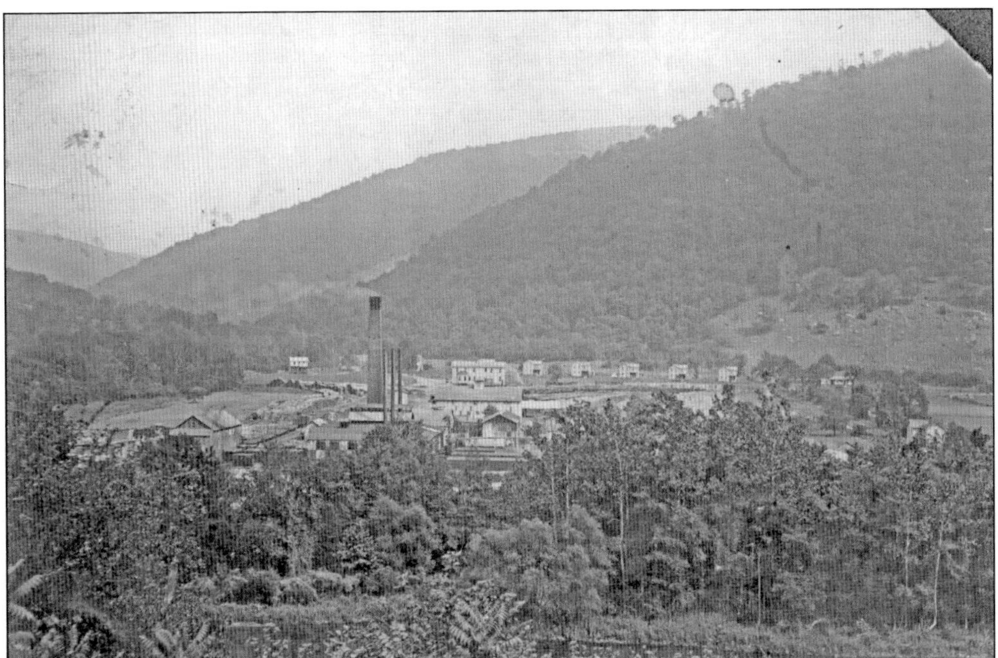

A panoramic view of the acid factory in Corbett, in the town of Colchester, with its smokestacks and piles of wood waiting to be consumed, is clearly visible. Note the houses for workers at upper right and the rail tracks of the Delaware & Northern at left. At far right can be seen the beginnings of a hillside denuded of its trees. The wood chemical industry produced products such as wood alcohol, creosote, charcoal, and formaldehyde.

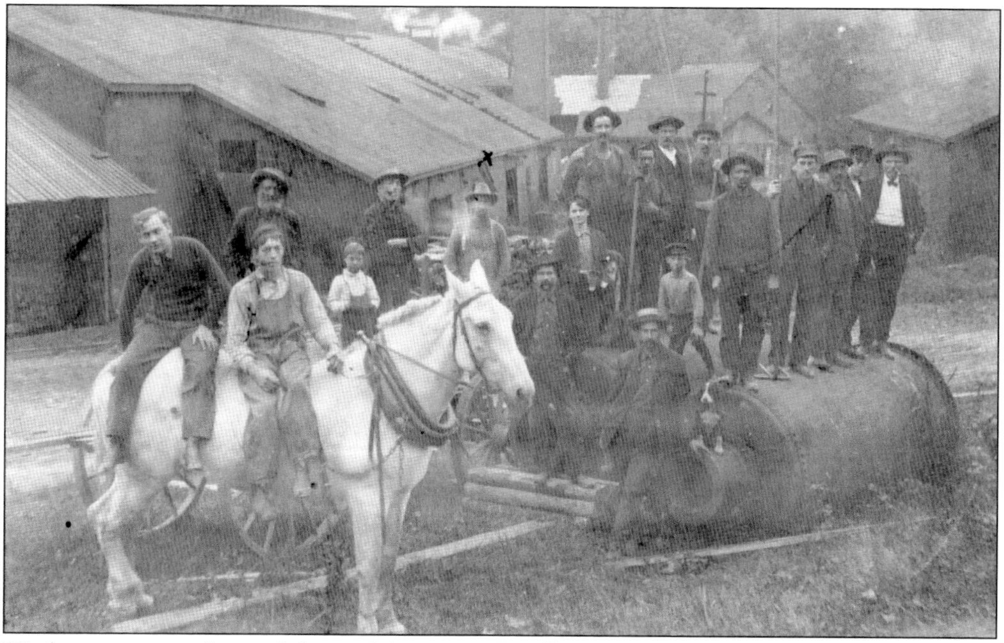

Workers posing in front of the acid factory in Readburn in the town of Hancock. This image appears to show the presence of at least two child workers. The wood chemical industry required enormous quantities of hardwood and water. Thus, Delaware County was an ideal location. Several communities in the region owe their names to the industry: Acidalia, Burnwood, and Methol.

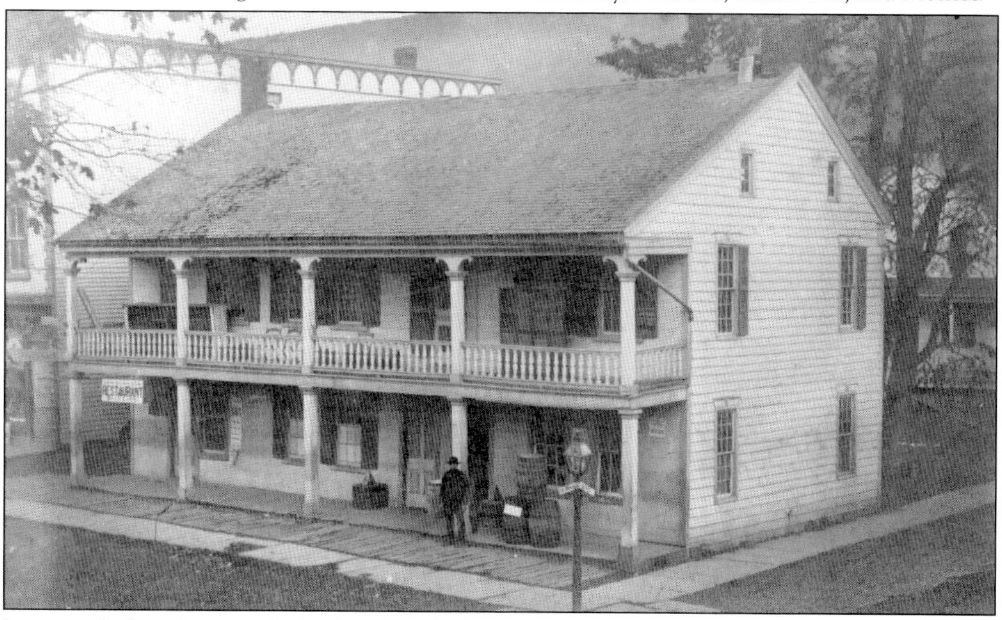

In an era before the arrival of railroads in Delaware County and the invention of the automobile, travel was painfully slow. Hotels and taverns thus played an important role in the daily lives of rural dwellers here and elsewhere; they provided places for weary travelers to eat and sleep. Here is an early view of Smith's Tavern in the village of Walton in 1856. The sign out front advertises the establishment as a restaurant, offering fresh oysters and clams. Smith's Tavern offered rooms on the upper floors.

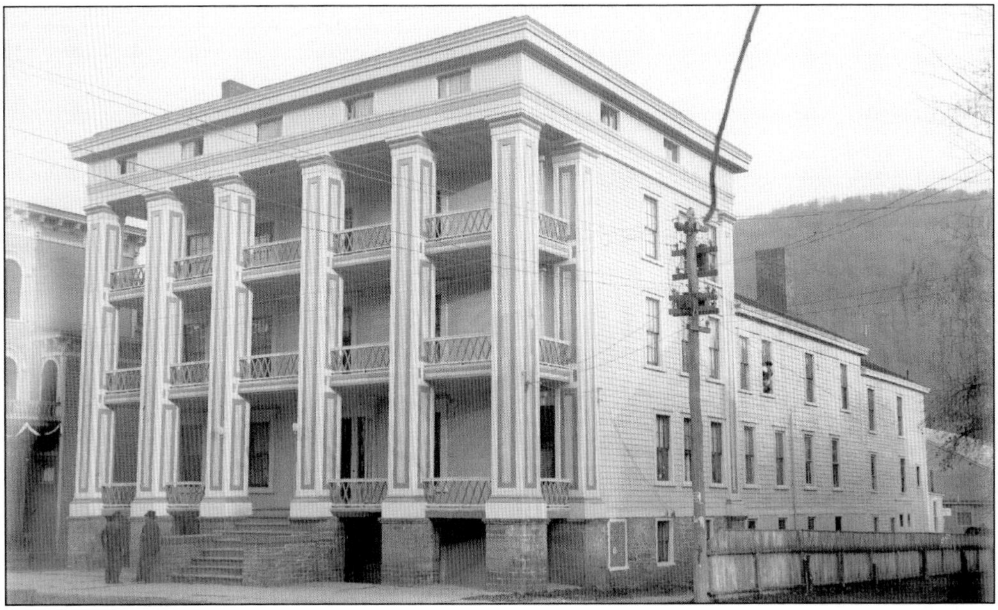

The Edgerton Hotel, located on Main Street in the village of Delhi, is seen around 1890. The hotel was owned and operated by numerous people over the years, but it retained the name "the Edgerton House" for most of its existence. Owners included a Mr. Griffis, John Dodds, and Marshall Arbuckle. In 1921, the hotel was briefly owned by L.D. Whitlock. In March 1928, a foreclosure sale was held, and in December 1928, Wilson Brothers started tearing down the structure.

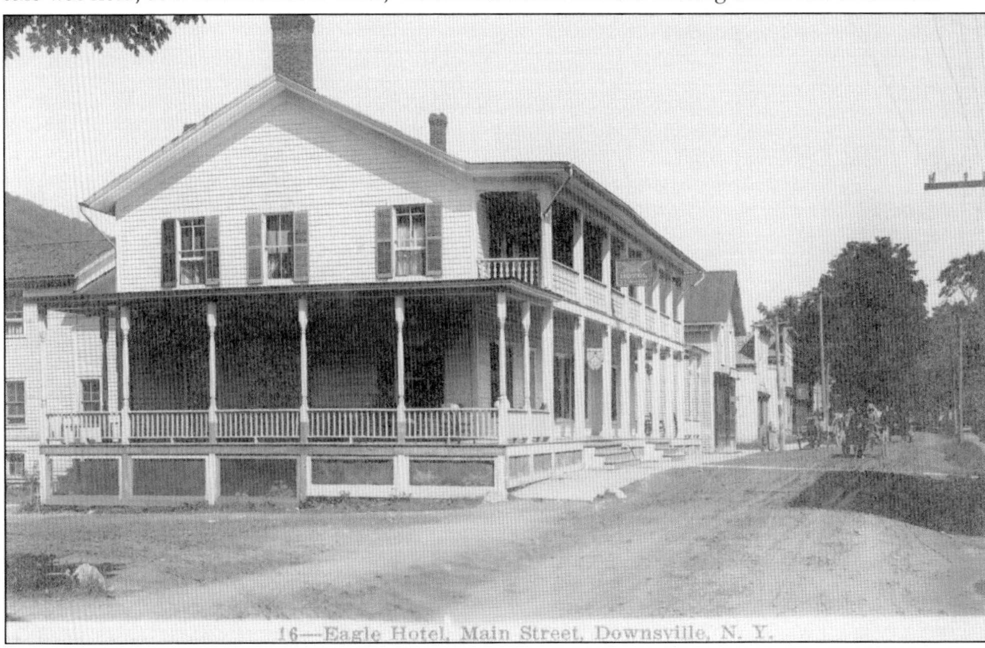

This is a view of the Eagle Hotel in Downsville in the town of Colchester. From the sign, one can ascertain that the proprietor of this 1890s image is E.T. Smith. Note the unpaved, rough nature of the road. The Eagle Hotel operated in Downsville until well into the 20th century. The business received a major boost in 1906 with the completion of the Delaware & Northern Railroad through the hamlet.

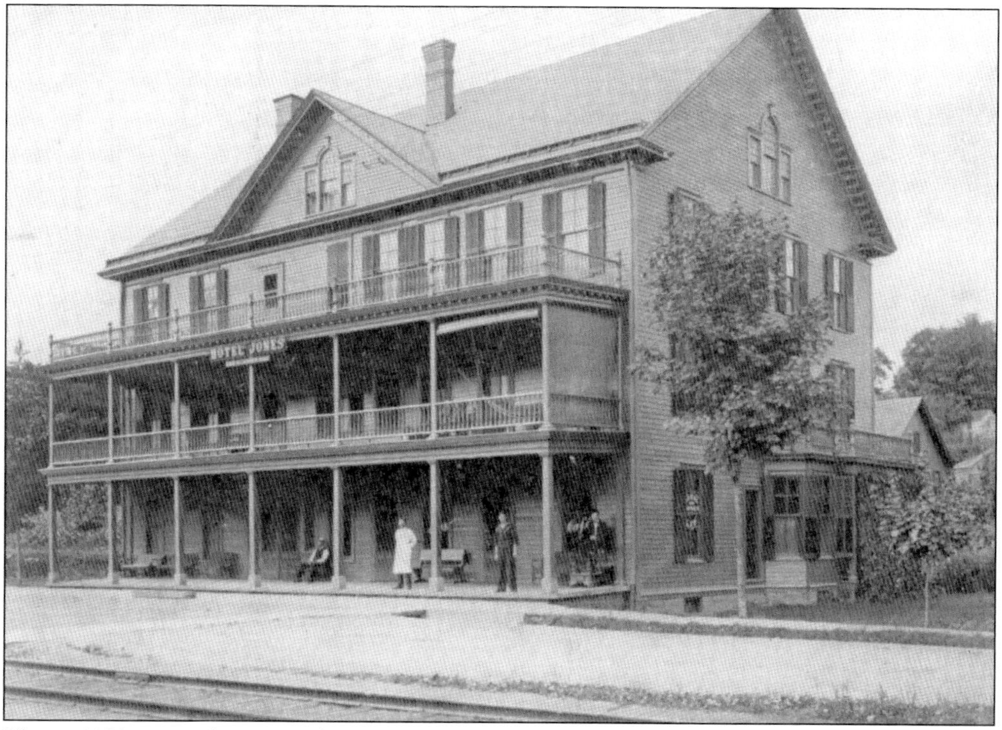

This c. 1900 image shows Hotel Jones in the village of Hancock. Note the tracks of the New York & Erie Railroad in the foreground. Hotels such as this one flourished in Delaware County after the arrival of the railroads. For the community of Hancock, this occurred somewhat earlier than the rest of the county, for the New York & Erie came through the village in 1848. During the 1860s, Hancock was an important embarkation point for soldiers leaving to fight in the Civil War.

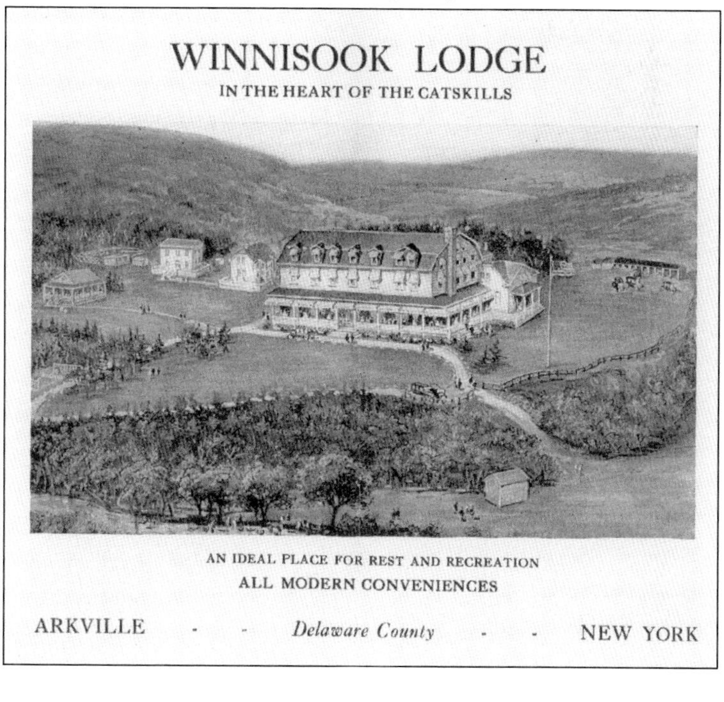

As stated in this early-20th-century advertisement, Winnisook Lodge was not only in the community of Arkville, town of Middletown, but also "in the Heart of the Catskills." Communities such as Arkville were reached by the railroads during the 1870s, specifically by the Ulster & Delaware in September 1871. The railroads and later the automobile proved the catalyst for a major Catskills tourism boom.

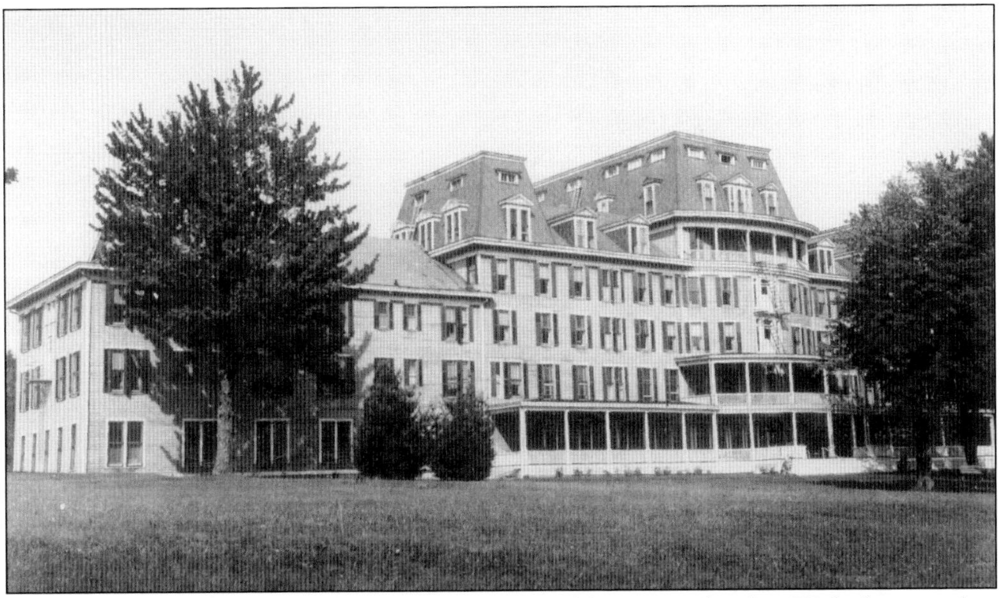

The venerable Rexmere Hotel in Stamford is pictured here in its heyday. With the arrival in Stamford of the Ulster & Delaware Railroad in 1872, the village soon became known as the "Queen of the Catskills." Largely the result of the energy of one man, Dr. S.E. Churchill, by 1905, there were 32 hotels in the community. Sadly, the Rexmere building, long used as an educational center, burned to the ground in March 2014.

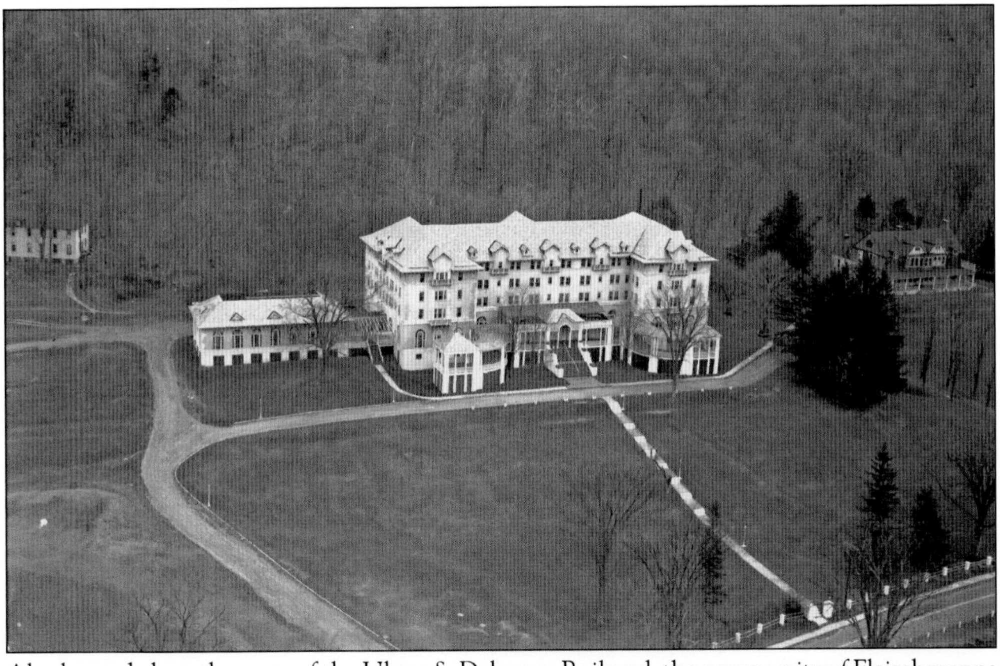

Also located along the route of the Ulster & Delaware Railroad, the community of Fleischmanns in the town of Middletown experienced its own tourism boom beginning in the 1870s. The Takanassee Hotel, shown here from the air in the mid-20th century, was one establishment built to accommodate the throngs of summer visitors to Fleischmanns. The hotel could accommodate up to 300 guests.

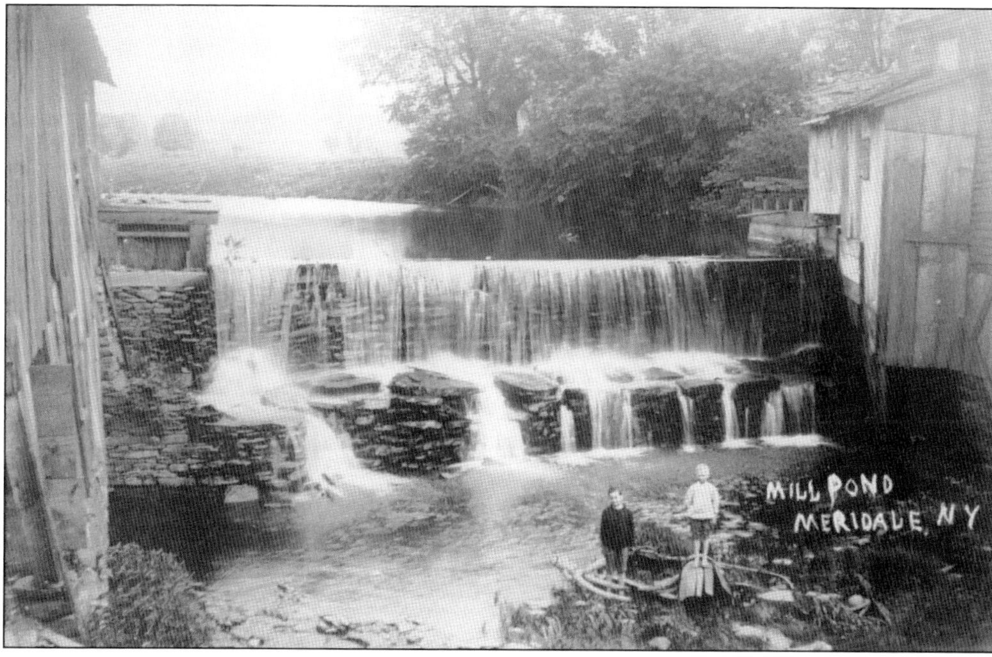

An early-20th-century view shows the upper millpond and millrace in the heart of the small hamlet of Meridale in the town of Meredith. Bruce Bouton and Ruez Bisbee are the two boys pictured in the foreground. Water-powered sawmills and gristmills were once a common sight in Delaware County and local residents often dammed streams and rivers to provide the power necessary for the machinery.

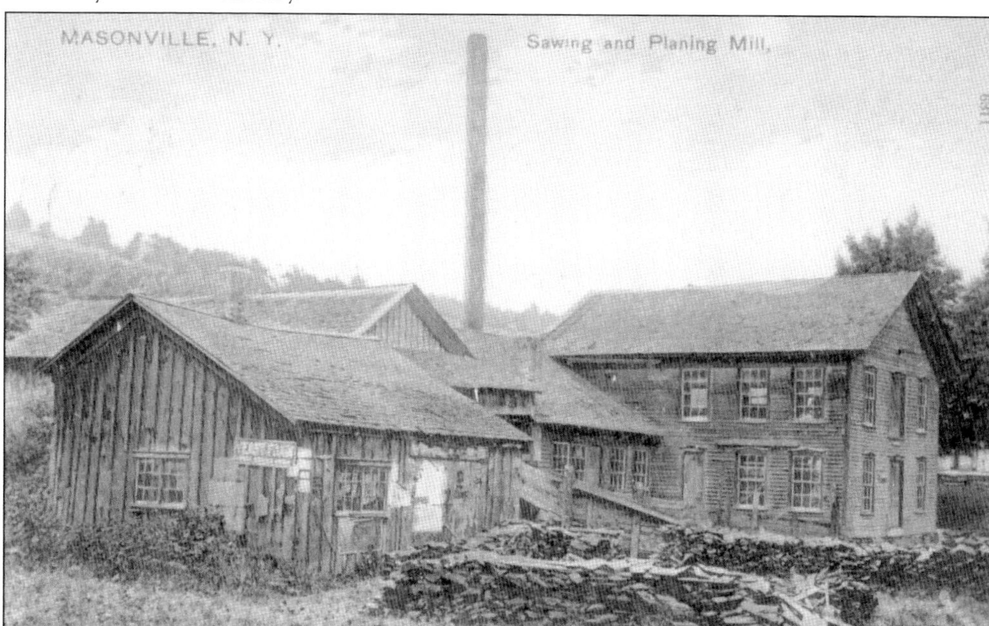

This is a sawing and planing mill in Masonville. Water-powered sawmills in Delaware County numbered some 54 in 1820 and over 160 by 1860. The following decade it was estimated that a full quarter of the industrial workforce was employed in sawmills.

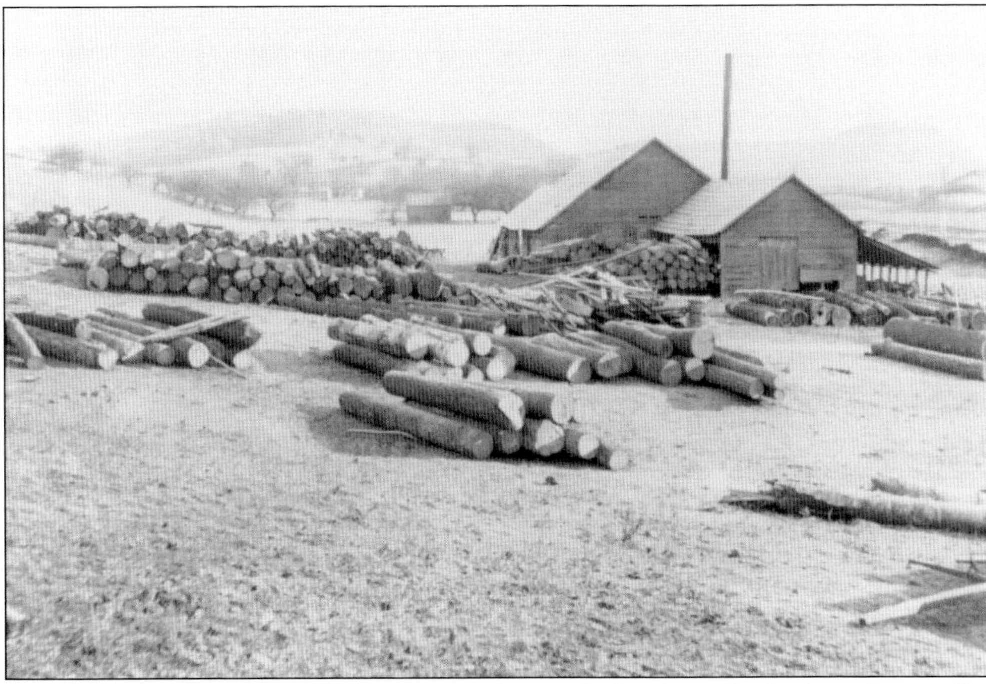

Depicted here in this mid-20th-century view are logs stacked in the yard at Lockwood's sawmill in West Davenport. The number of water-powered mills reached their zenith in 1870 but thereafter declined, largely due to having reached the limits of their efficiency. By the 20th century, mills such as this one were using some combination of water and steam to power their machines.

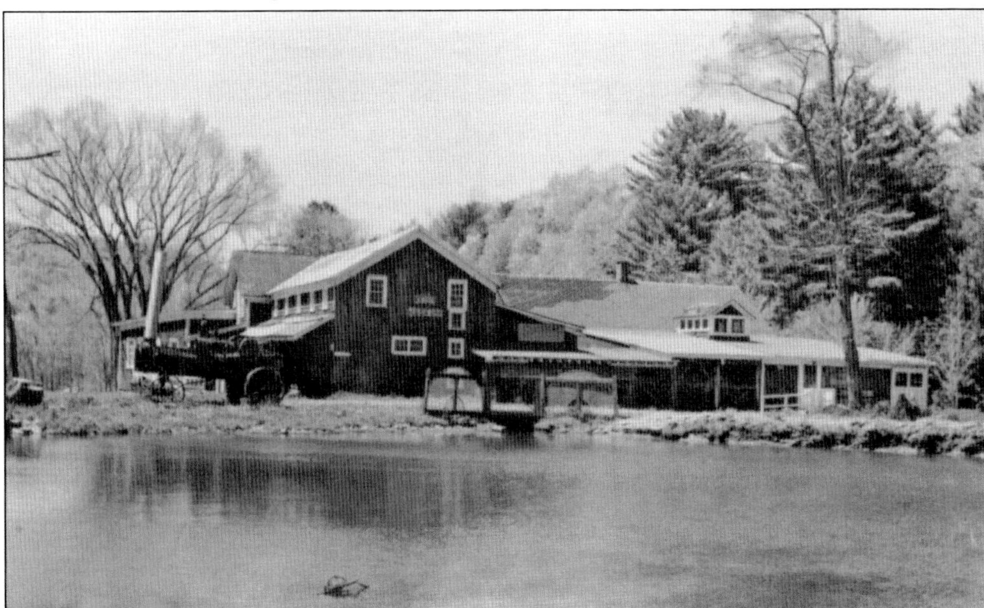

This East Meredith sawmill, in operation since 1846, was owned and operated for many years by the Hanford family. The mill was powered by the nearby Kortright Creek and then by steam and gasoline engines. By the end of the 19th century, the mill sat immediately adjacent to the tracks of the Ulster & Delaware Railroad. The mill is still in operation today as Hanford Mills Museum.

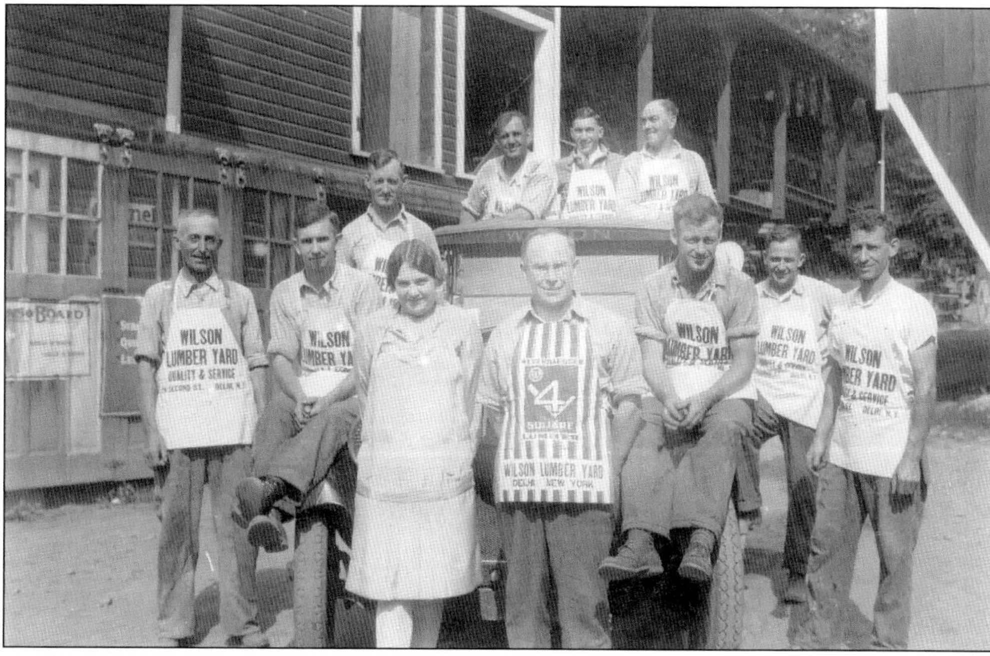

Workers pose around a company delivery truck at Wilson Lumber Yard in Delhi. Located along Second Street opposite the Baptist church, the remnants of this once thriving business can still be seen in old foundations. Pictured in front of the truck are, from left to right, Edna Elliot, Bob Wilson, and Charlie Elliot.

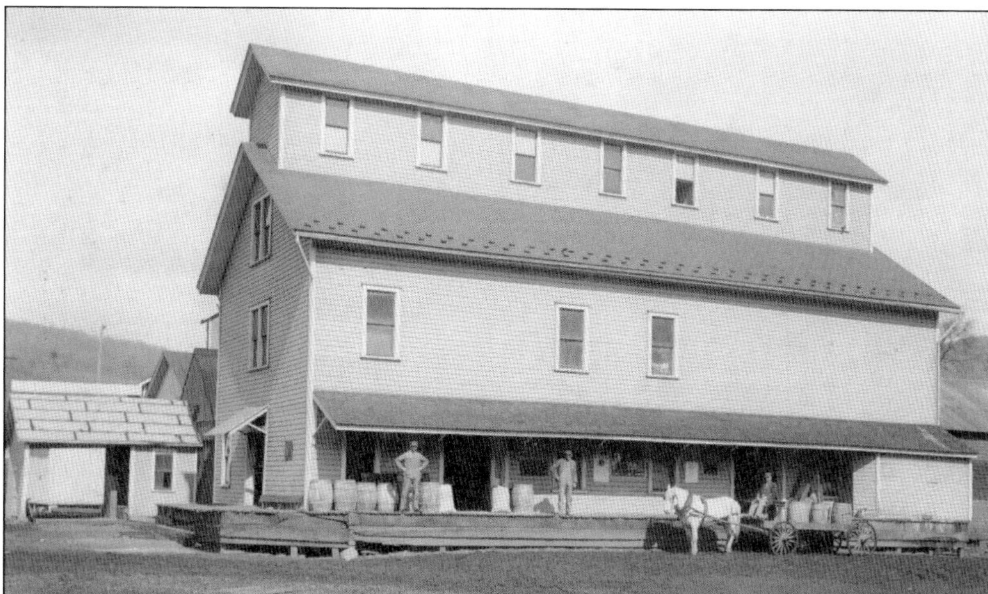

Here is a late-19th-century view of the Smith and Penfield Milling Company in Delhi. Established in 1824 as the Delhi Woolen Mill, the business was acquired by O.J. Penfield and Company in 1865, becoming Smith and Penfield in 1870. The building depicted in the photograph was constructed soon after Smith and Penfield was incorporated. It was last used commercially as a storeroom for the Wickham's car dealership.

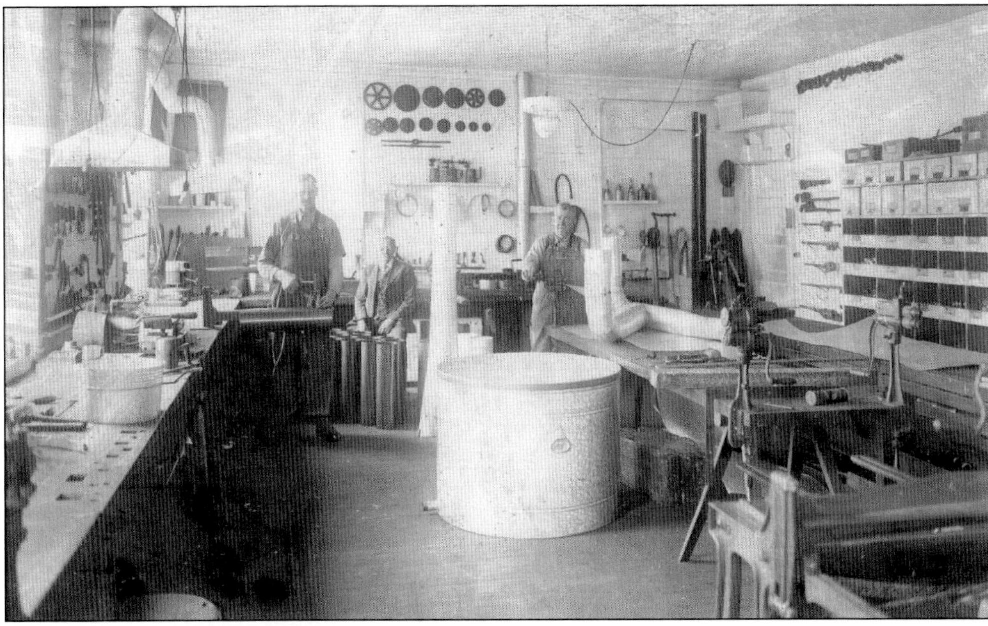

Although dairy farming became the mainstay of the local economy after 1850, not everyone was directly involved in agriculture. This image depicting the rear of a hardware store (possibly Jester's Hardware) in Cannonsville at the end of the 19th century highlights the fact that county residents were engaged in numerous occupations; some were directly related to the dairy industry, others not.

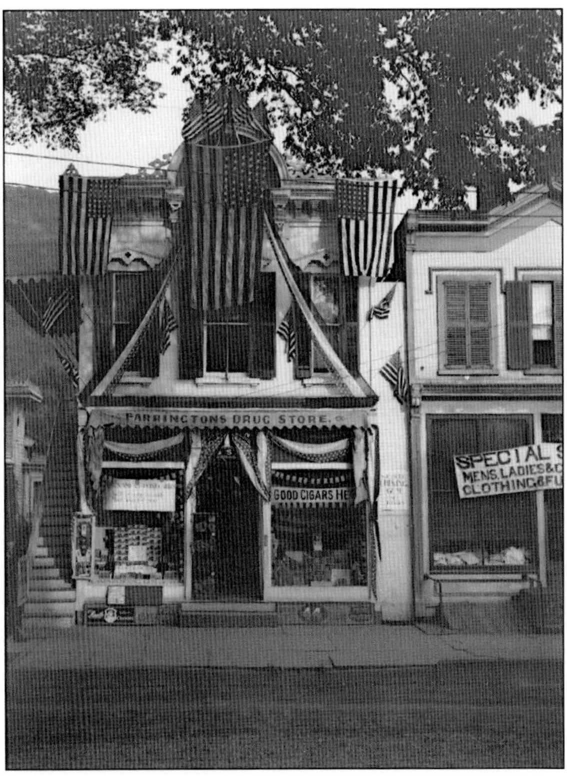

Shown is an early-20th-century view of Farrington's Drugstore on Main Street in Delhi. This structure is adjacent to where today's Delhi Diner now stands. In 1865, Dr. John Calhoun purchased the building, and in 1868, he opened a drugstore and office there. The drugstore continued under his name until 1878, when it was sold to Maurice Farrington. Farrington's store continued to operate in this location until 1911. The building still exists today at 93 Main Street.

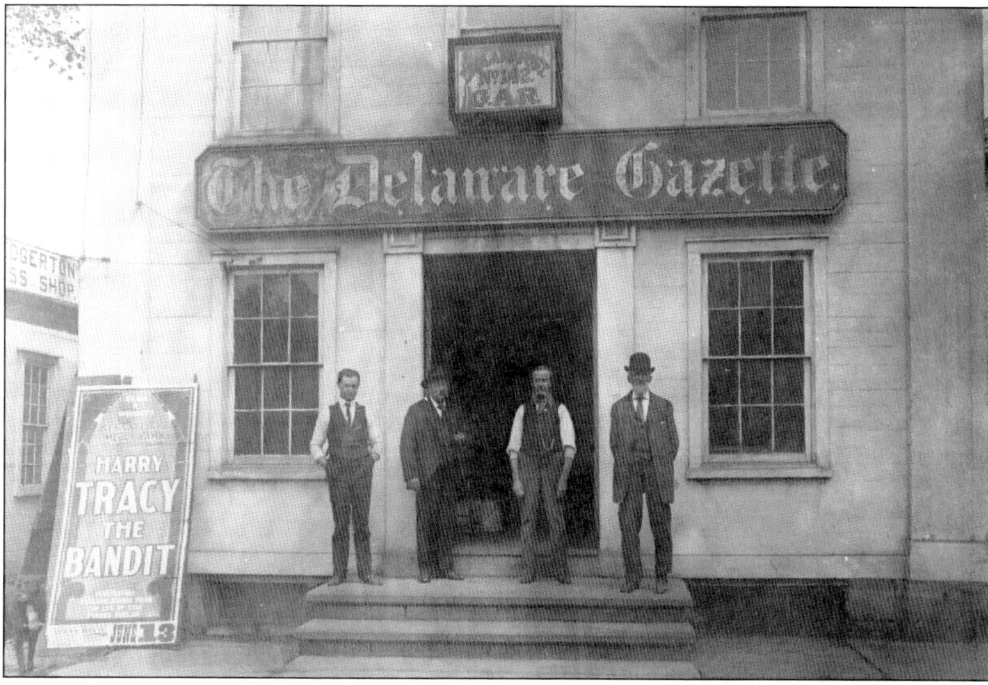

The offices of the *Delaware Gazette* newspaper are seen here on Main Street in Delhi. Dating back to 1819, the *Gazette* was the first newspaper established in Delaware County. Nineteenth-century newspapers were very political. The *Delaware Gazette* started out as "independent" and then came to support the Democratic-Republican Party before turning Democrat. It stood by its principles, and when the 1915 elections did not go its way, the paper folded. As shown in this photograph, the upper floor of the building housed the Theodolpholus England Post of the veterans' organization, the Grand Army of the Republic.

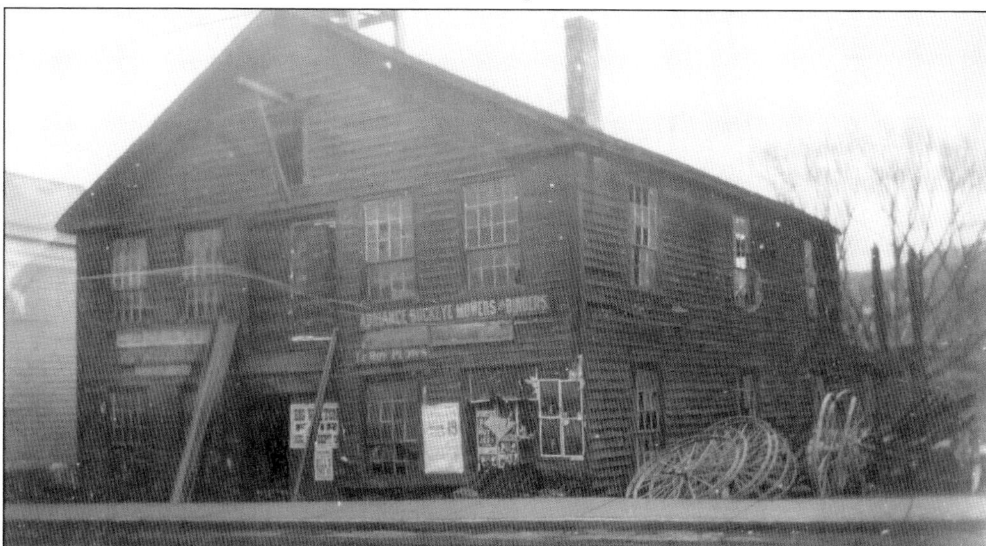

John Robinson's foundry on Main Street in Hobart is depicted here at the end of the 19th century. On the 1869 *Beers Atlas of Delaware County*, Robinson's is listed as a foundry, machinists, and manufacturer of agricultural implements. Note the wagon wheels to the right of the building.

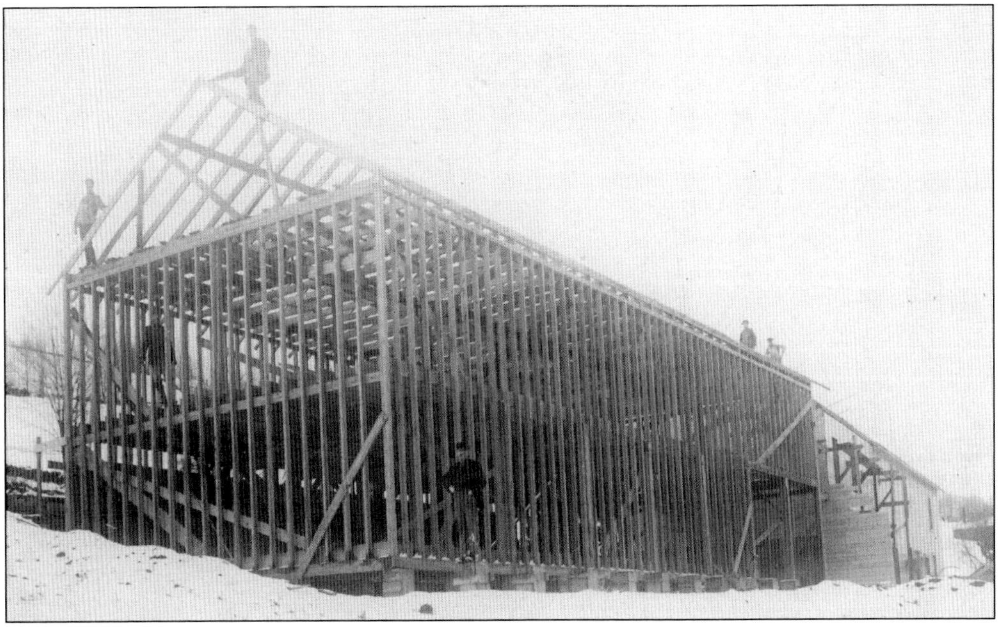

This wintery image from the early 20th century depicts construction at W.C. Oliver's Andes Feed Store. The boom in dairy farming in Delaware County after the 1870s gave rise to a similar increase in those industries and services related to agriculture. Feed stores such as this one began to show up all over the region, in addition to other companies selling machinery and implements to local farmers.

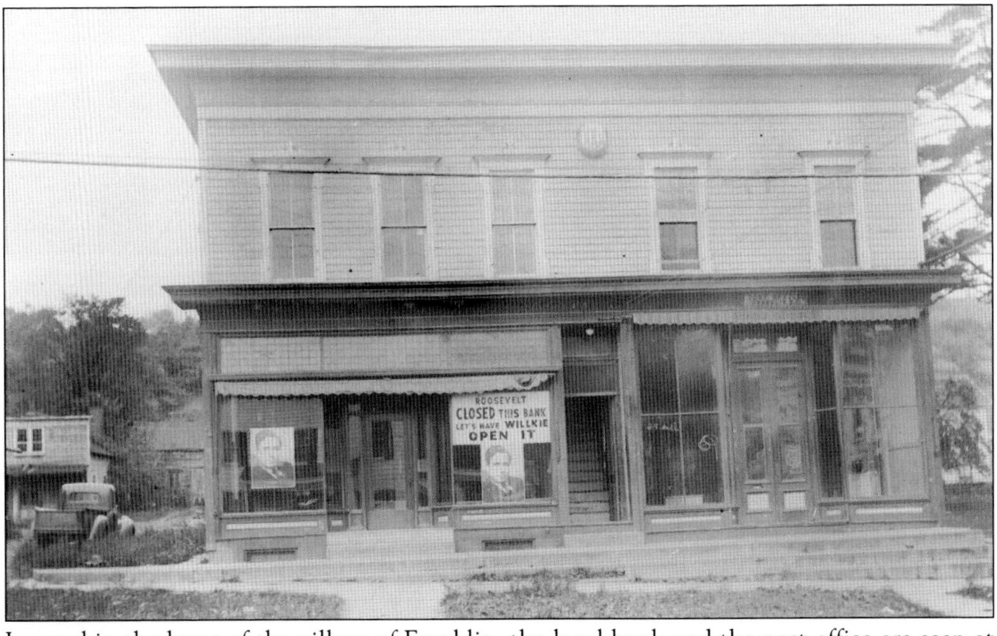

Located in the heart of the village of Franklin, the local bank and the post office are seen at the height of the Great Depression in the early 1930s. Note the politically charged poster on the bank's window. This building is still recognizable and was once home to Robinson's Department Store. What once housed the bank has been a vacant storefront for some time. The post office is currently the home of a local woodworking studio.

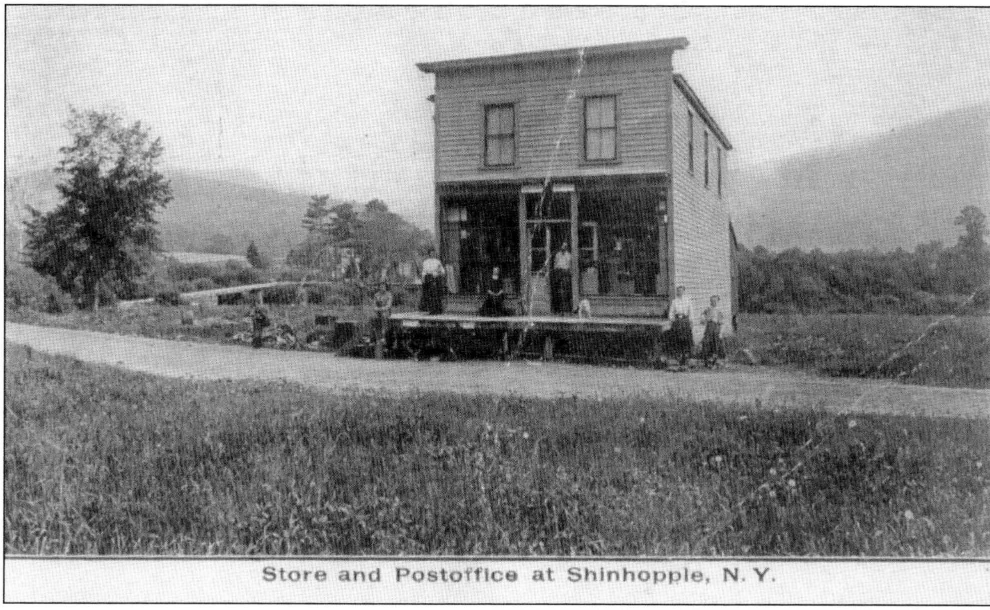

The general store and post office at Shinhopple are seen in the 1890s. Shinhopple, located on the East Branch of the Delaware River in the town of Colchester, was a bustling place in the 19th century lying as it did in close proximity to several acid factories. The store and post office, commonly housed in one establishment, serviced the needs of local farmers and the workers at the nearby plants. Note the bridge spanning the Delaware River in the left background.

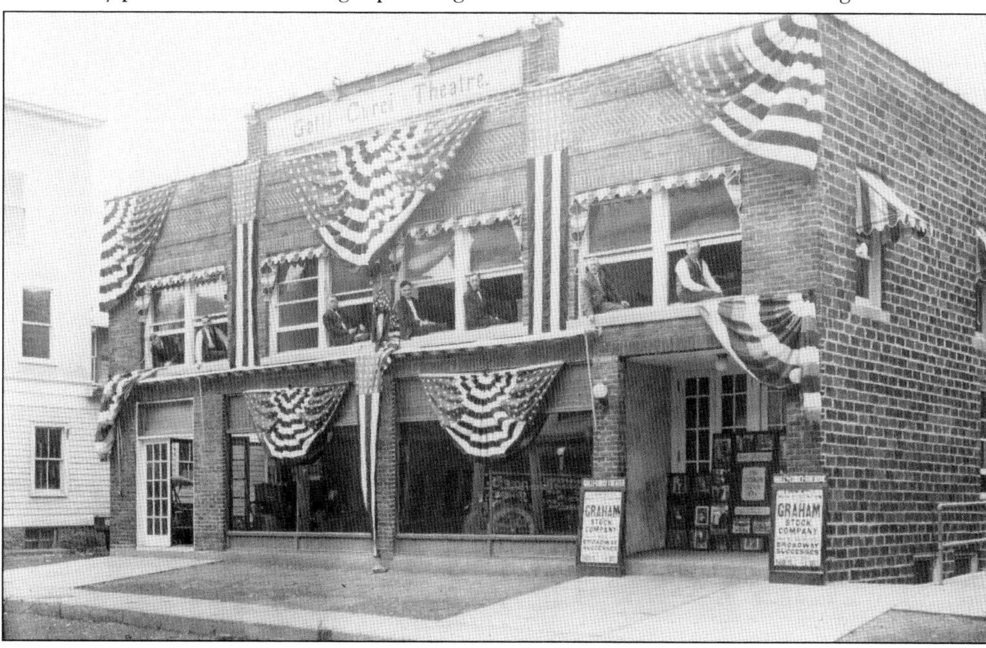

Shown here is the opening of the new Galli Curci Theater in Margaretville in 1922. The theater was named after renowned Italian opera singer Amelita Galli Curci, who was a regular summer resident of the village. The upper story housed offices of the Delaware & Northern Railroad. Pictured are, from left to right, D&N employees James J. Welch, Charles A. Snyder, Ira F. Terry, James Walsh, Harry J. Miller, Andrew Benjamin, and Harry G. Eckert.

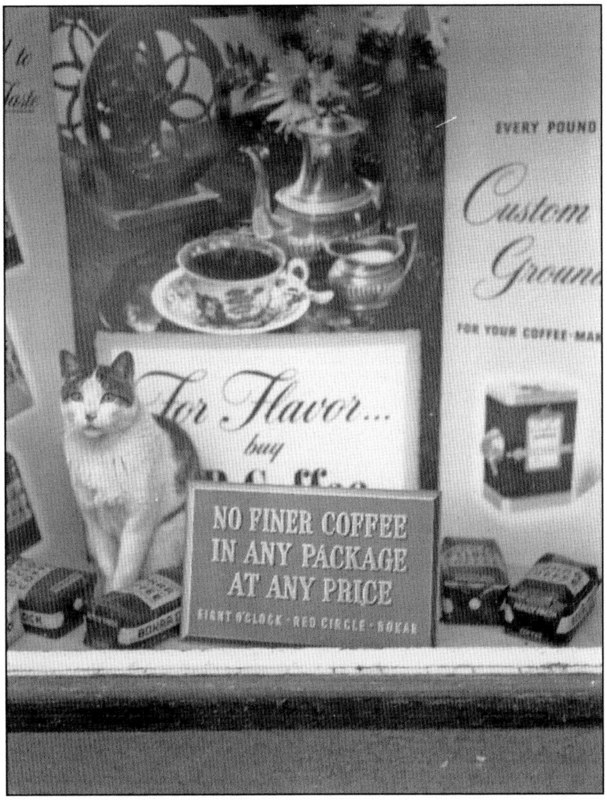

A cat sits serenely in a storefront window along Delhi's Main Street in the 1930s.

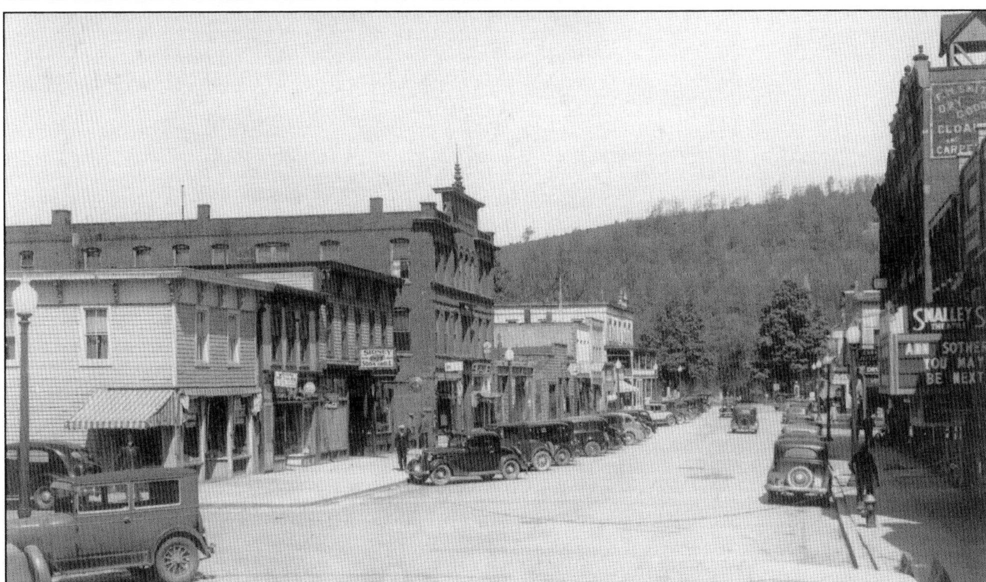

The village of Sidney was already a bustling place in this mid-1930s view of the downtown shopping district. Sidney owed much of its economic well-being to its situation along the Susquehanna River and the fact that it lay at the crossroads of two railroad lines. Sidney received an added boost during World War II when military orders poured in to the Scintilla Magneto, Bendix Aviation Corporation.

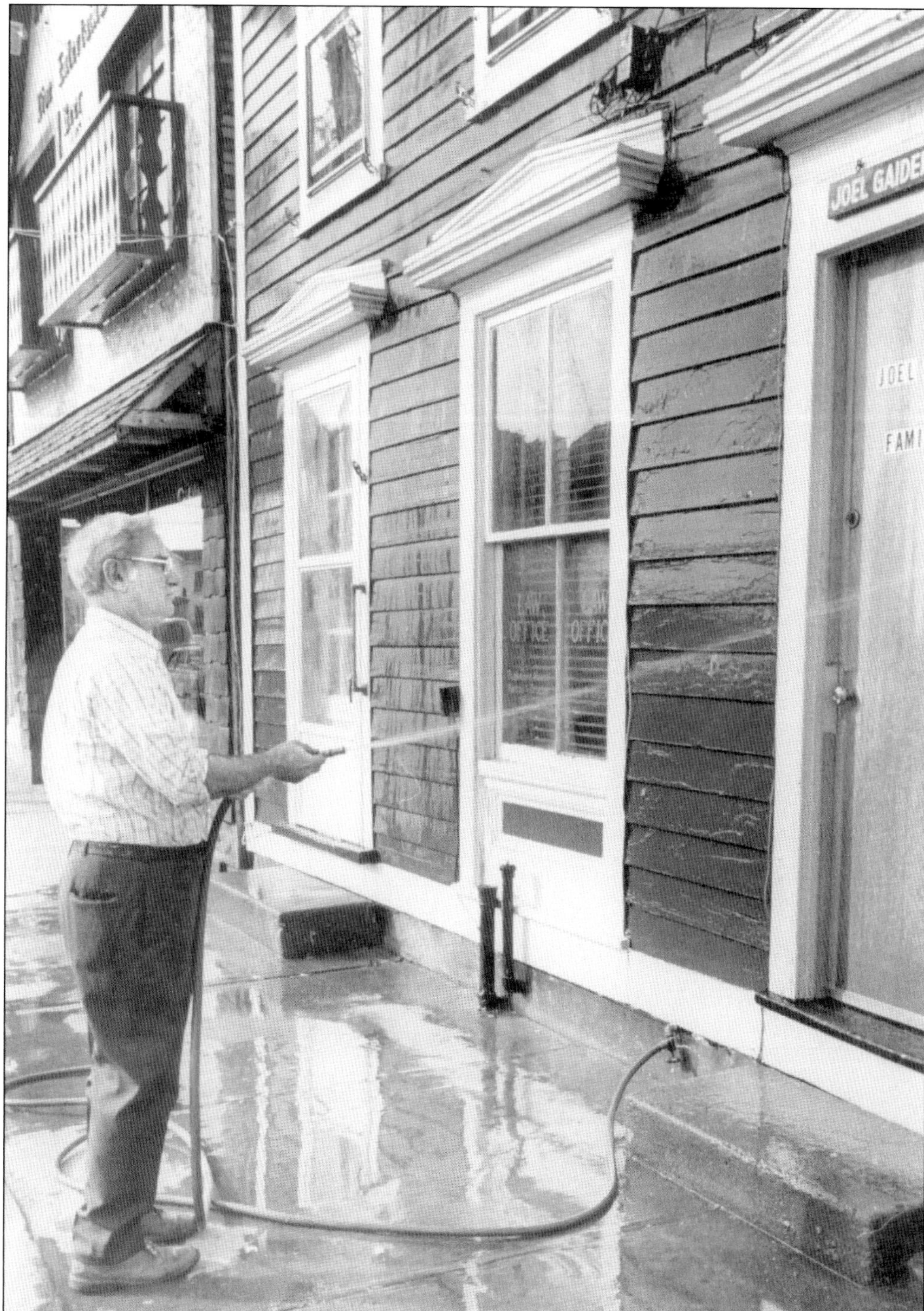

Prominent Delhi resident and local attorney John Crocker is seen giving the Main Street facade of his Delhi office a cleaning. In addition to his legal career, Crocker was an avid collector of historic images of the county. Many of those images have since been donated to the collections of the Delaware County Historical Association.

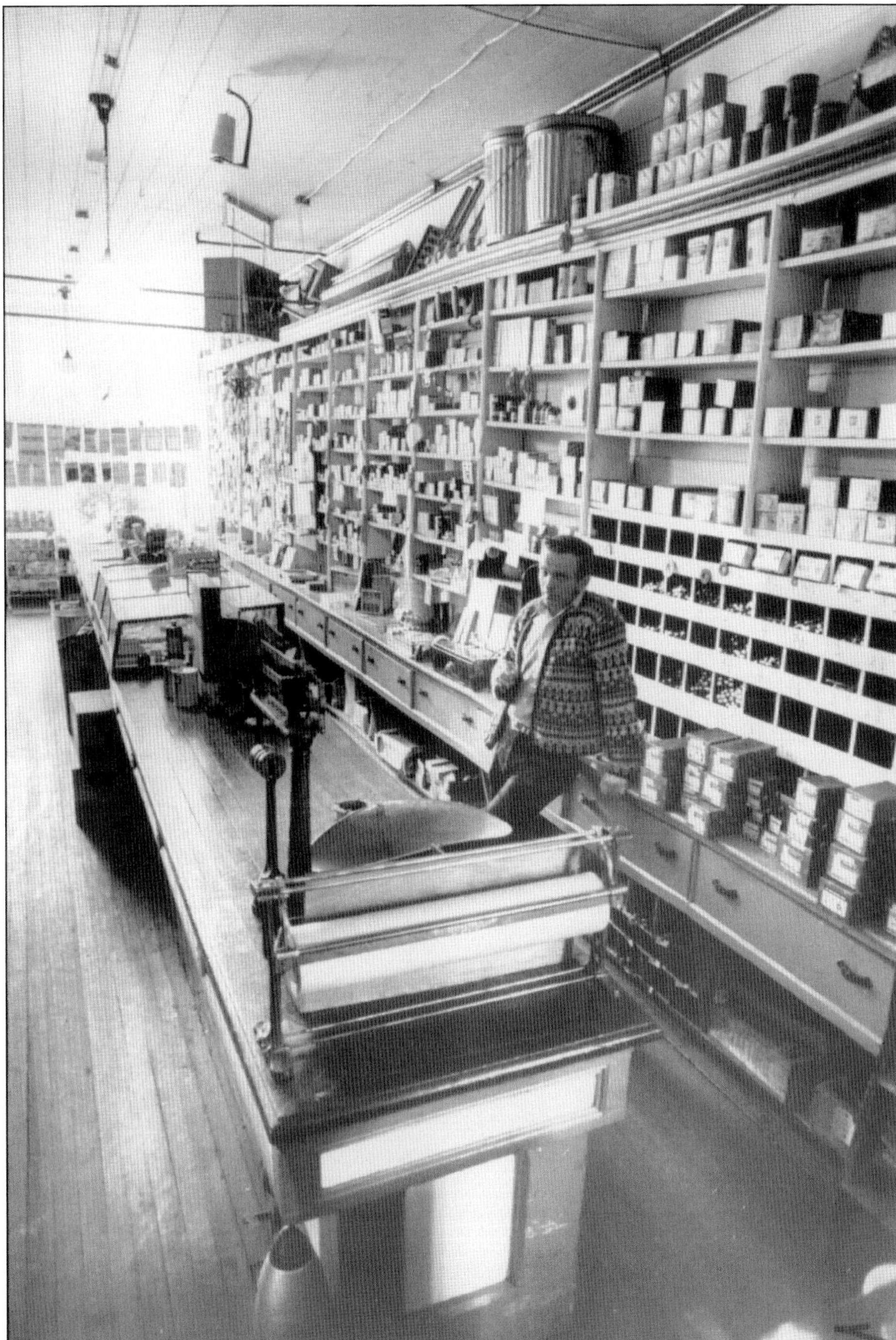

The interior of the Hamden General Store is seen in 1973. This building today houses the store of the Lucky Dog Organic Farm. The Lucky Dog is one of many newly established alternative agricultural enterprises, and, as such, it highlights the move away from traditional dairy farming toward organic and sustainable forms of agriculture. The Lucky Dog store is an example of successful repurposing of a historic building in the heart of a Delaware County village.

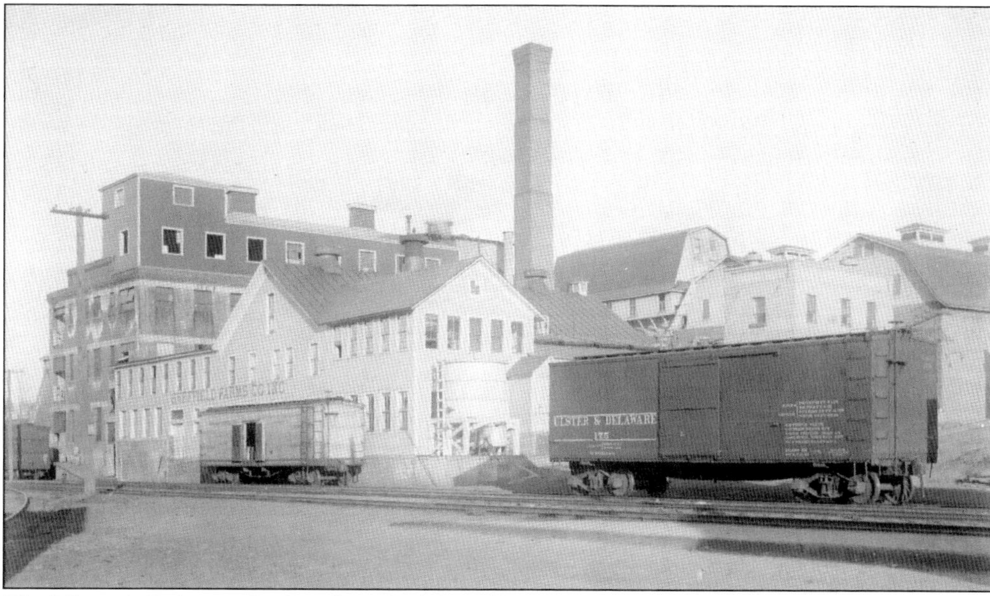

The Ulster & Delaware Railroad reached the village of Hobart in 1884 and then continued south to Bloomville, which was reached in 1891. The line provided an almost immediate economic boost to farmers and others along its route, including the Sheffield Farms Company. In 1892, the company opened the nation's first milk pasteurization plant in the United States at Bloomville. By 1912, Sheffield Farms boasted 35 plants in Delaware County and surrounding counties, including the one pictured here at Hobart.

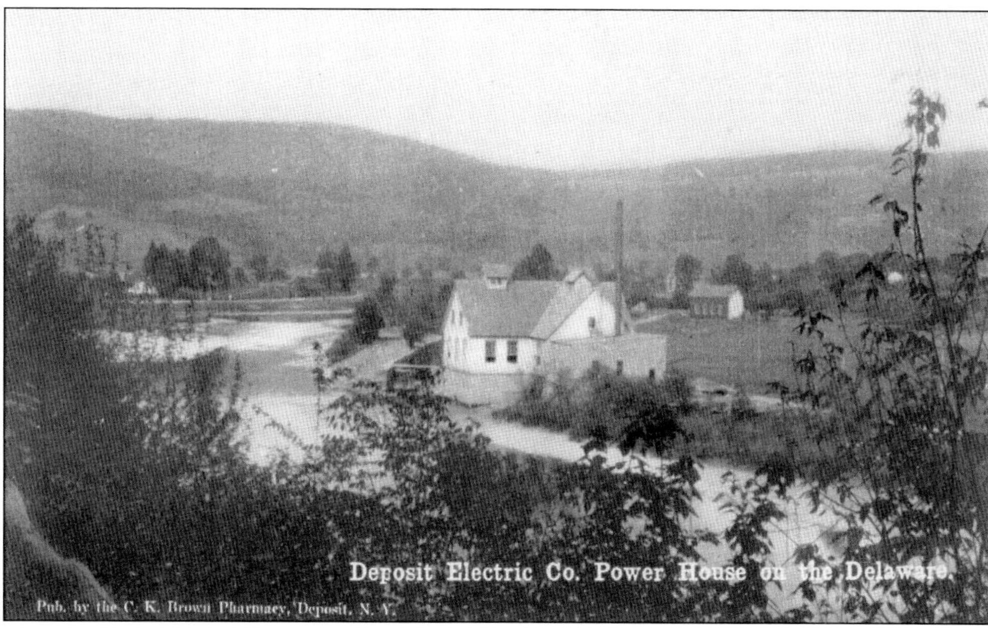

A great many local communities utilized the power of rivers to generate their own electricity at the end of the 19th century. Shown here is the Deposit Electric Power Plant along the West Branch of the Delaware River. Among other places, Hanford Mills in East Meredith once provided hydroelectricity to the small community around it, while Treadwell once had an "electric light pond."

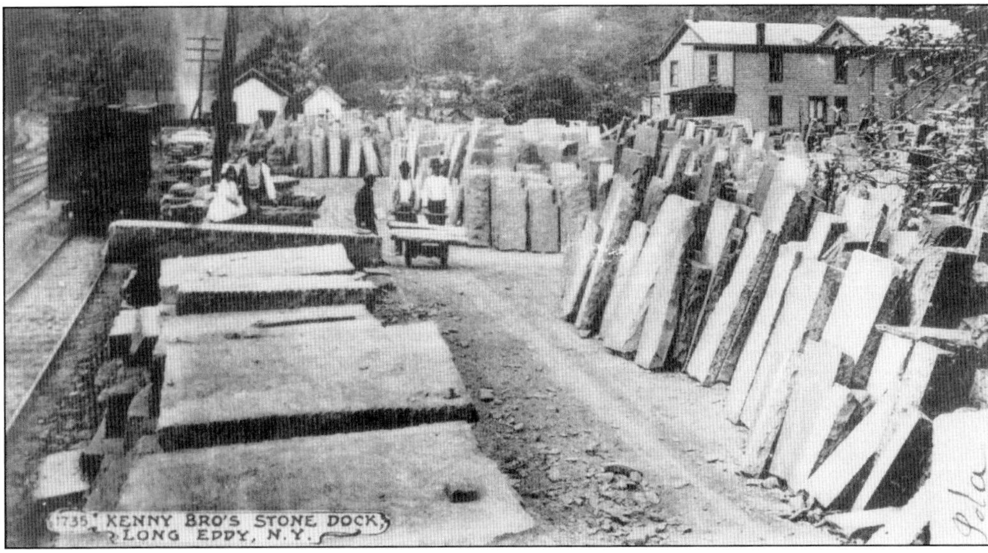

This is a view of Kenny Brothers' Stone Dock in Long Eddy, town of Hancock. Located along the route of the New York & Erie Railroad, Long Eddy is the most southerly community in Delaware County, straddling the Sullivan County line and just across the Delaware River from Pennsylvania. The town of Hancock is still an important location for the quarrying of bluestone, and the Hancock Public Library features a room devoted to this important industry.

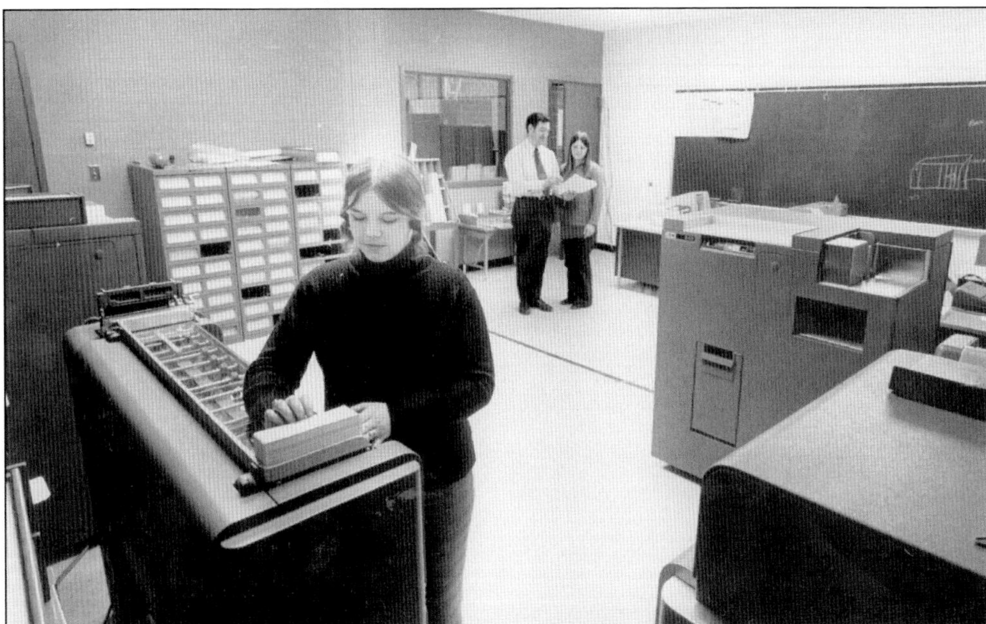

In 1972, construction of a new campus was completed along State Route 206 in the Delaware County town of Masonville. This image, taken in May of the same year, depicts the data processing center at the new facility, known at its inception as the Western Delaware Educational Center and now as the Robert W. Harrold Campus. The campus today forms a part of the Delaware-Chenango-Madison-Otsego Board of Cooperative Education (BOCES). In the foreground is Holly Miller of Sidney, and in the background are instructor Richard Courtney and Sharon Danowski of Walton.

Five

Community and People

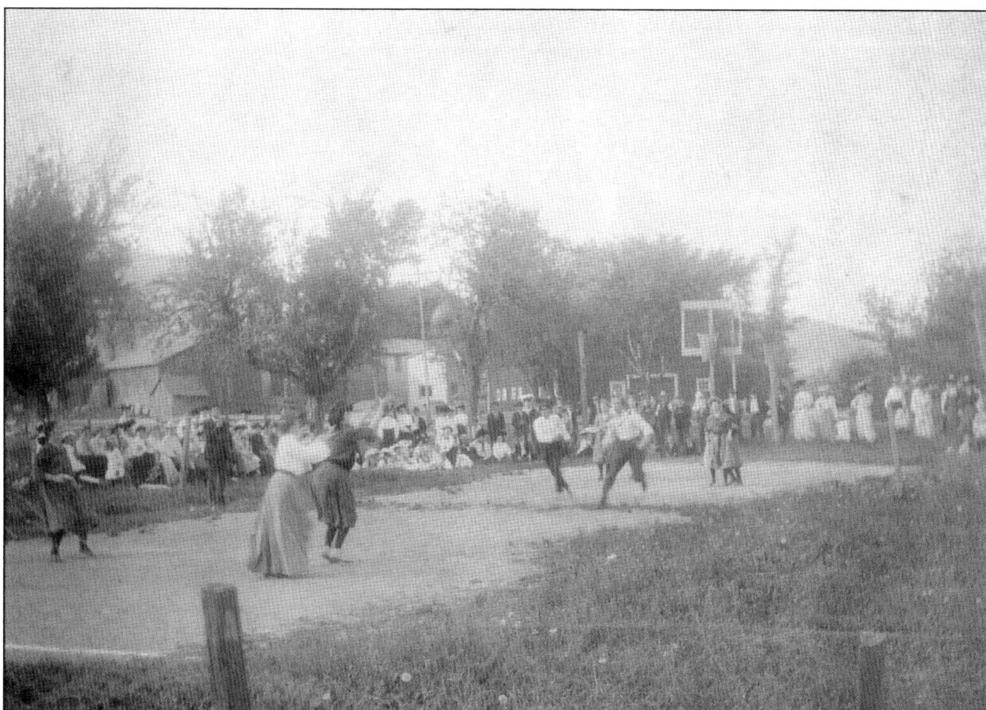

A 1906 outdoor basketball game features both young men and women. It must have been very difficult—and not very comfortable—playing an exerting game of hoops wearing those clothes!

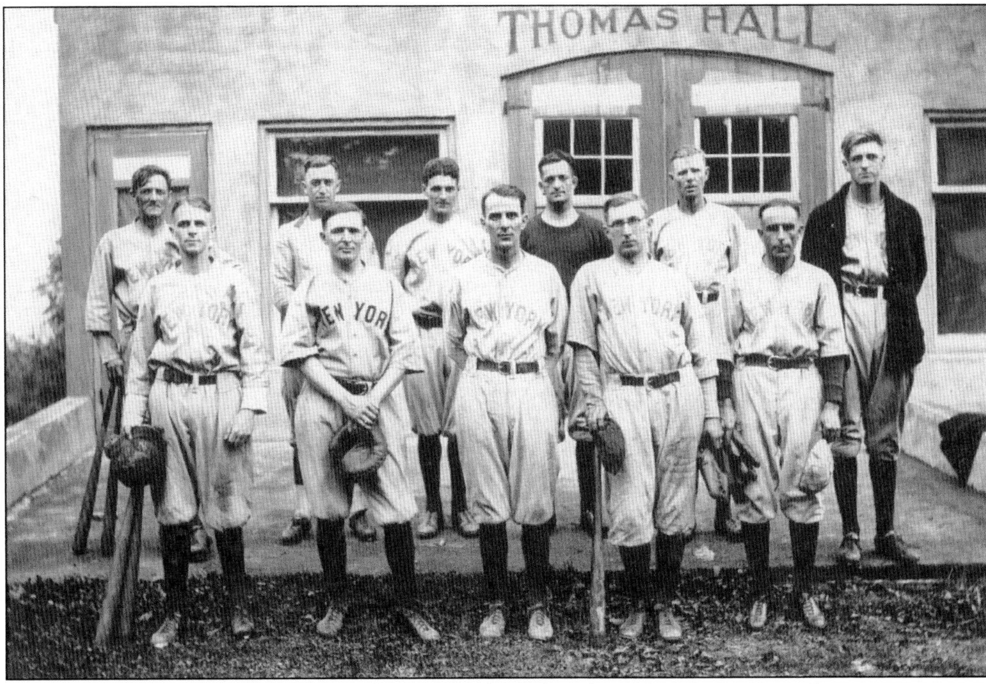

Baseball was a popular pastime in the late 19th and early 20th centuries, with many town and village teams competing against each other, such as this team from Downsville.

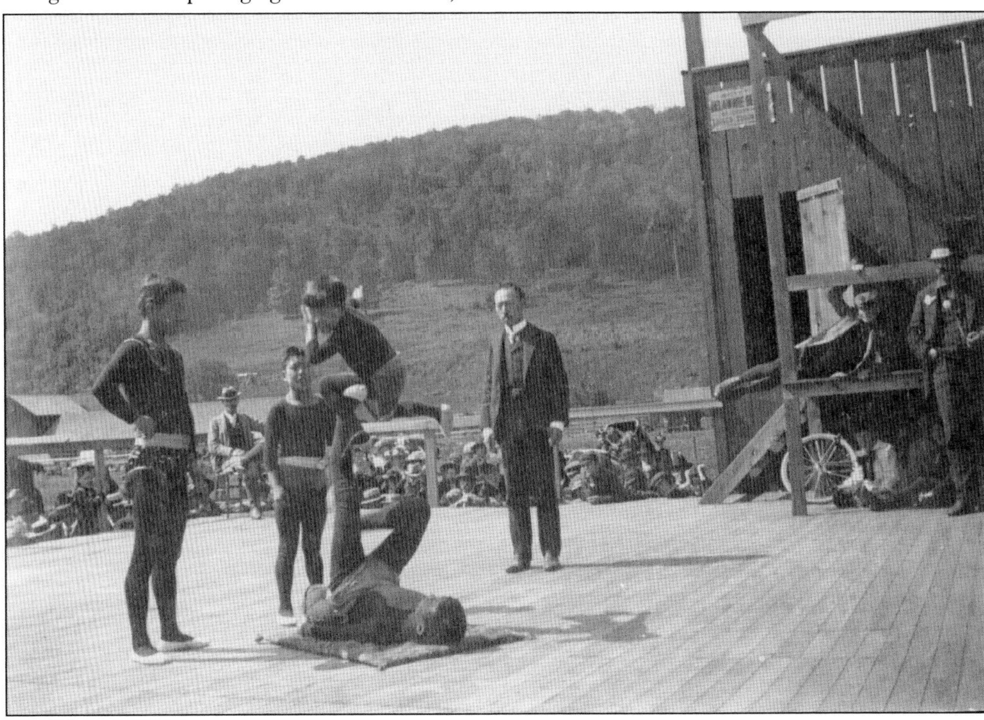

The county fair provided an opportunity for performers to strut their stuff, and they came from near and far. Here, Chinese acrobats perform on the stage before an audience at the 1899 Walton Fair.

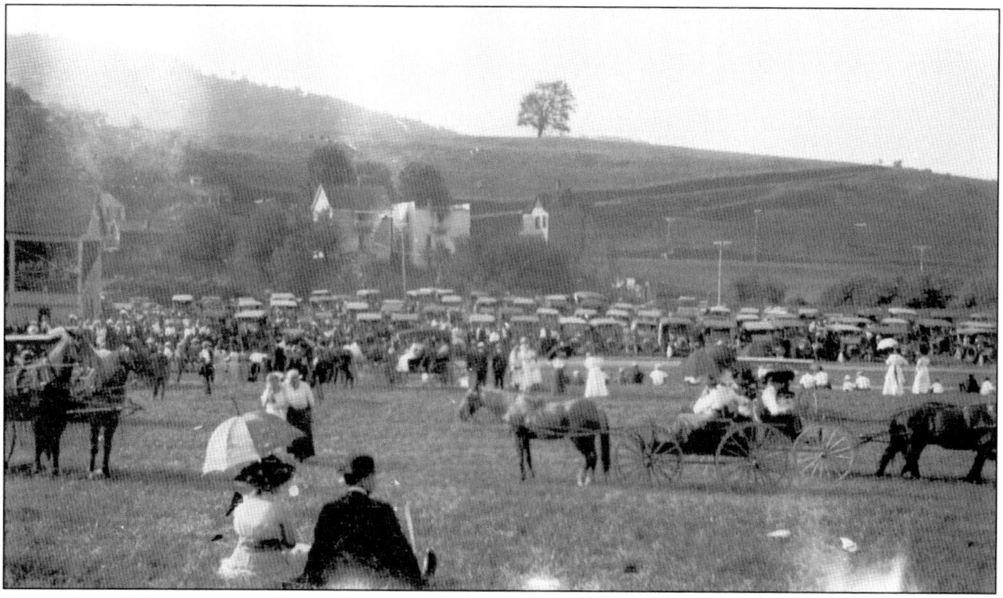

Agricultural fairs attracted a wide variety of people. This view of one such fair in Delhi likely dates from the 1910s or 1920s. People were traveling by automobile, but some still relied on equine-powered transport.

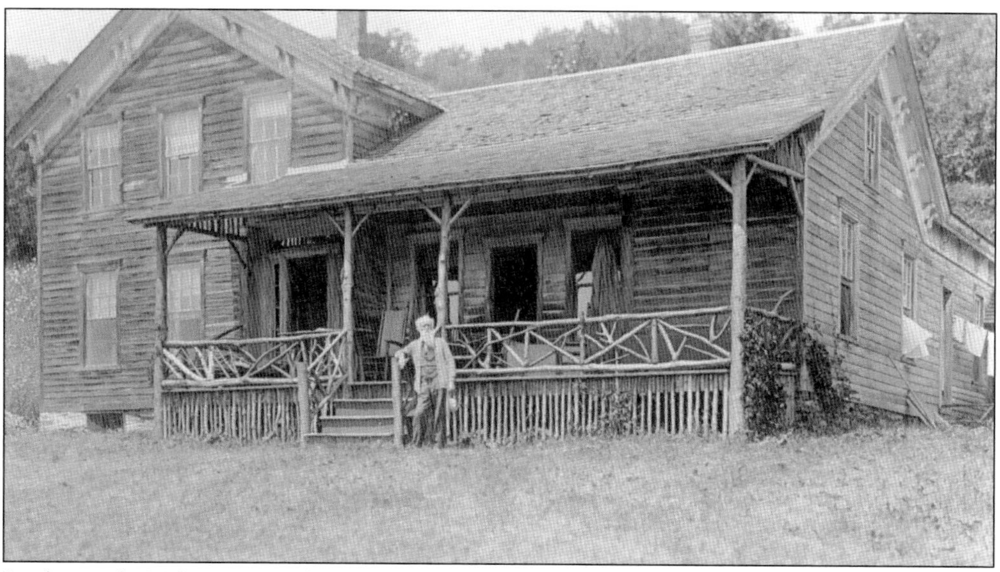

In this early-20th-century photograph, John Burroughs poses outside his Delaware County retreat, Woodchuck Lodge, in the town of Roxbury. Burroughs was born and raised in Roxbury before launching a career as one of America's preeminent naturalists. As a youth in Delaware County, he was a friend and neighbor of Jay Gould, later a renowned Wall Street tycoon and railroad magnate.

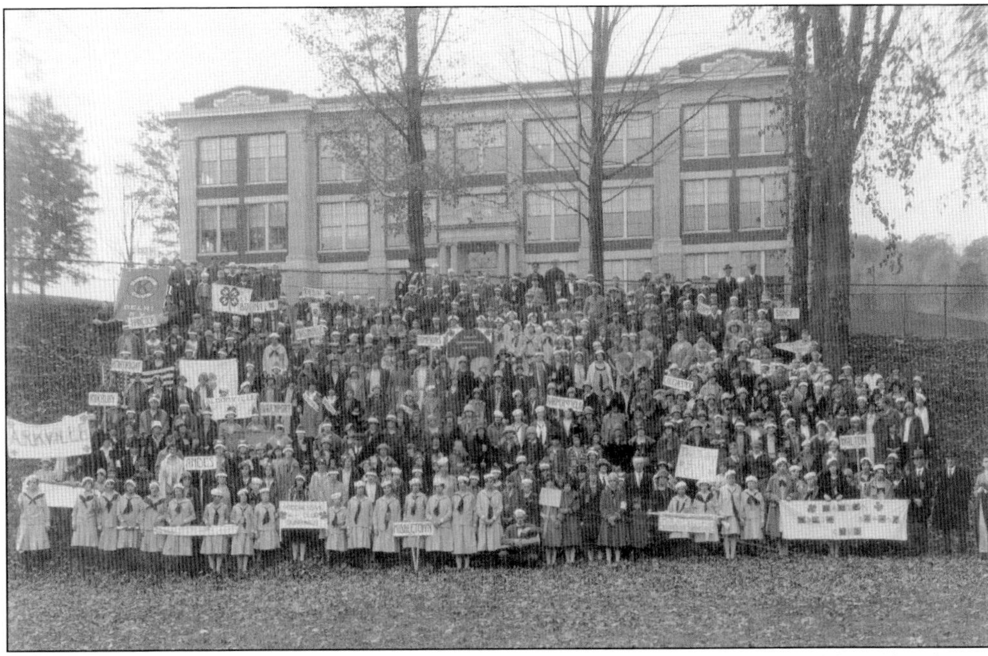

A gathering of 4-H Club members from around Delaware County poses in front of the old Delaware Academy building in Delhi in this c. 1930 image.

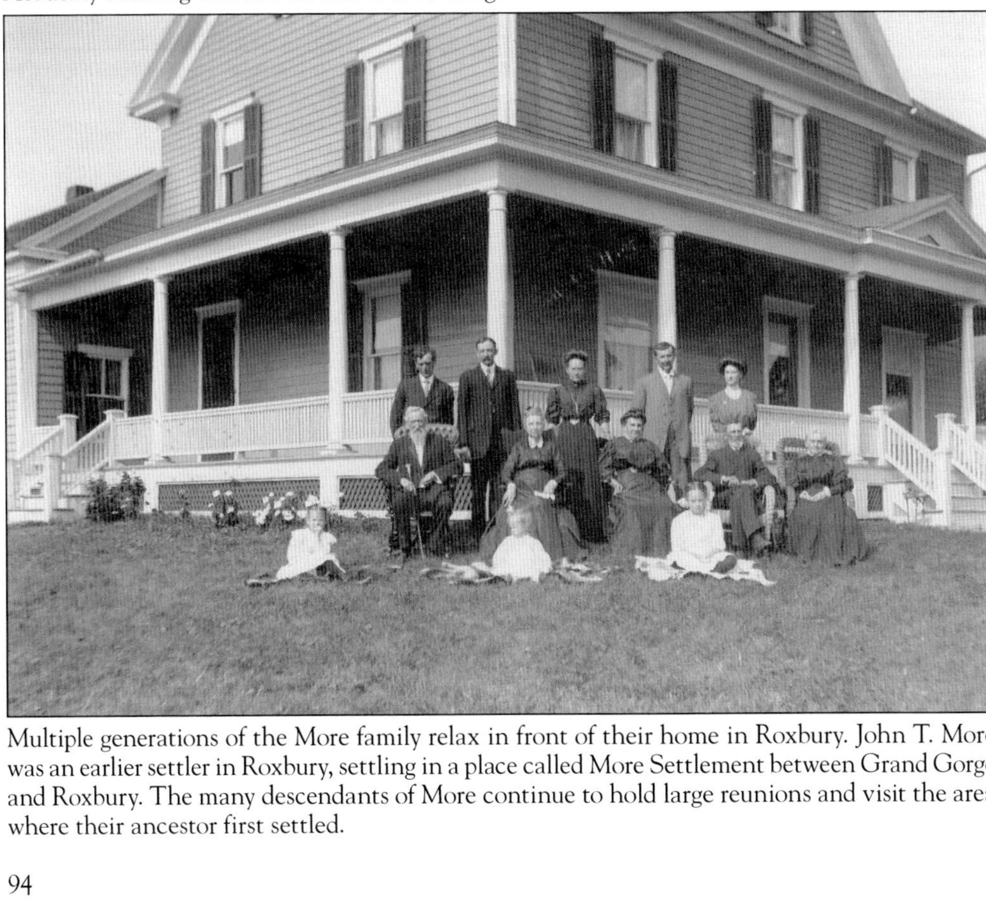

Multiple generations of the More family relax in front of their home in Roxbury. John T. More was an earlier settler in Roxbury, settling in a place called More Settlement between Grand Gorge and Roxbury. The many descendants of More continue to hold large reunions and visit the area where their ancestor first settled.

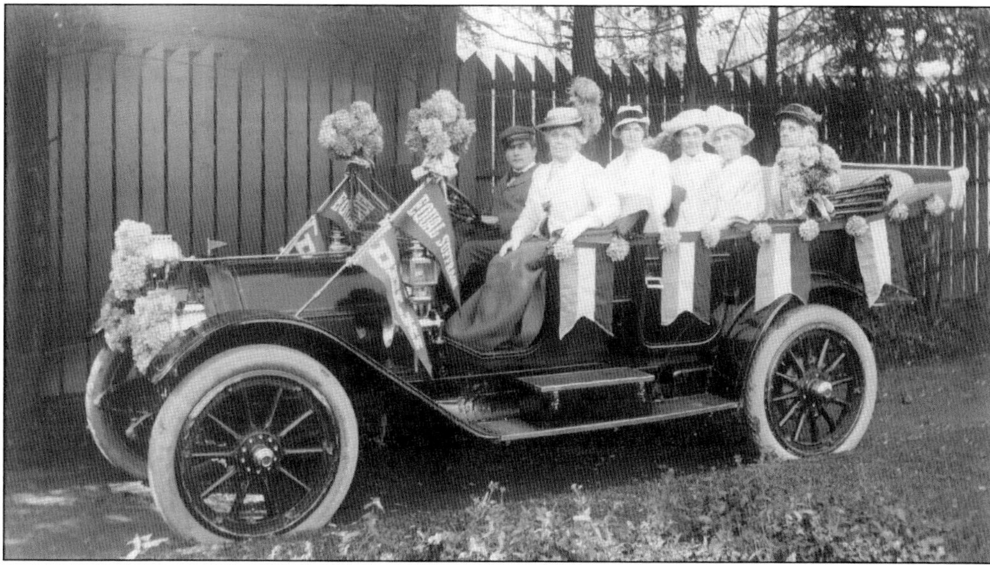

Jennie (Curtis) Cannon was active in the women's suffrage movement. She chaired the Delaware County Committee of the New York Woman Suffrage Association. She also was the vice president of the National American Woman Suffrage Association. Cannon was instrumental in holding a mass meeting at the Delaware County Courthouse Square in the fall of 1915. This image of her in her car decorated to promote women's suffrage dates from 1918 or 1919.

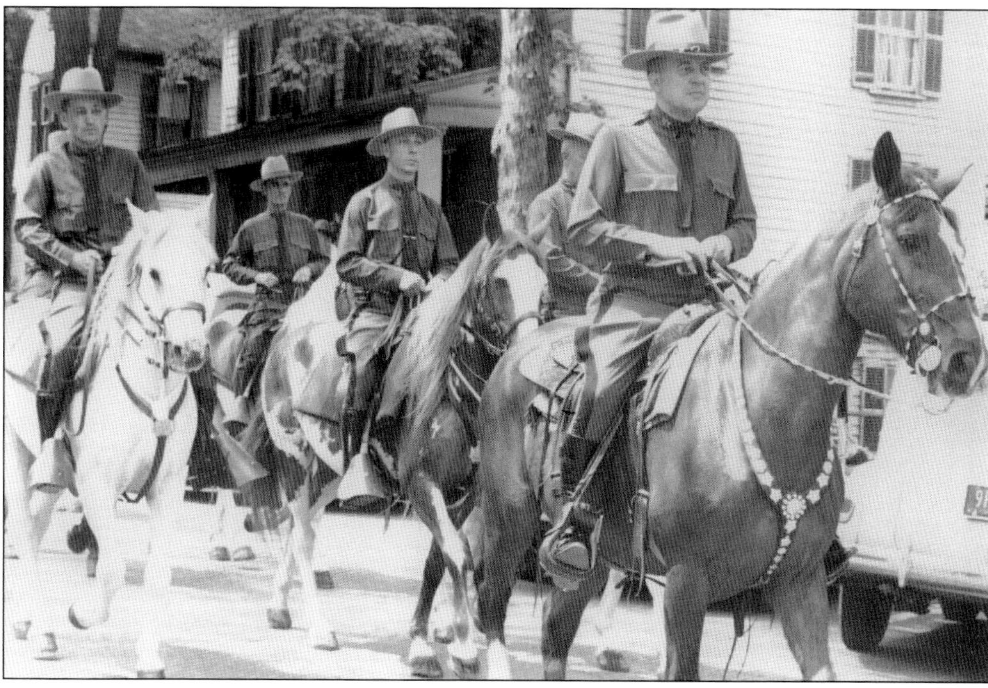

Led by Capt. Daniel E. Fox, the "Rough Riders" of Troop C of New York State Troopers parade down a street in Sidney around 1930. Fox joined the state police in 1917 and rose quickly through the ranks, becoming captain of Troop C in Sidney, which covered most of the southern tier. The troop was especially noted for its work on horseback, using the animals to patrol 10 counties. The Rough Riders were internationally known for their riding skills.

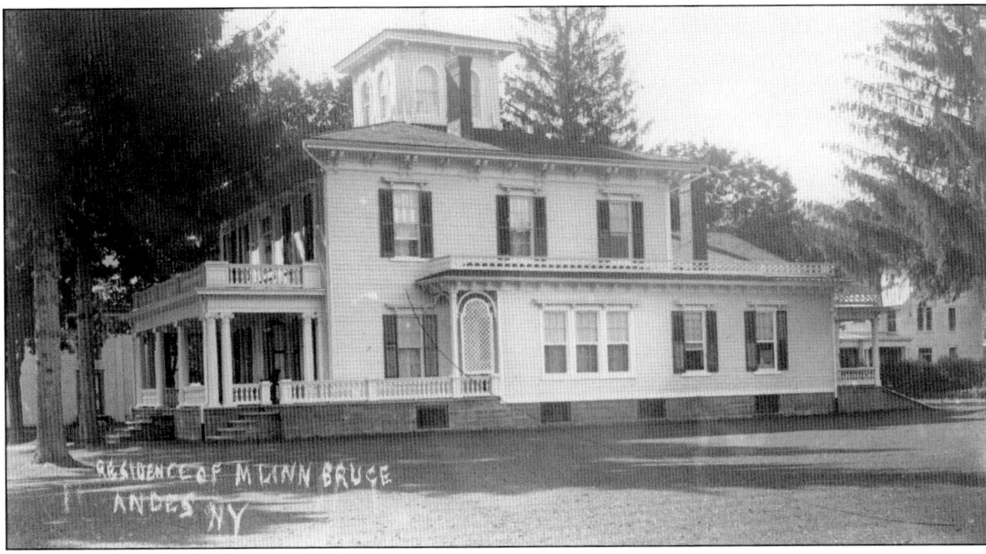

The Bruce Mansion in Andes was built in 1854 by Duncan Ballantine, who owned a bank and a general store. The house was later named after M. Linn Bruce, who lived there off and on from the early 1900s until his death in 1936. M. Linn Bruce was born in Pennsylvania in 1860 and was educated at the Andes Academy. He served one term as New York State's lieutenant governor (1905–1906). He also served briefly on New York's Supreme Court. Bruce is buried in Andes.

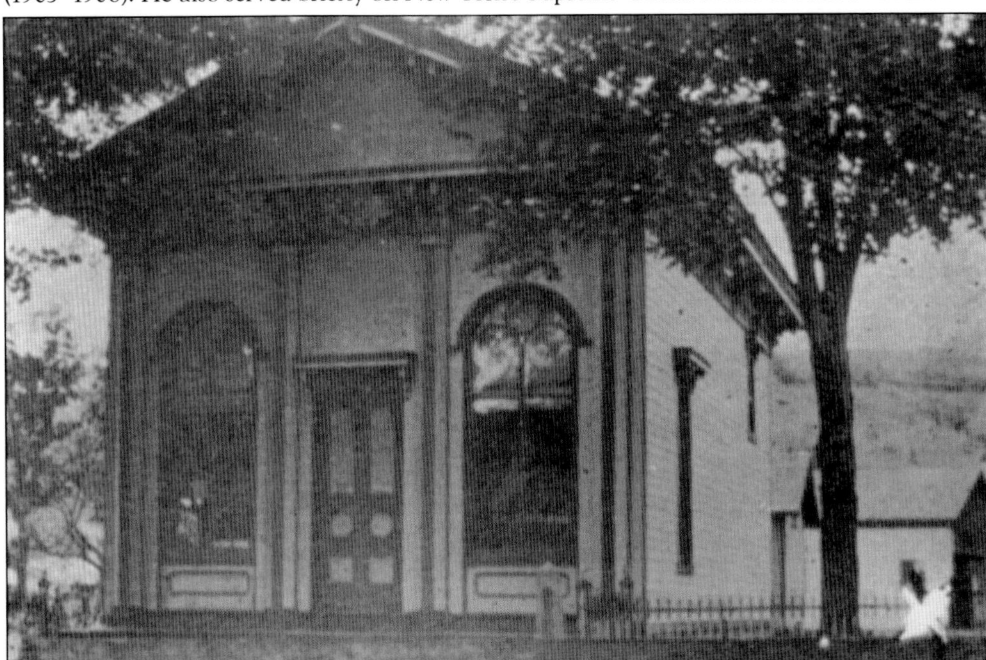

On the night of October 28, 1905, a bank robbery occurred in the village of Andes during which young resident Frank Graham was fatally shot. Graham had been walking home from a dance with a friend when he pointed out a light in Ballantine's bank. The robbers heard him, made him put up his hands, then shot him. Graham died later of his wounds despite being tended by a New York City doctor sent by Commodore Gerry from Lake Delaware. The robbers had been attempting to blow up the safe but were unsuccessful. They were never captured.

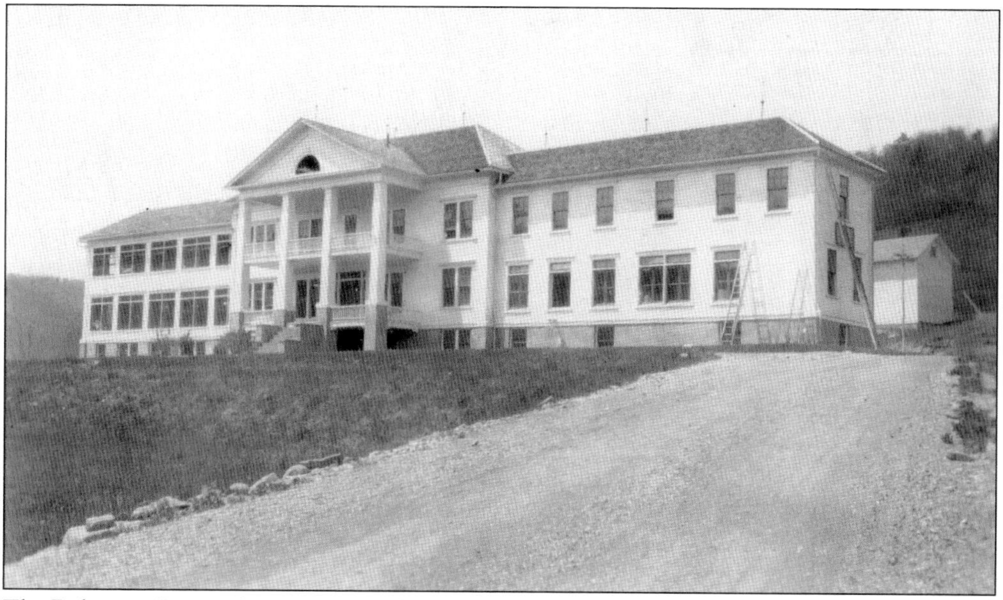

The Delaware County Sanitorium was built in Delhi in the 1860s and served in various capacities, including for many years as a tuberculosis sanitorium. In its last capacity, it was used as the county infirmary. When a new county infirmary was constructed adjacent to the old building in the 1960s, the 19th-century sanitorium/infirmary was torn down.

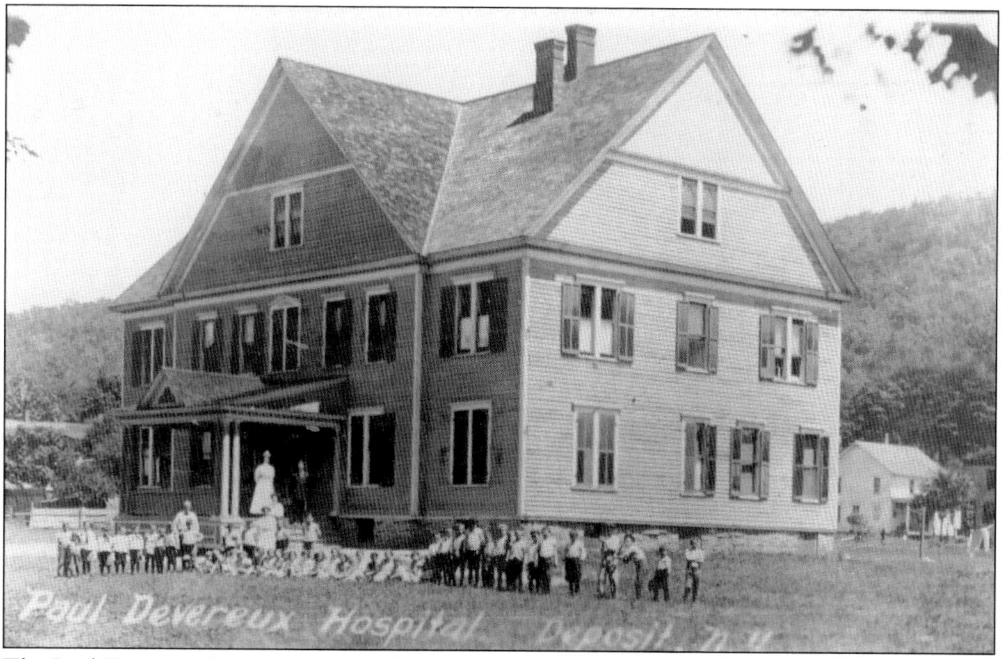

The Paul Devereux Hospital in the village of Deposit was built by Alvin Devereux as a memorial to his son, who had died young of tuberculosis. The construction was completed in 1898. Paul Devereux had expected the village to run the hospital and supply personnel, but this never happened. The *Herald Tribune*'s Fresh Air Fund rented it starting in 1900, and it continued to host children from New York City during summers well into the 1930s. The building was demolished in the 1950s.

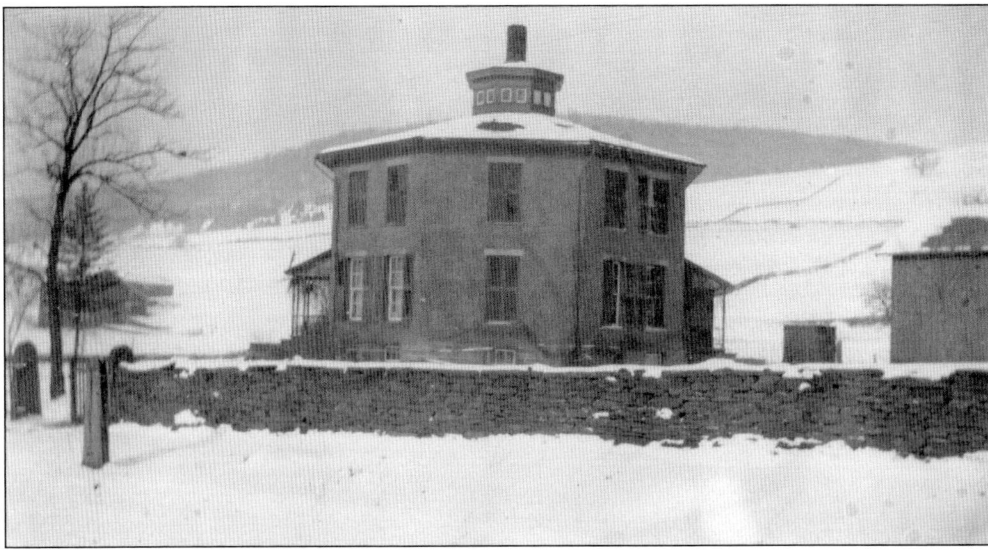

One of the notable homes in the town of Hamden is the Octagon House. It was built by John Hawley in the 1850s, using locally quarried stone to mimic houses he had seen in his native England. Several of the property's outbuildings have similar stonework in their foundations. Twenty years later, it was raised four feet and veneered with brick. Owned for a number of years by the Ploutz family, it now serves as a bed-and-breakfast.

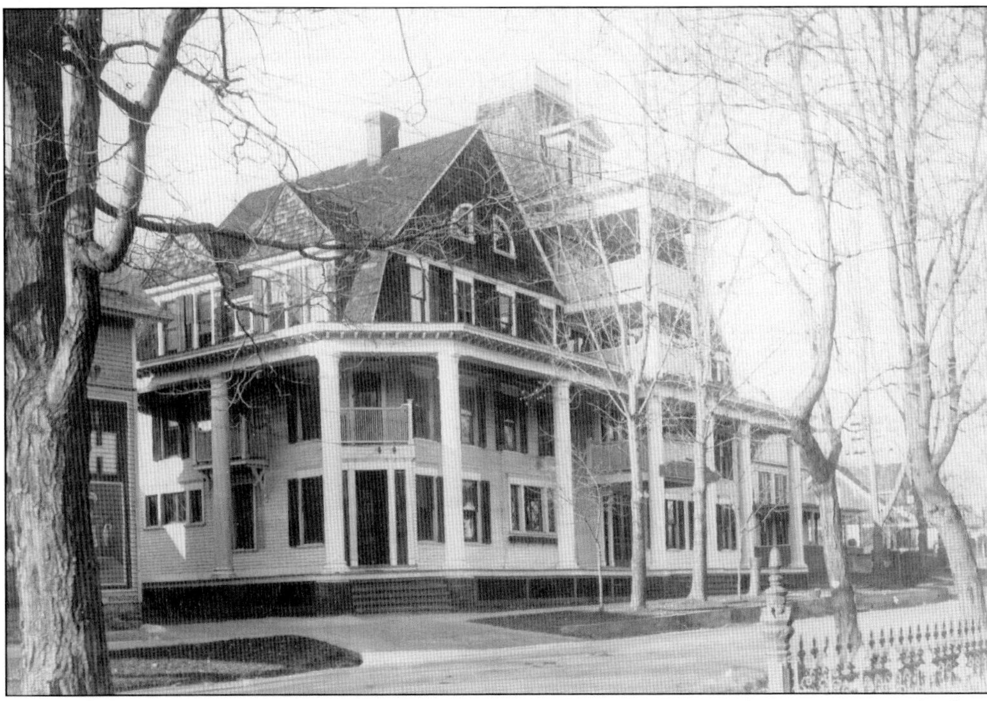

This hotel was located in Hobart and known by several names over the years. It was built in 1900 to replace Green's Hotel, which had burned down the previous year. Known as the Mansion House Hotel for a few years and the New Hobart Hotel for a longer period, it later was known as the Drake Hotel. A fire in 1941 destroyed the top two floors. The building served as the Hobart Community Hall for a number of years.

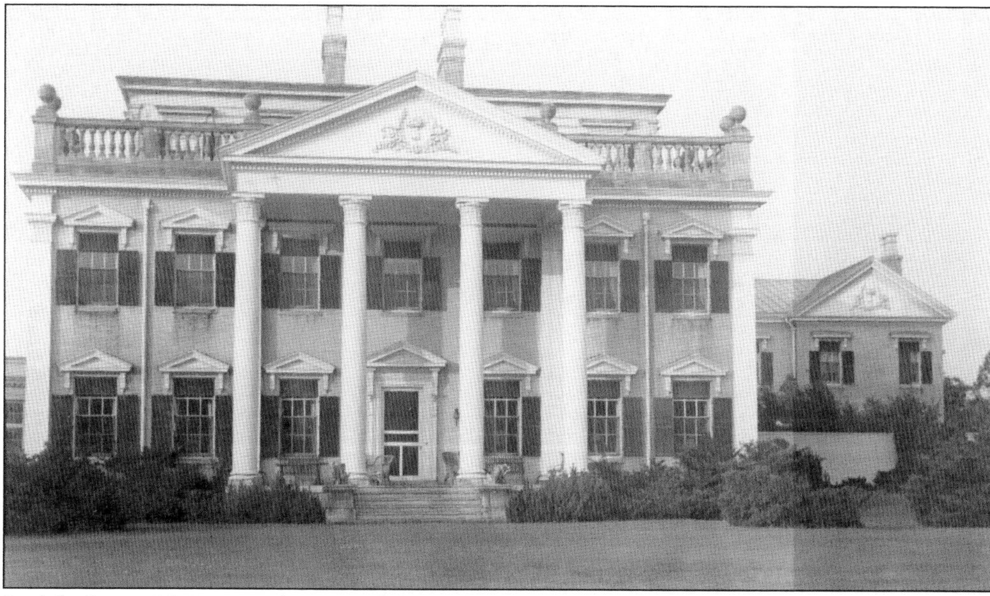

Built by James McLean at the turn of the 20th century, the McLean Mansion in South Kortright was the scene of many important events during the 1930s and 1940s when his daughter Alice McLean lived there. She hosted a large barbecue to which all area residents were invited in the late 1930s and the International Assembly of Women in 1946, at which Eleanor Roosevelt was a featured speaker. The mansion, until recently, was the home of Phoenix House, a drug and alcohol treatment program.

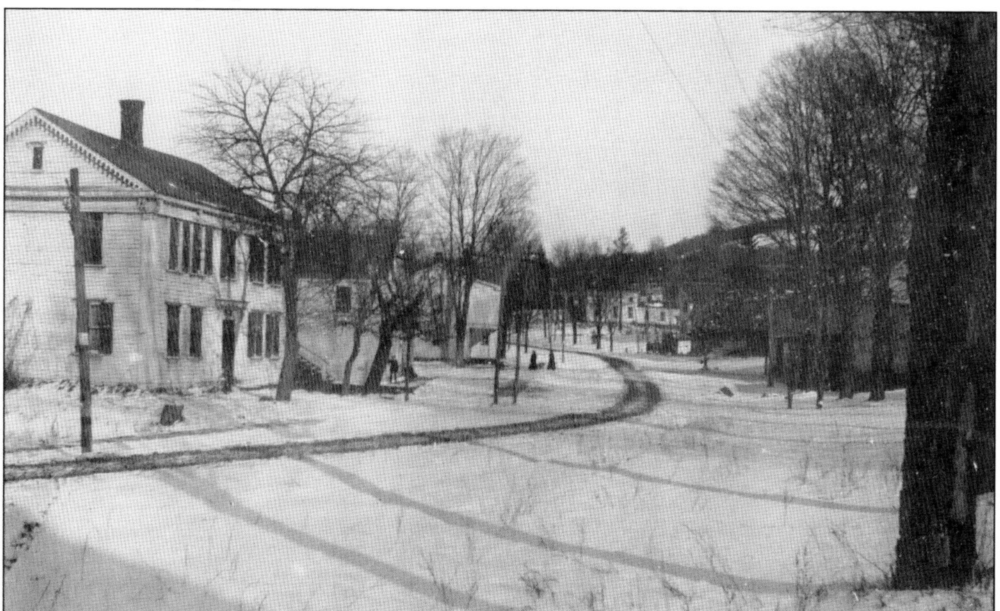

Shown is an early-20th-century view of Treadwell, a hamlet of the town of Franklin. The hamlet was originally known as Croton but had to change its name in the mid-19th century at the behest of the US Post Office so as not to be confused with the town of the same name in Westchester County, New York. Treadwell was named after the first postmaster and local tavern-keeper Minor Treadwell.

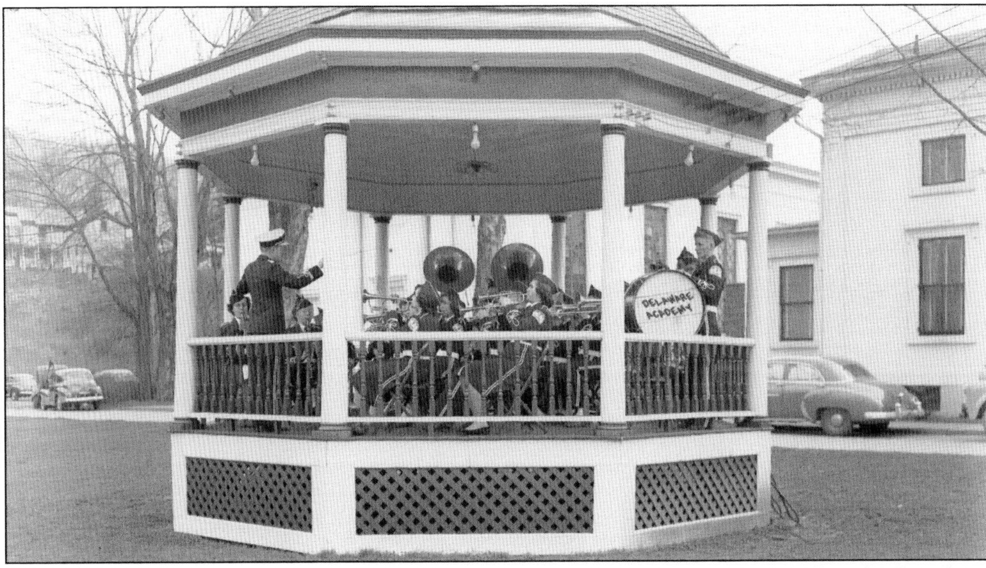

The high school band is playing on the gazebo on Courthouse Square in Delhi; the band and gazebo gained national attention in July 1951 when both appeared in a painting on the cover of the *Saturday Evening Post*. This photograph, taken in March 1951, is one of several believed taken to assist artist Stevan Dohanos.

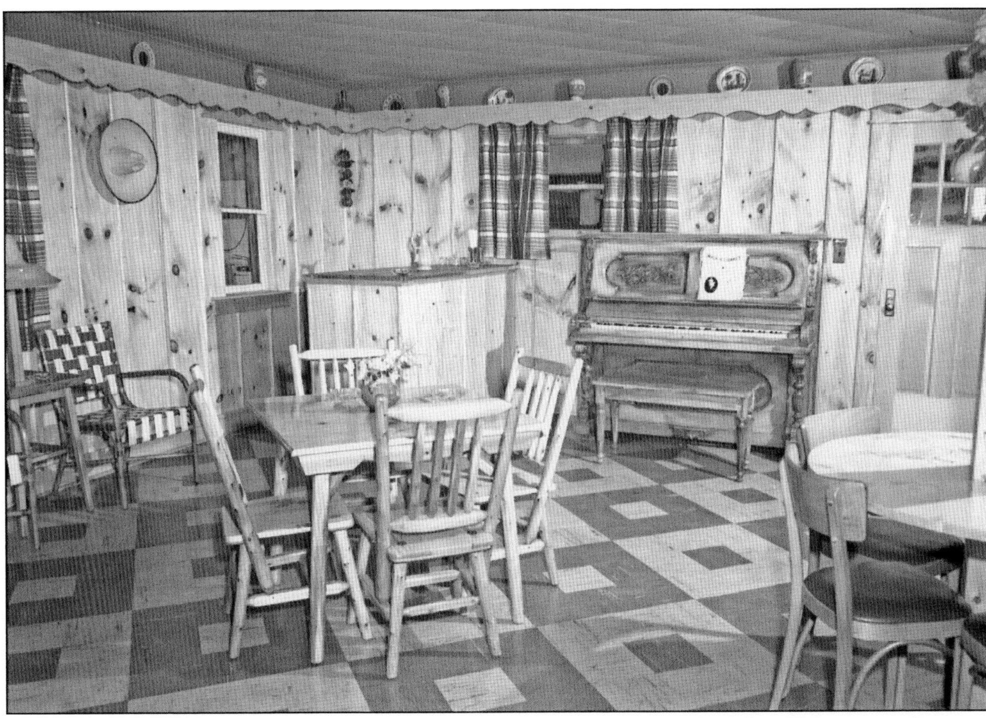

Shown is the interior eatery of the Round-Up Ranch in Downsville. This Western-style resort was created by Dr. Charles T. Markert and opened in the spring of 1947. The ranch grew over the years, offering horseback riding and many other activities, including tennis, swimming, golf, and badminton. The ranch also was noted for its regular Saturday night rodeos. Sold in 1985, it closed soon after, and most of the buildings were demolished.

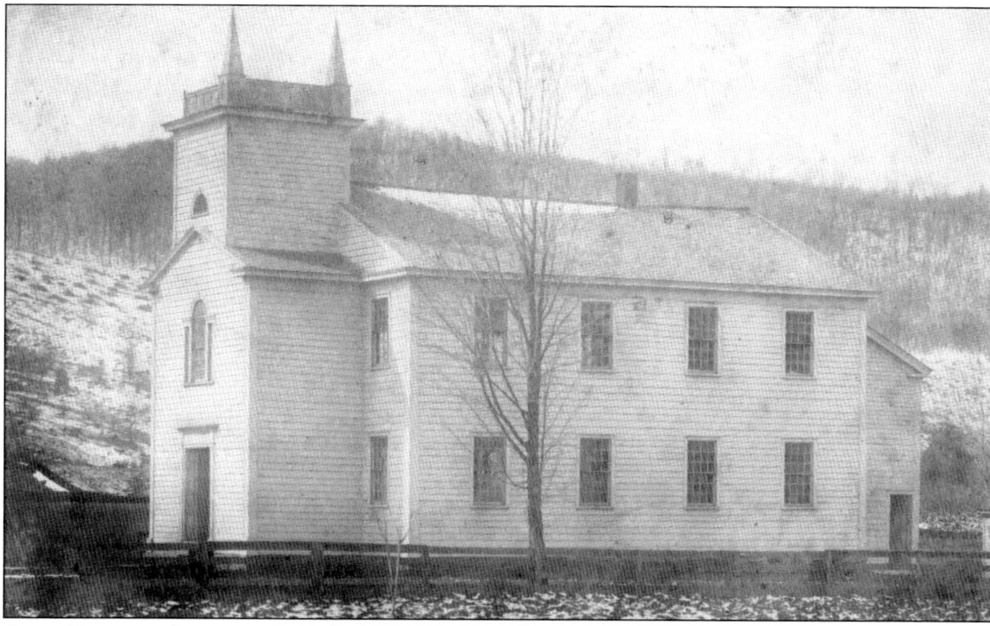

A small group of pioneers, mostly from Scotland, first worshipped in a barn situated on the flats along the Delaware River below the village of Delhi; the congregation was later known as the First Presbyterian Church of Delhi. In 1811, this church was built and was used until the 1880s, when it was determined that a larger building was needed for the growing congregation. The new church was built in the village of Delhi on Clinton Street and still operates today.

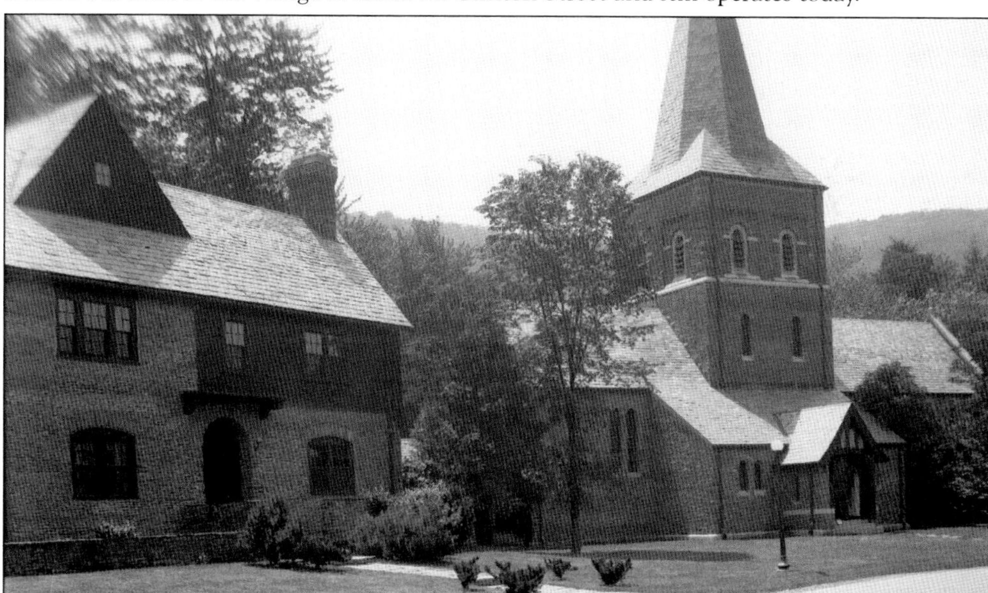

In the spring of 1914, a small house in "the Hook" area of Bovina, also known as Lake Delaware, was leased and prepared for use as a house of worship by Mabel Gerry. In the early 1920s, her sister Angelica was determined to build a new chapel and hired the noted American church architect Ralph Adams Cram of Boston. Construction began in the spring of 1922, with first services held the next year and consecration in 1924.

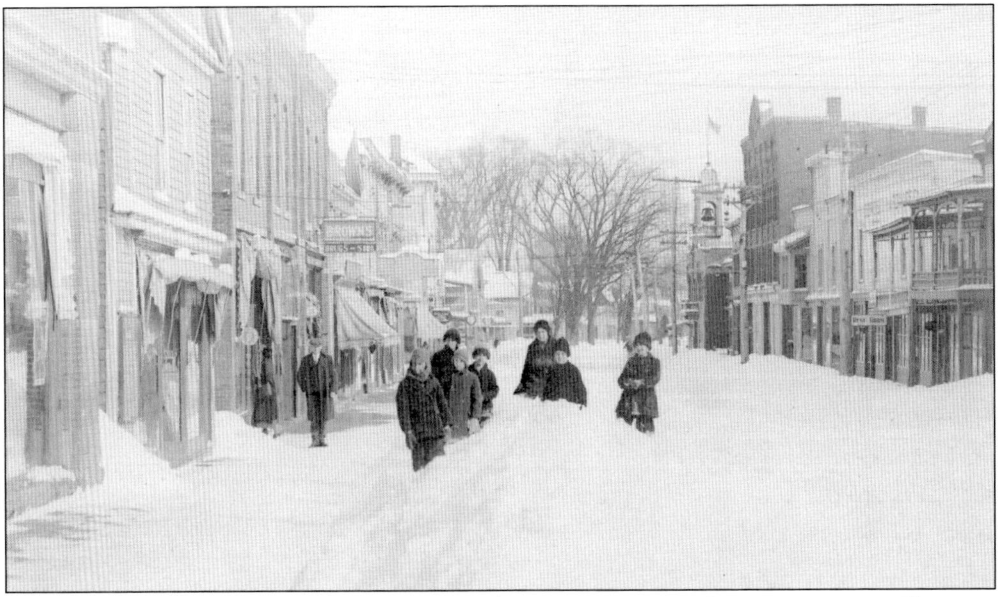

Due to its location in the Catskill Mountains, Delaware County is used to snowy winters. However, sometimes the amount of precipitation can be a bit overwhelming. The famous blizzard of 1888 paralyzed much of the Northeast, though people in Delaware County soldiered on through this and later snowstorms. As seen in this undated photograph from Deposit, children were particularly good at taking advantage of the circumstances.

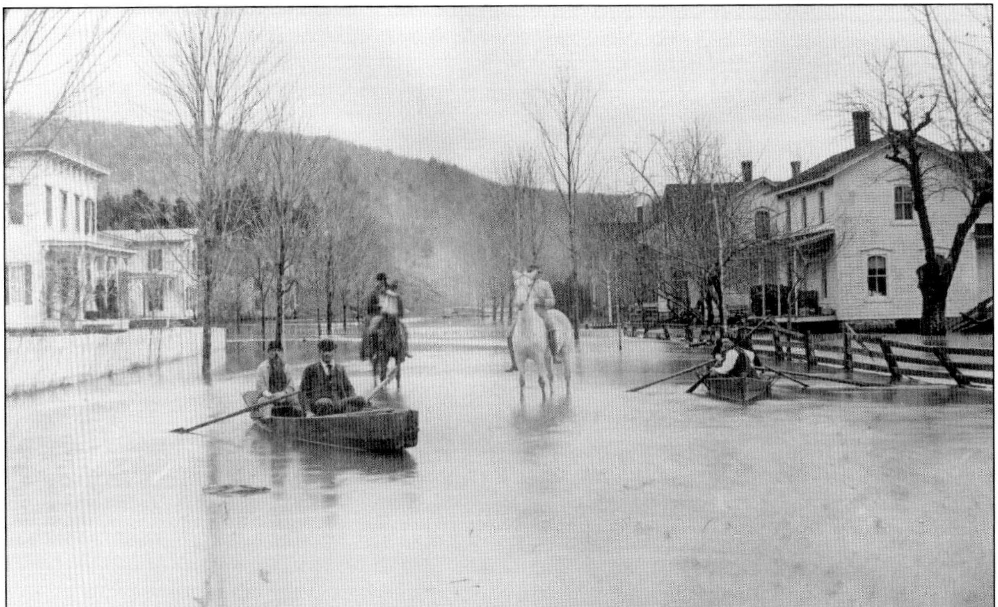

While having numerous rivers and streams has been an advantage for Delaware County, it also has led to occasional flooding. In 1895, as shown above, Downsville was hit with flooding, and it would not be the last time. There have been several subsequent floods in the area, including "The Great Pumpkin Flood" of October 1903 and floods in 1926 and 1933. There also were several floods in the 1940s. The late 20th and early 21st centuries saw further flooding, including floods caused by Tropical Storm Ivan in 2004 and Hurricane Irene in 2011.

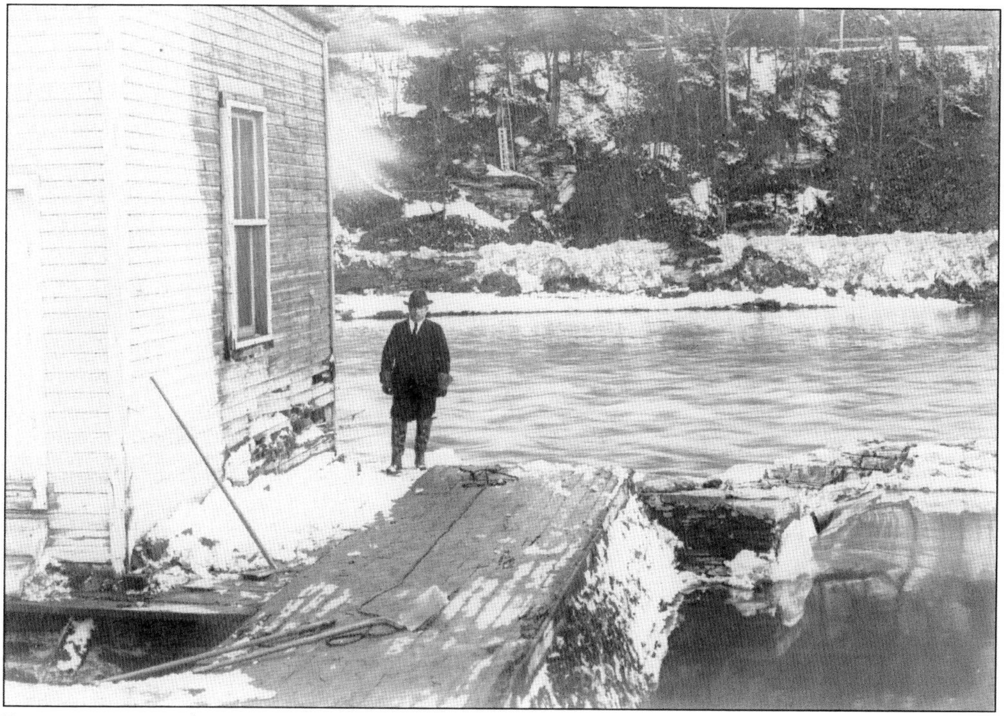

Deposit, given its location where the West Branch of the Delaware passes through and along the Pennsylvania border, also is prone to flooding, such as this flood in 1919. Deposit was hit hard during Hurricane Irene in 2011.

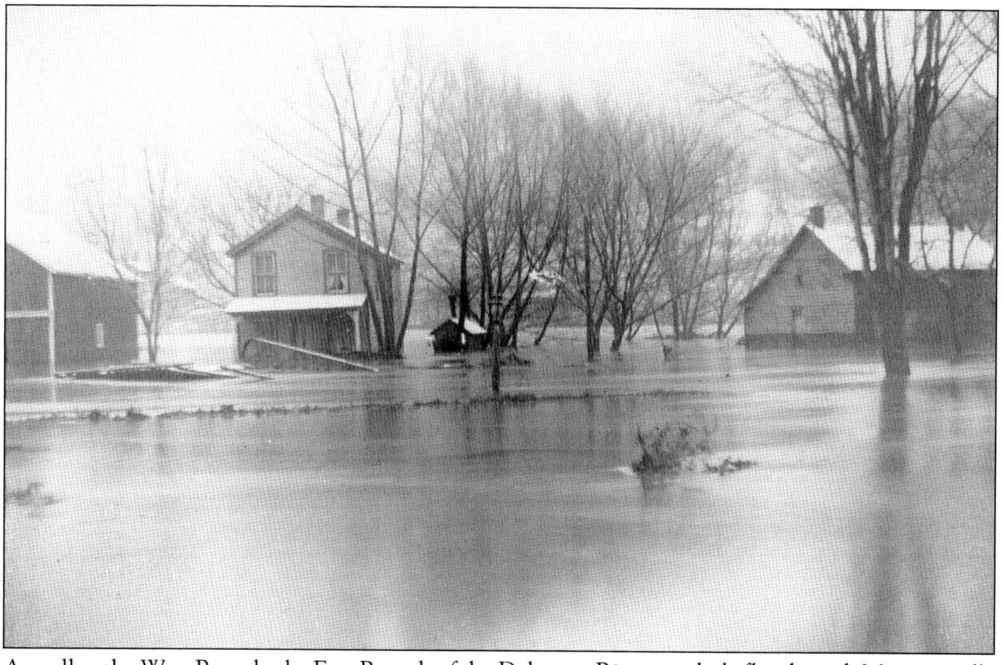

As well as the West Branch, the East Branch of the Delaware River regularly floods, with Margaretville being hit numerous times, including this flood in 1933. The village was particularly hard hit in 1996 and again by Hurricane Irene in 2011, with major damage to the business district.

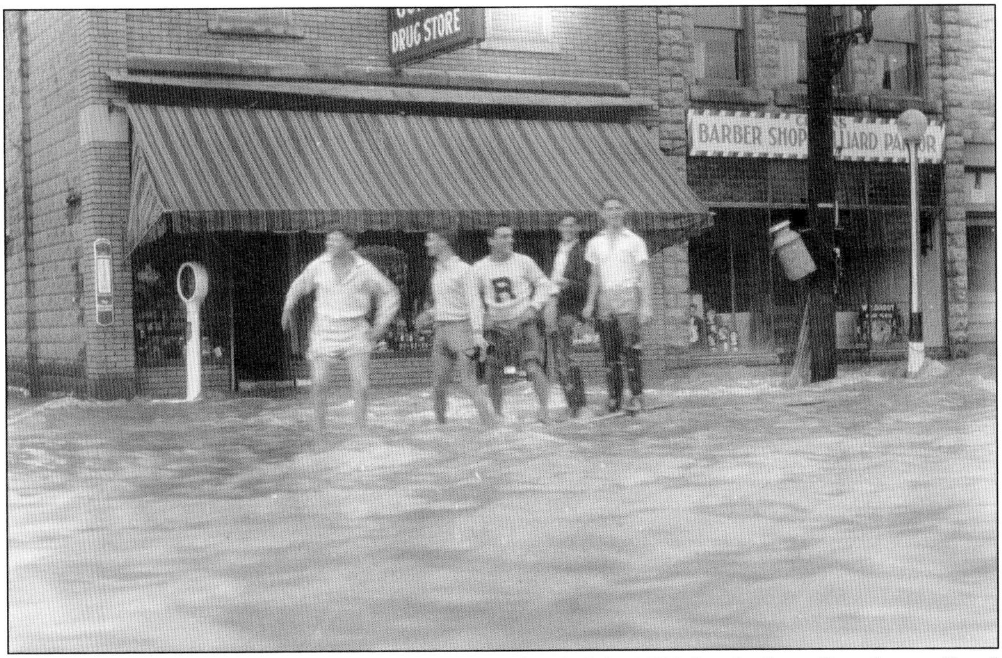

While these young men seem to be enjoying Walton's July 1935 flood, the village has suffered from this and other floods before and after this date. This was a history-making flood until the flood of January 1996, which did severe damage and killed several people. In 2011, Tropical Storm Leo caused more flooding in Walton.

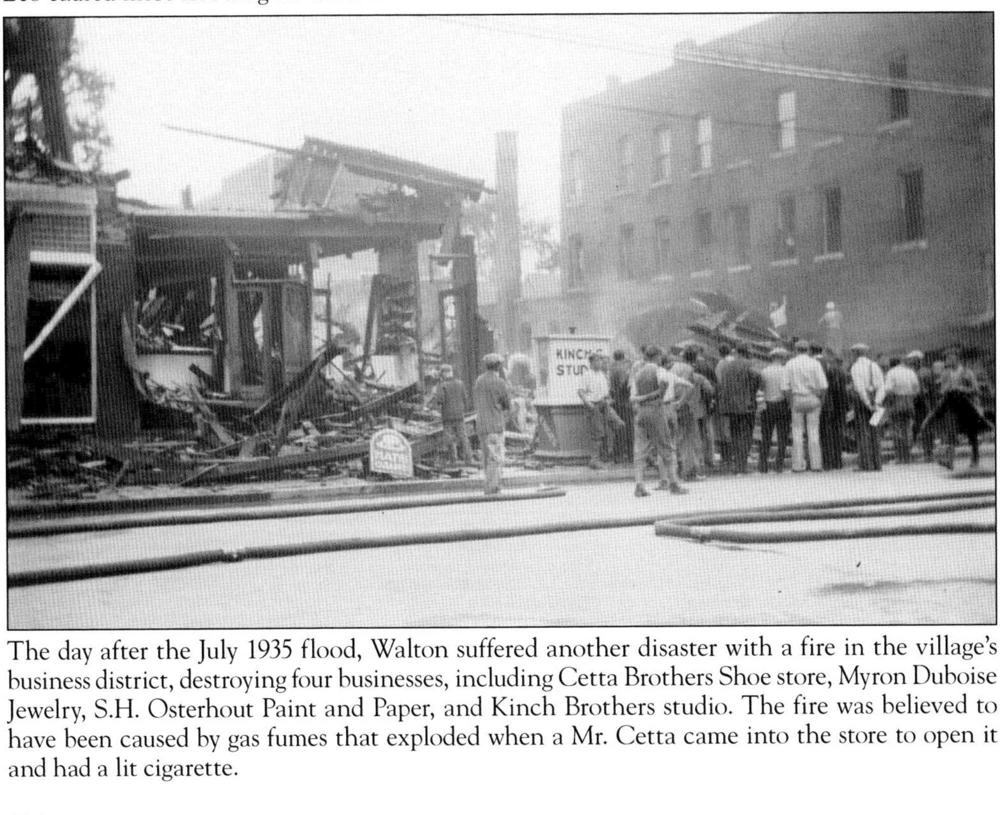

The day after the July 1935 flood, Walton suffered another disaster with a fire in the village's business district, destroying four businesses, including Cetta Brothers Shoe store, Myron Duboise Jewelry, S.H. Osterhout Paint and Paper, and Kinch Brothers studio. The fire was believed to have been caused by gas fumes that exploded when a Mr. Cetta came into the store to open it and had a lit cigarette.

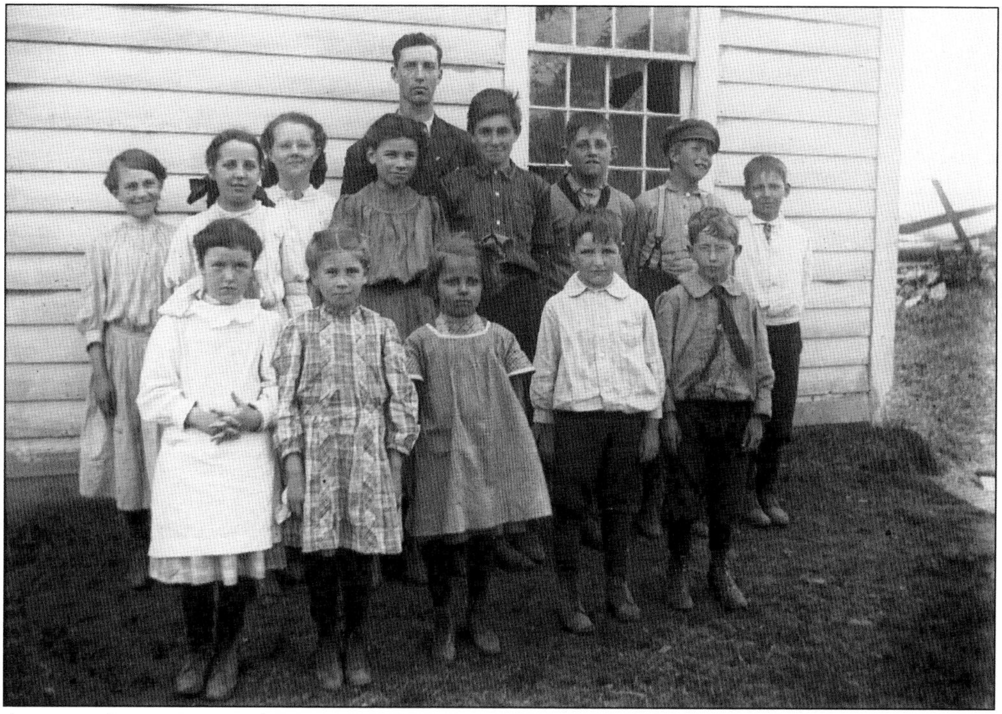

As typical in most rural counties, education was provided through the system of one-room schoolhouses, organized as common school districts. This system was established by the state in 1812. Each town had numerous districts. Even a small town like Bovina had over 10 districts in the 1860s while towns like Franklin and Middletown had over 20. The one-room schools usually taught students through the eighth grade.

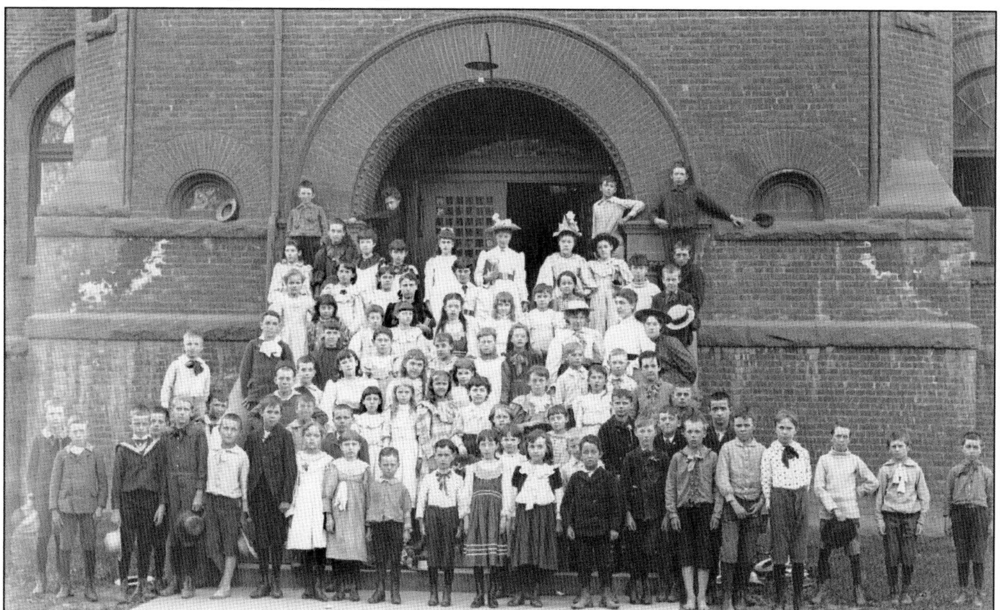

In the center of villages with more concentrated populations, larger schools were possible, such as this school in Walton.

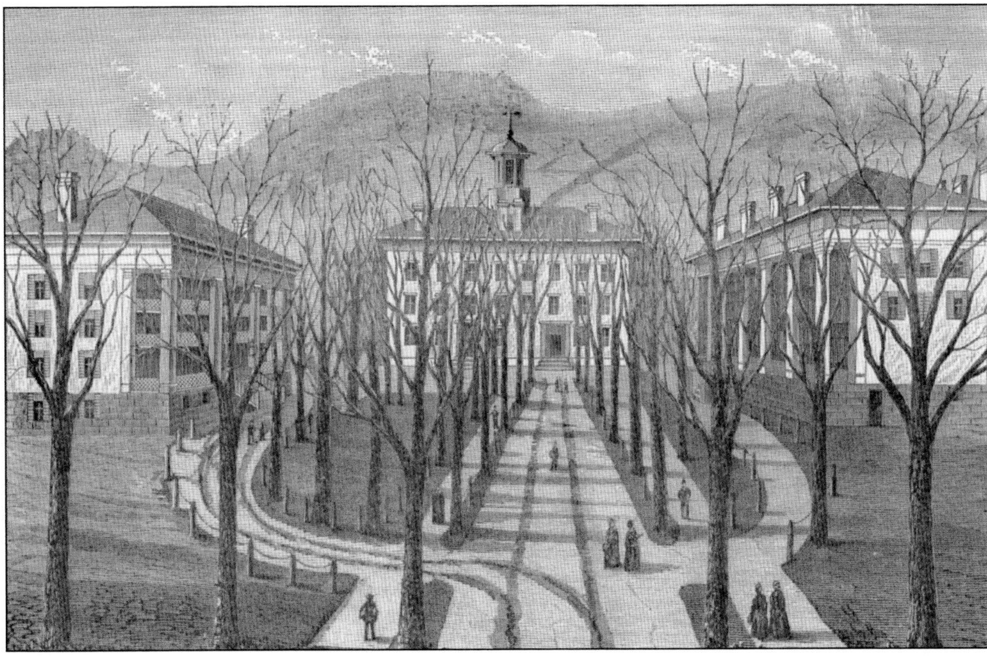

The Delaware Literary Institute was established in Franklin in 1835 and operated as a "literary institution for the instruction and education of youth of both sexes," with a primary aim of educating ministers and missionary teachers. Enrollment began to fall after the Civil War, and in 1902, the institute closed, with the buildings subsequently being used as a Union Free school. Chapel Hall today is used by the Franklin Stage Company as a theater.

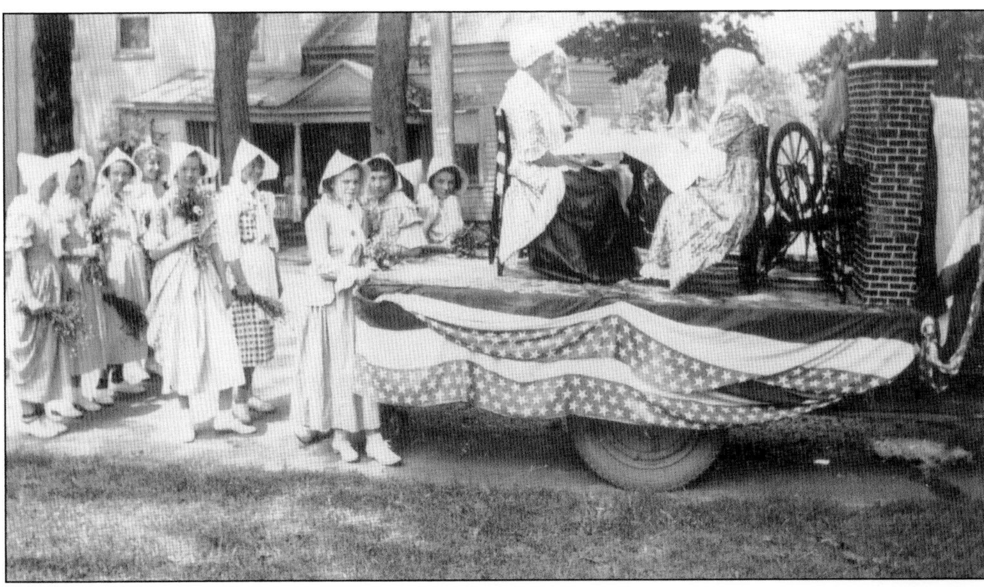

To mark the centennial of the founding of the Delaware Literary Institute in 1935, Franklin held elaborate celebrations. Here, a group of local school girls follows a decorated truck down a village street. The scene is intended to depict Franklin life in 1835.

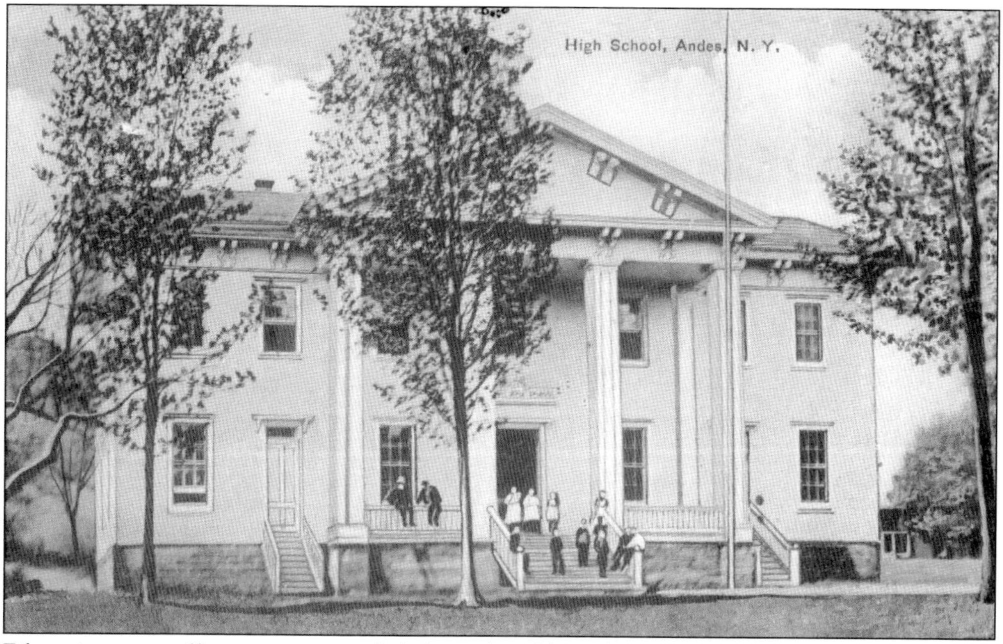

Education generally was not provided through public schools after the eighth grade. Several communities saw the creation of high schools, such as this one in Andes. Students attending these schools often boarded with friends or relatives during the week.

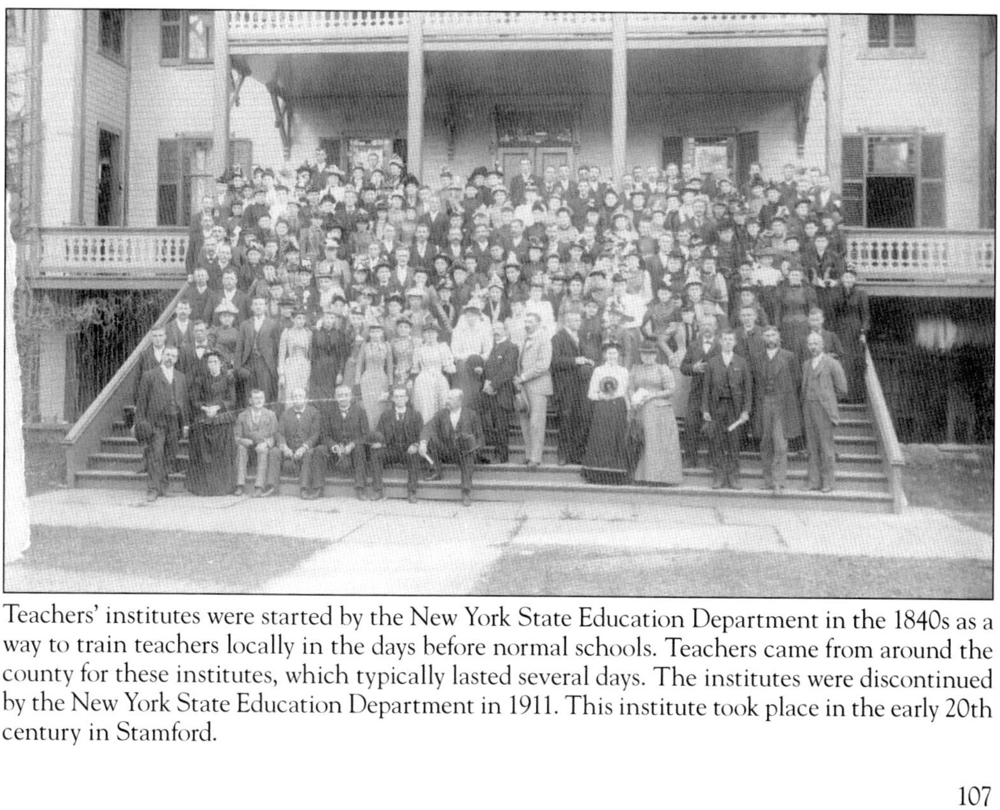

Teachers' institutes were started by the New York State Education Department in the 1840s as a way to train teachers locally in the days before normal schools. Teachers came from around the county for these institutes, which typically lasted several days. The institutes were discontinued by the New York State Education Department in 1911. This institute took place in the early 20th century in Stamford.

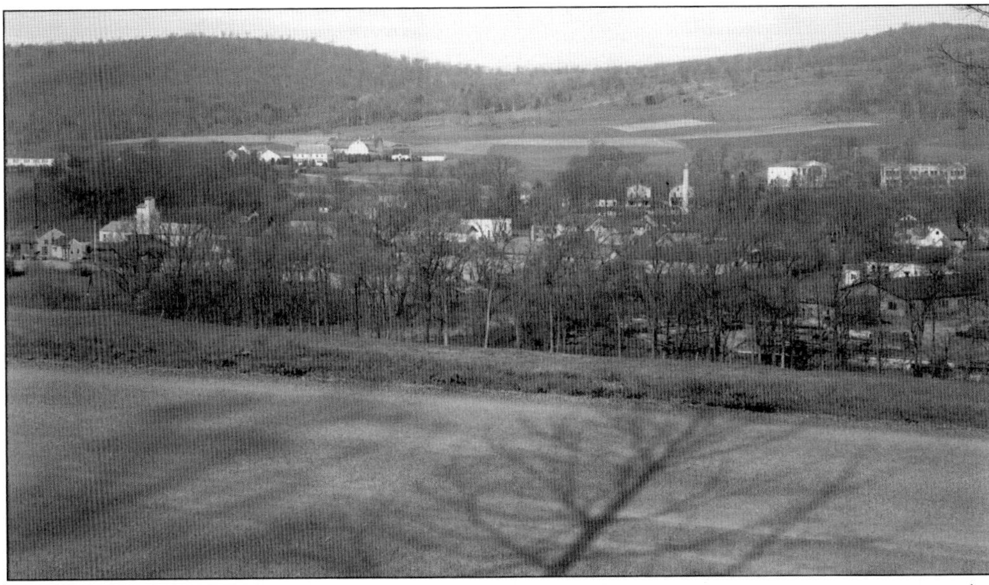

The campus of the State Agricultural School is seen across the valley in this 1930s image. Founded in Delhi in 1913 as an institute for higher learning, State University of New York (SUNY) at Delhi has experienced tremendous growth over the past decades. Known in the 1960s and 1970s as Delhi Tech, the college expanded its programs and now offers both two- and four-year degree programs. It is the only institution devoted to higher education in Delaware County.

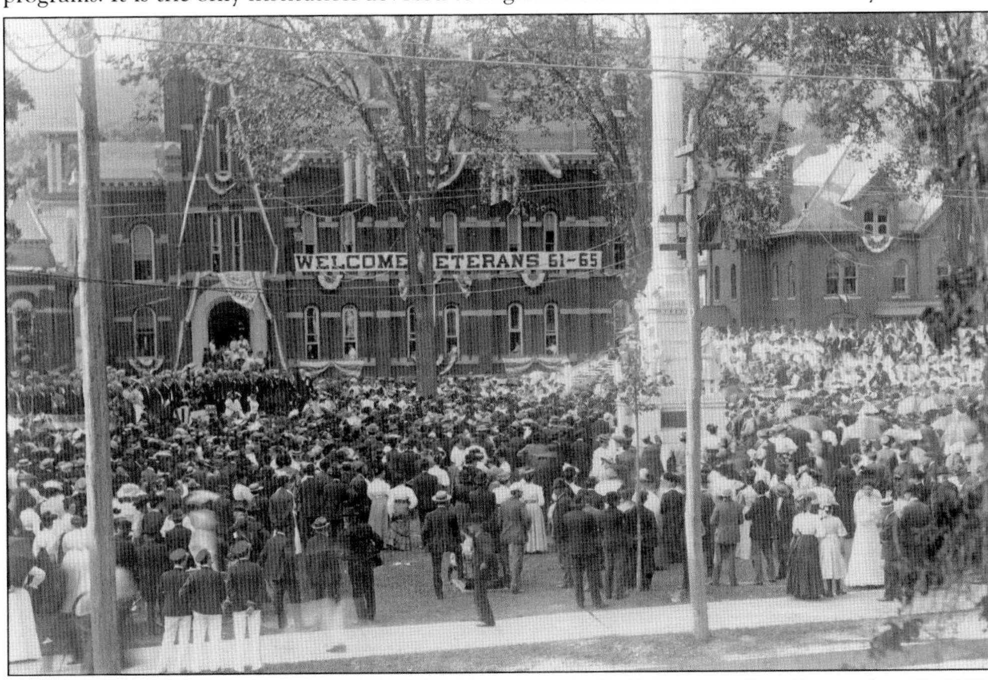

Dedication of Delaware County's Civil War monument in Delhi occurred on September 18, 1906. Although the Civil War had ended over 40 years earlier, memories of the war and the sacrifices made remained strong in the early 20th century. Numerous veterans of the war and their families were in attendance at the monument's unveiling on Delhi's Courthouse Square. Military veterans are still honored today with ceremonies held adjacent to the monument each November 11.

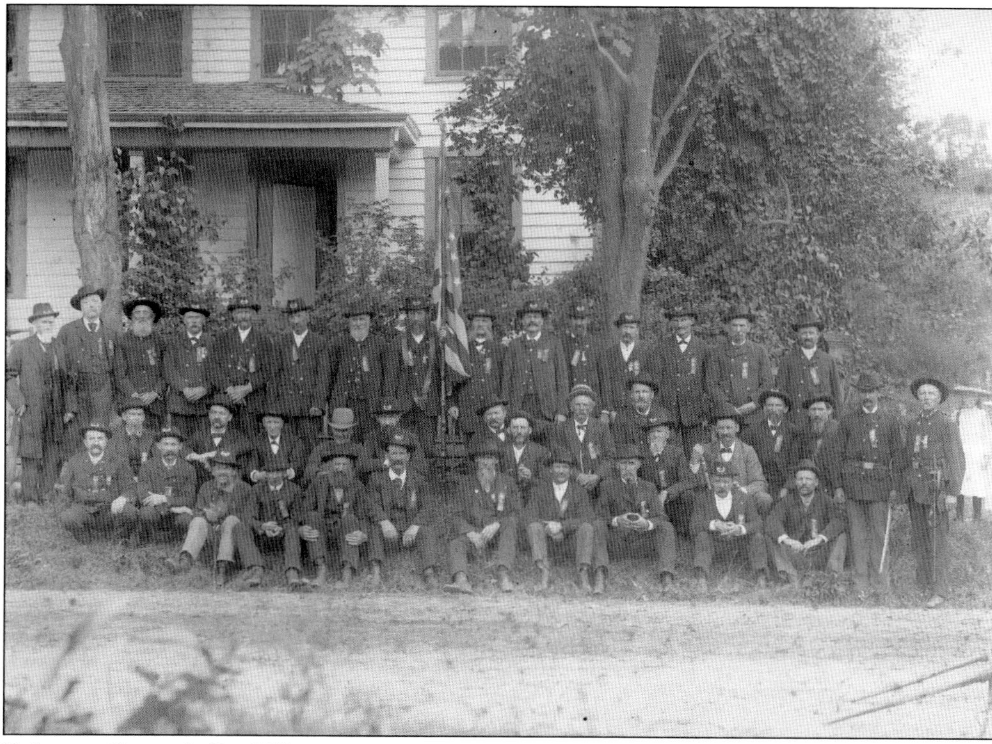

Delaware County's Civil War veterans gathered frequently for reunions and to remember their fallen comrades. The national Grand Army of the Republic was the Union Civil War veteran organization. There were 13 chapters in Delaware County, including the Ben Marvin Post in Walton and the Theodolpholus England Post in Delhi. This reunion of "old soldiers" took place in Hancock, likely in the late 19th century, and included soldiers from the 72nd and 144th Infantry Regiments.

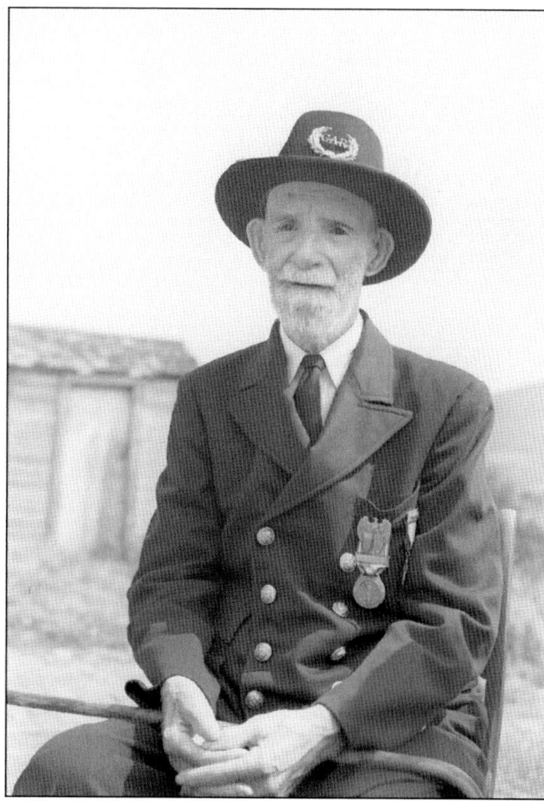

Delaware County's last surviving old soldier was George Dugan. He had served for three years in the 51st New York Infantry regiment, incurring a wound in his leg during that time. After the Civil War, Irish native Dugan had lived in several places around Delaware County, settling for some time in Harpersfield. Photographed by Bob Wyer in the spring of 1941 for his 102nd birthday, Dugan died at the end of that year in Roxbury.

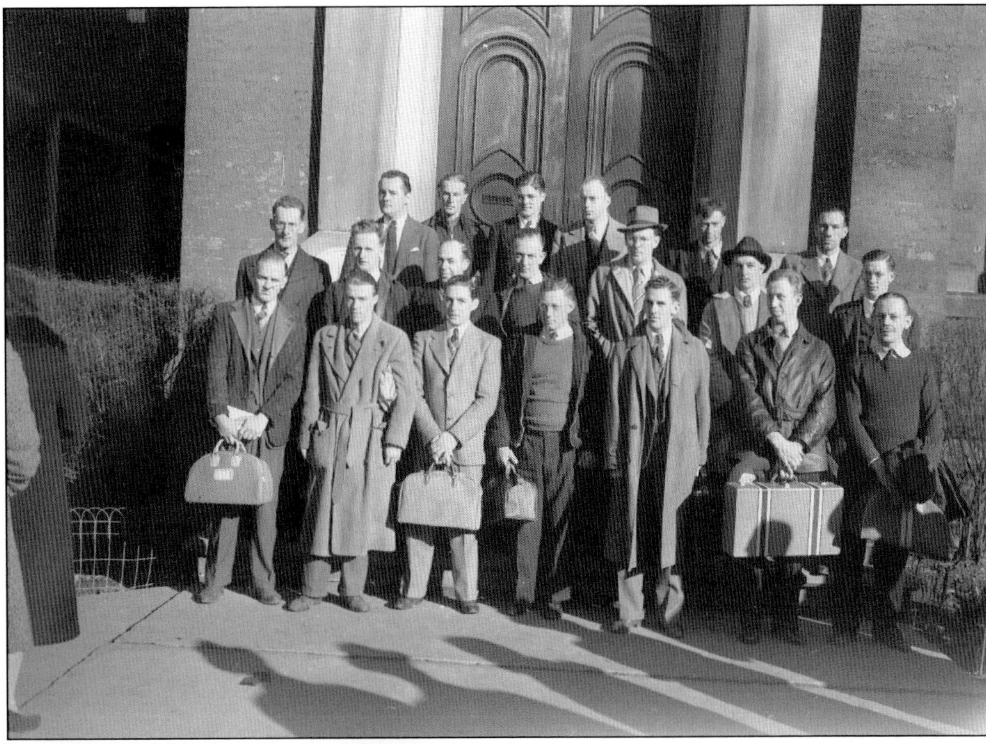

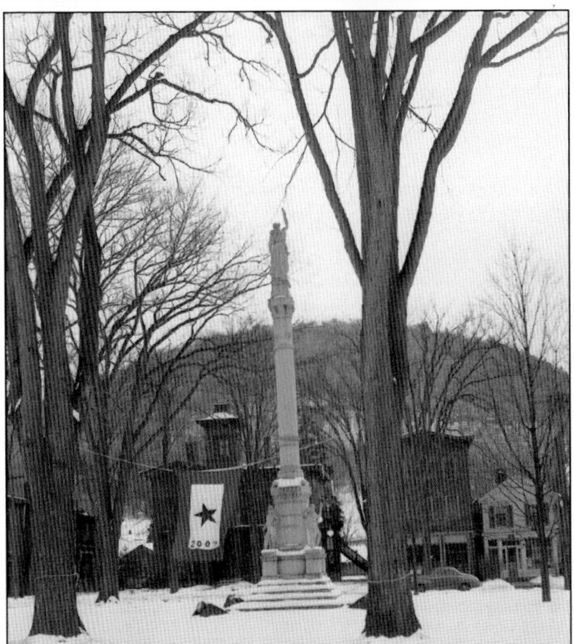

With the attack on Pearl Harbor on December 7, 1941, young men (and some women) from Delaware County stepped in to do their part. Early in 1942, Bob Wyer photographed numerous groups of inductees, like this group here, approved for service and ready to head out for their training. This group is posing in front of the county courthouse in Delhi.

During World War II, this flag was hung at the Courthouse Square in Delhi with the number of service men and women from the county. The number changed frequently as the enlistments continued. (Photograph by Bob Wyer.)

Six

SINCE 1945

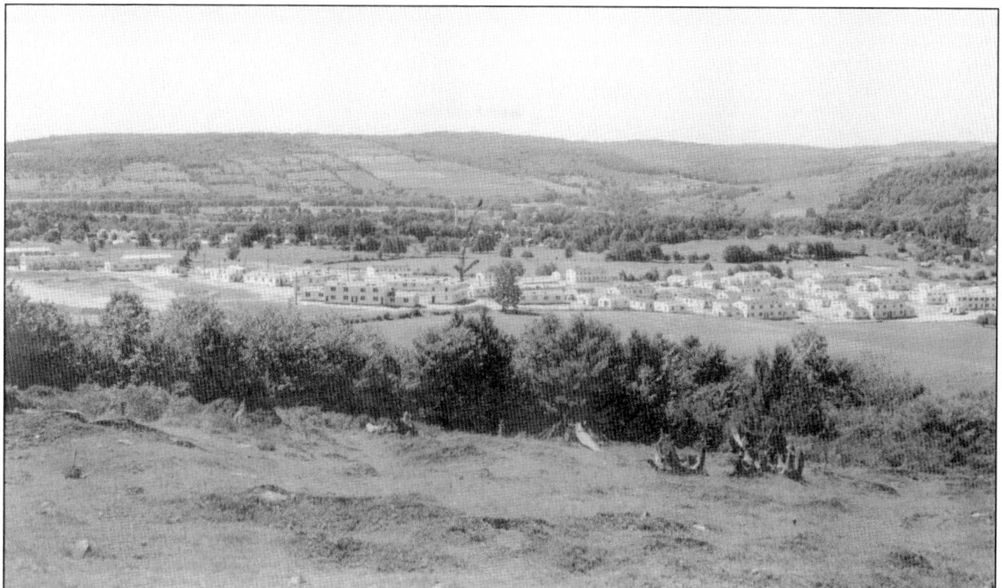

72—Defense Housing Project, "Sherwood Heights", Sidney, N. Y.

Sidney today is the largest incorporated village in Delaware County. Much of its growth in the 19th century was propelled by the two railroads whose tracks crossed in the village, the Ontario & Western and the Delaware & Hudson. World War II provided a major population boost, with military-related industries such as the Scintilla Magneto, Bendix Aviation Corporation plant attracting thousands of workers from near and far. The Sherwood Heights complex was constructed during the war to house the influx.

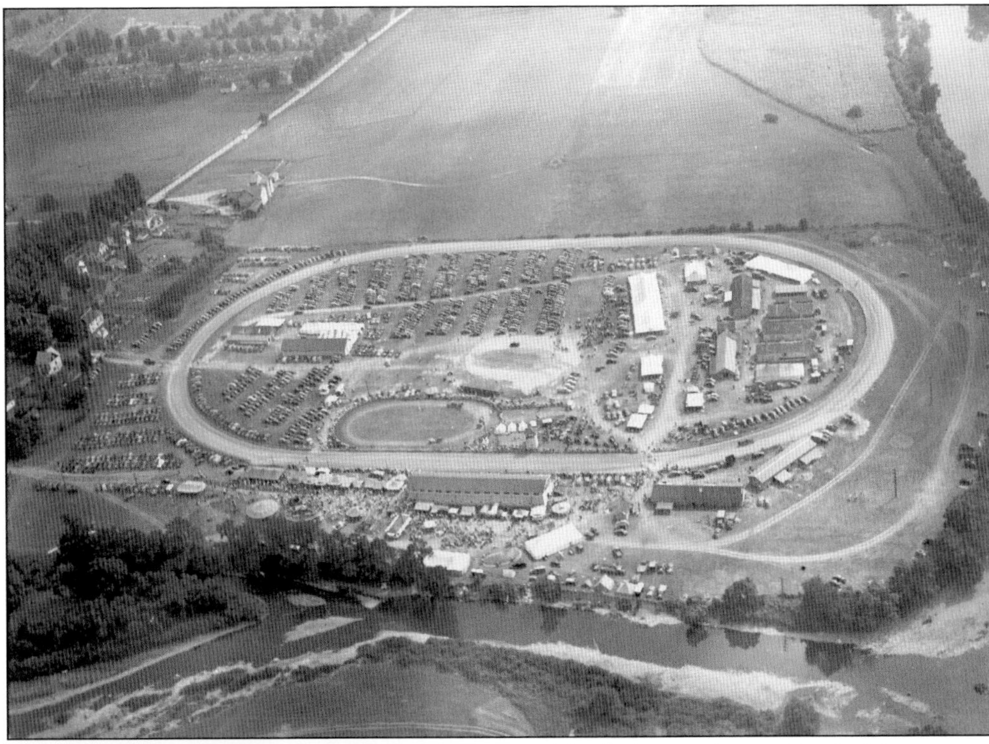

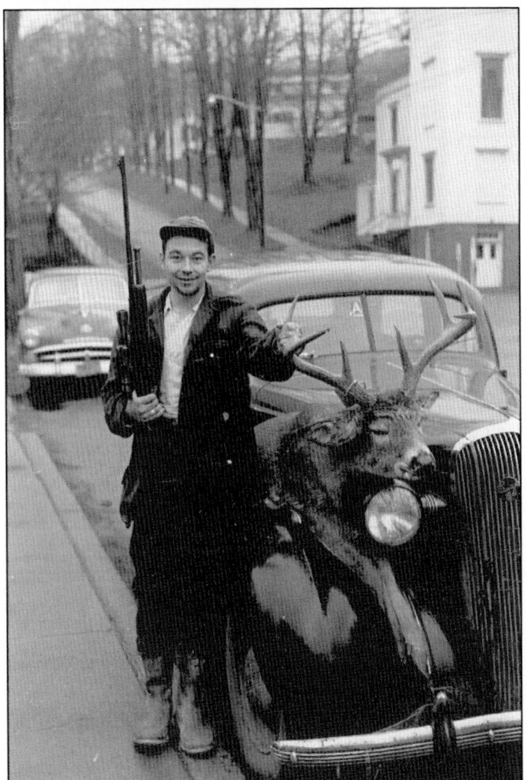

The Delaware County Fair had its start in the 19th century and was held in a number of towns during that century, including Walton, Franklin, Delhi, and Andes. During the 1920s, the county fair was firmly established in Walton, where it remains today. This aerial photograph of the fairgrounds dates from the 1940s, showing the same location in which the fair is still held each August. The West Branch of the Delaware River meanders through the foreground of the view.

For centuries, the Catskills Mountains were utilized by the Lenni Lenapé and the Mohawk Indians as a vast hunting ground. Those tribes are now gone, but the hunting tradition continues. Over the course of the past century and a half, Delaware County has attracted local and visiting hunters during deer season, which usually takes place in November and December. This photograph shows John Bramley of Delhi with his buck in November 1952. Man and deer are posing on Court Street in Delhi outside the studios of noted local photographer Bob Wyer.

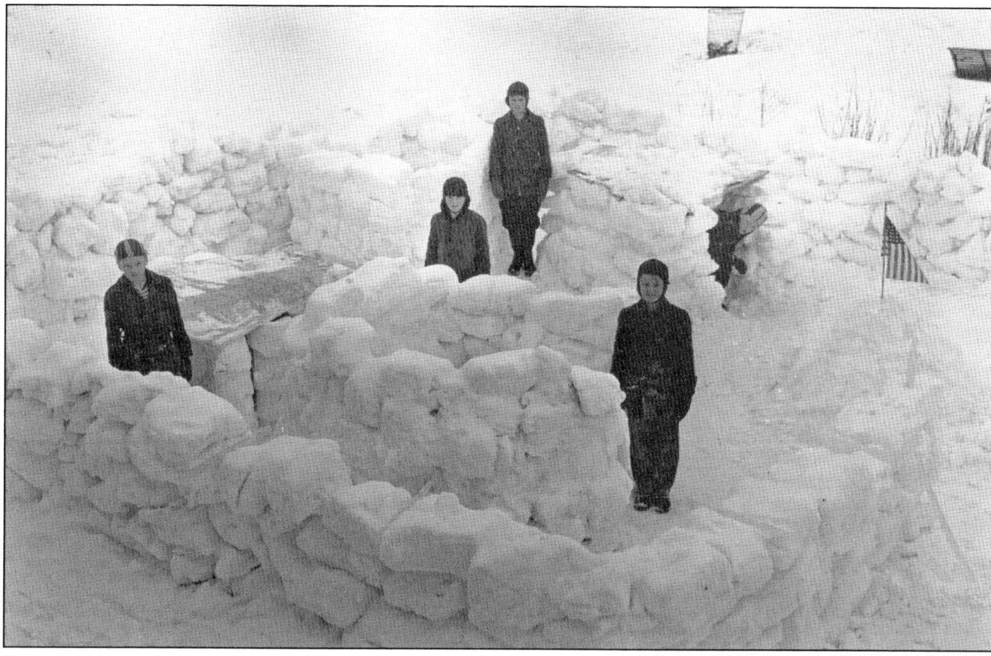

Winters are usually long and harsh in the Catskills. However, the colder months of the year can often be a time for lots of fun, as this image of a group of five young pals in the 1950s clearly shows. The group has evidently spent considerable time creating this snow fort and now poses proudly for the photograph. (Photograph by Bob Wyer.)

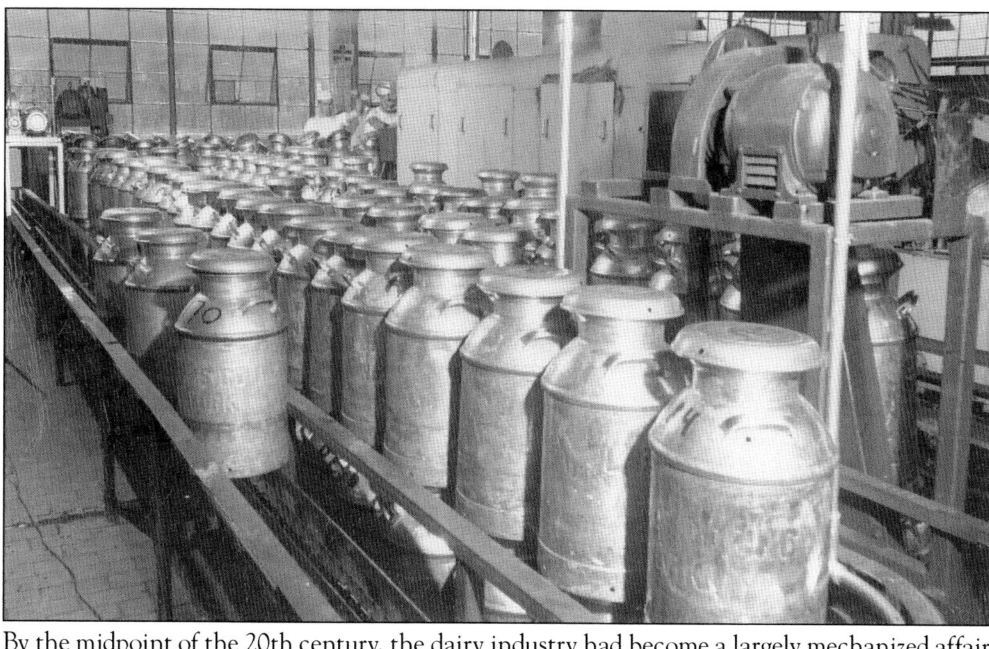

By the midpoint of the 20th century, the dairy industry had become a largely mechanized affair. Whereas 50 or 75 years earlier, farmers churned most of their milk into butter and cheese and then packed it into barrels for longevity, by the middle of the 20th century, milk from area farms was transported daily by trucks to creameries such as the one shown. Here, milk churns run along the conveyor at the Co-op Creamery in Delhi around 1950.

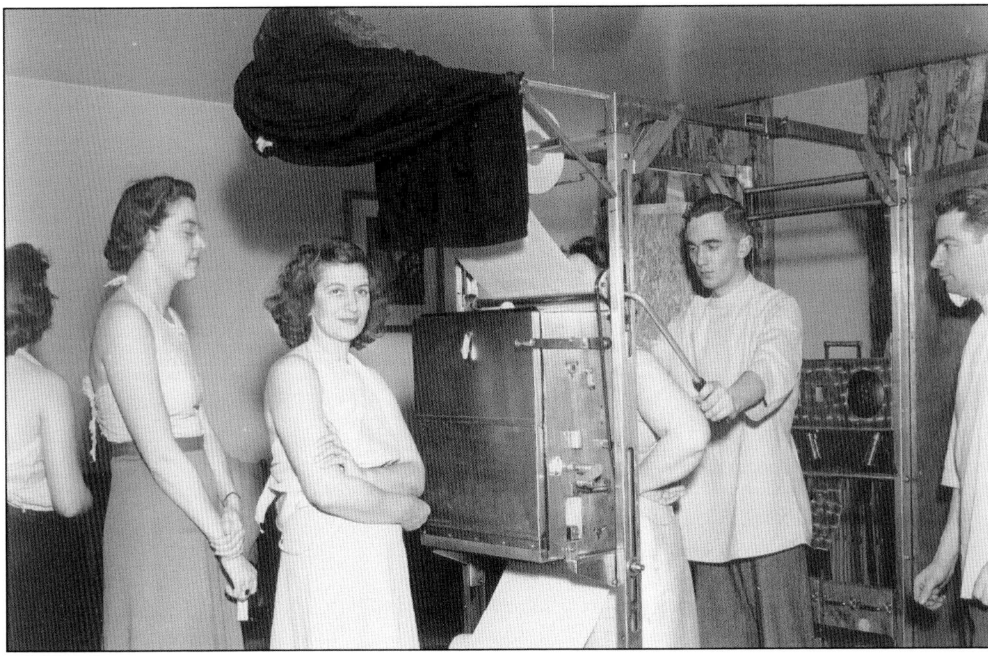

"Letting X-Ray Say O.K." was the caption on this photograph of company employees in Sidney, provided by the public relations department of the Scintilla Magneto, Bendix Aviation Corporation. The group pictured here on September 12, 1950, is having chest X-rays to screen for tuberculosis.

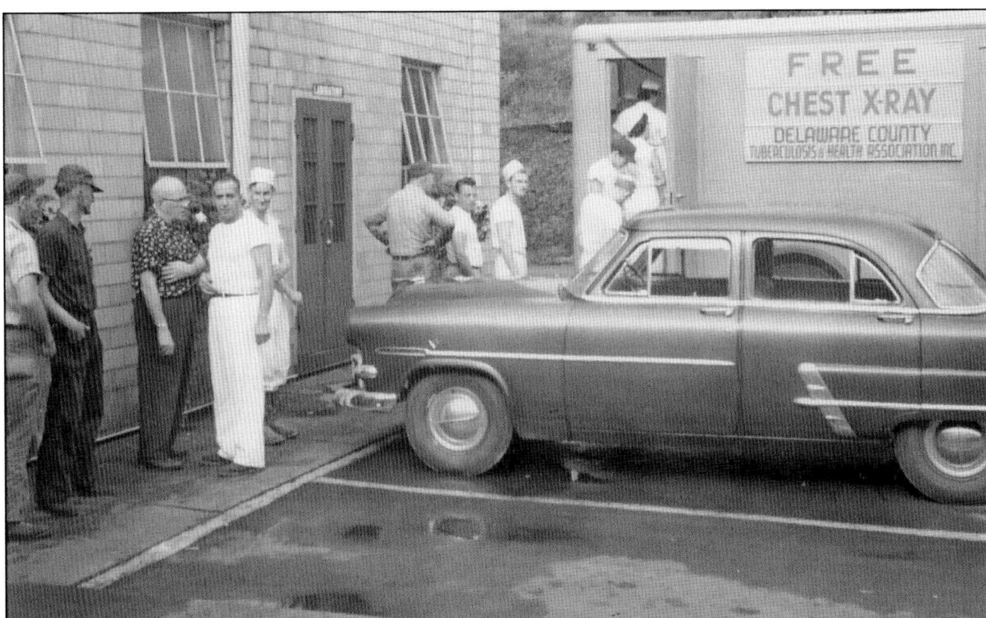

A total of 1,992 employees of Scintilla Magneto received chest X-rays on September 12, 1950, during a one-day program conducted at the Sidney plant's first-aid department under the sponsorship of the Delaware County Tuberculosis and Health Department. Here, the mobile van has parked and is receiving more employees awaiting their turn.

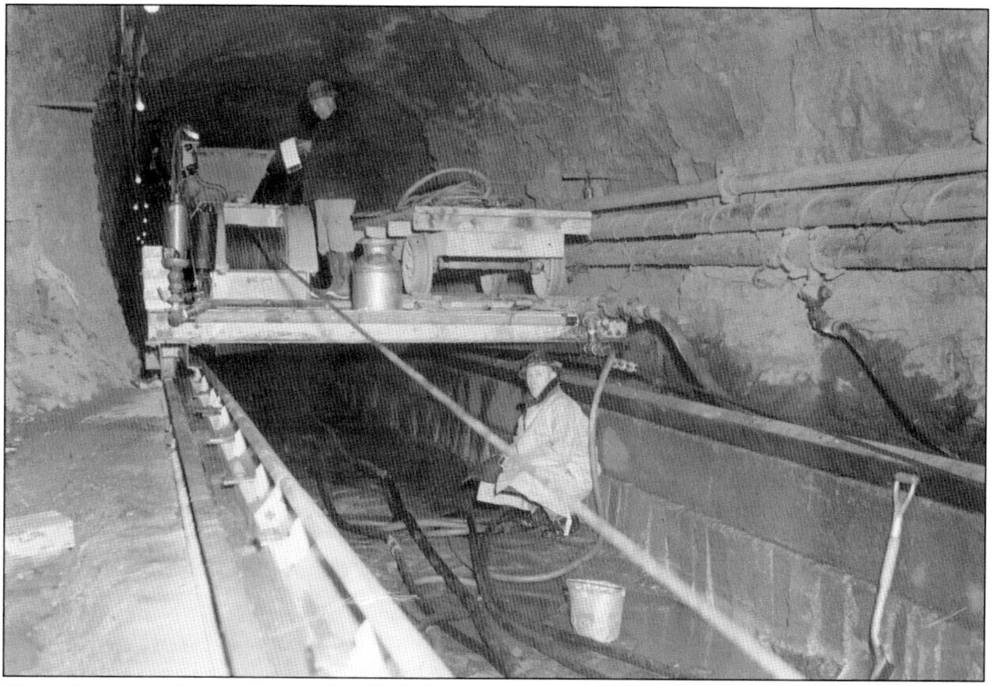

These images, taken on September 7, 1950, shows tunnel laborers working below ground on the Pepacton Reservoir intake tunnel, East Delaware Tunnel, Beaverkill Division. Walsh Construction Company won the contract for much of the work done on the Pepacton Reservoir project. Depicted here are workers of that company and those of another company, B. Perini & Sons, Inc. Shown above, rails were laid to aid the construction of the tunnels. Below, a drilling crew is at the head of the tunnel. Note the steel roofing at the very top of the picture.

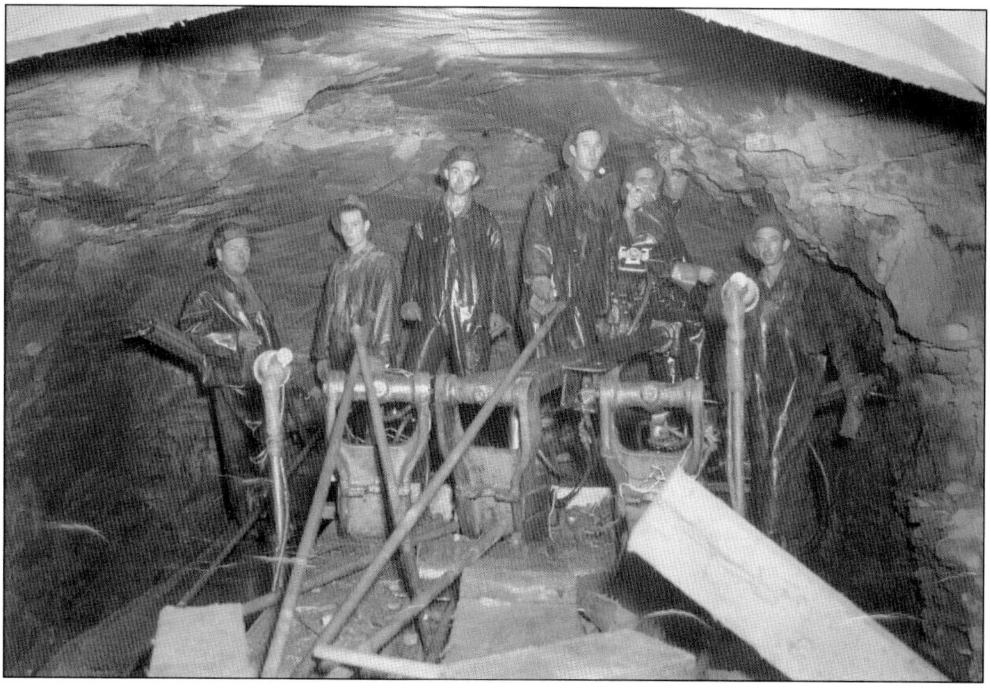

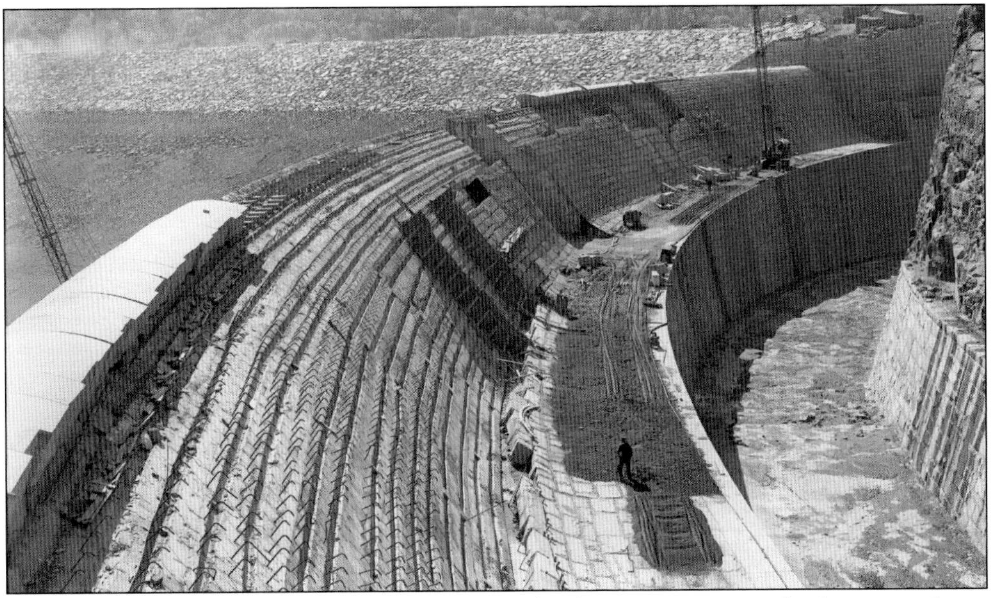

As New York City's population grew, it began to seek other sources to provide clean water for its many millions of residents. In the 20th century, the city cast its eyes on Delaware County and the East and West Branches of the Delaware River. Scheduled to begin in the late 1930s, construction of the Pepacton Reservoir was delayed by World War II. The project was a truly massive undertaking and included construction of this coffer dam outside of Downsville. The dam, built to hold back the waters of the East Branch of the Delaware River, was completed in 1949.

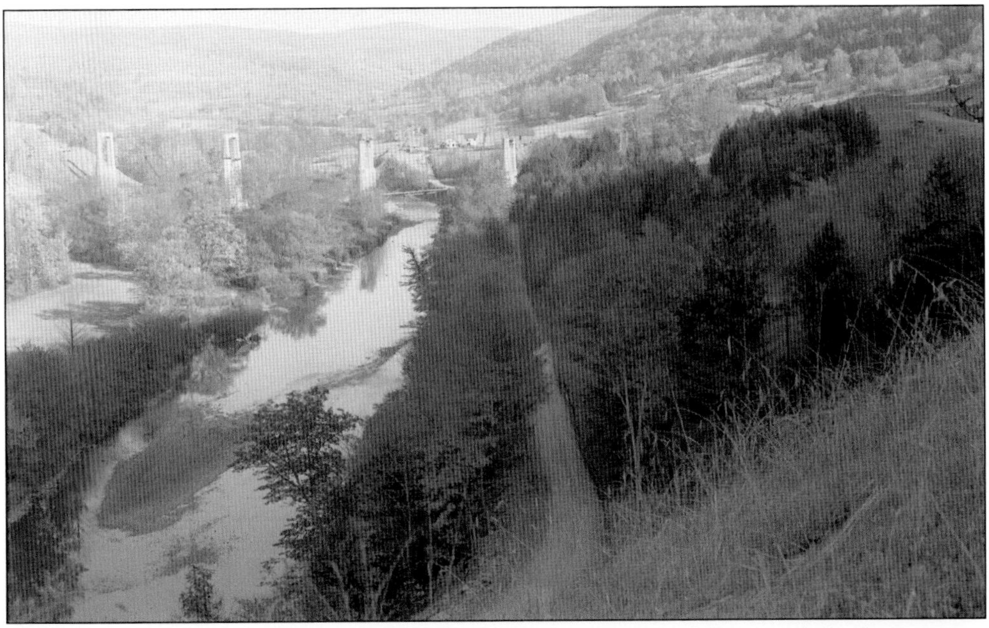

Work on the demolition of the communities and the construction of the tunnels for the Pepacton Reservoir continued into the 1950s. Work also included the construction of the Shavertown Bridge over the reservoir as pictured here. The Pepacton Reservoir began to fill in the fall of 1954 and was full by April 1956. In total, four communities disappeared under the rising waters: Arena, Pepacton, Shavertown, and Union Grove. In addition, much farmland was lost.

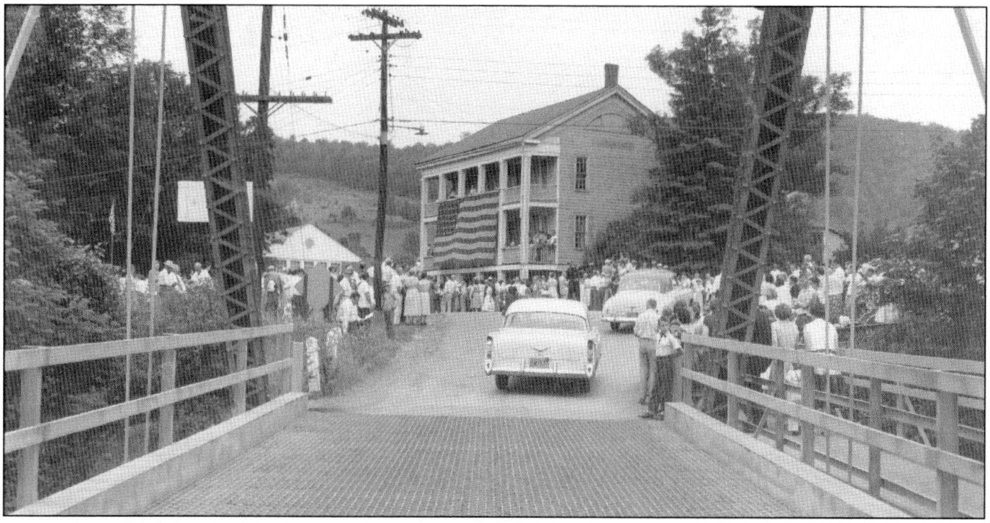

As work moved forward on the Pepacton Reservoir in the mid-1950s, the city moved ahead with plans for another reservoir utilizing the West Branch of the Delaware River. Local communities fought to stop the project, as did county politicians and officials, but they were ultimately overpowered and overruled. Work on the Cannonsville Reservoir project started in 1954. In July 1956, Cannonsville, one of the communities slated to be demolished, held its last Old Home Day. Pictured here is the rear of a parade passing over the bridge leading into the village.

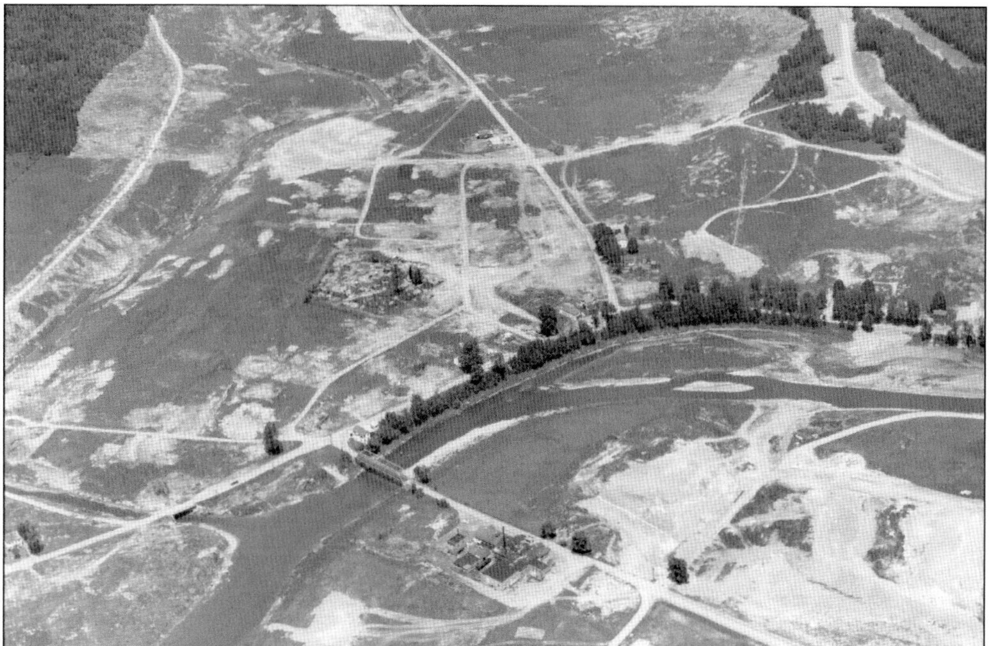

By 1963, much of the demolition of the communities of Beerston, Cannonsville, Granton, Rock Rift, and Rock Royal had been completed. This aerial photograph was taken in July 1963 as demolition was being completed in the Cannonsville hamlet. The bridge depicted in the previous photograph (and on the cover) is still visible in this view. The Cannonsville Reservoir was filled and eventually placed in service in 1965.

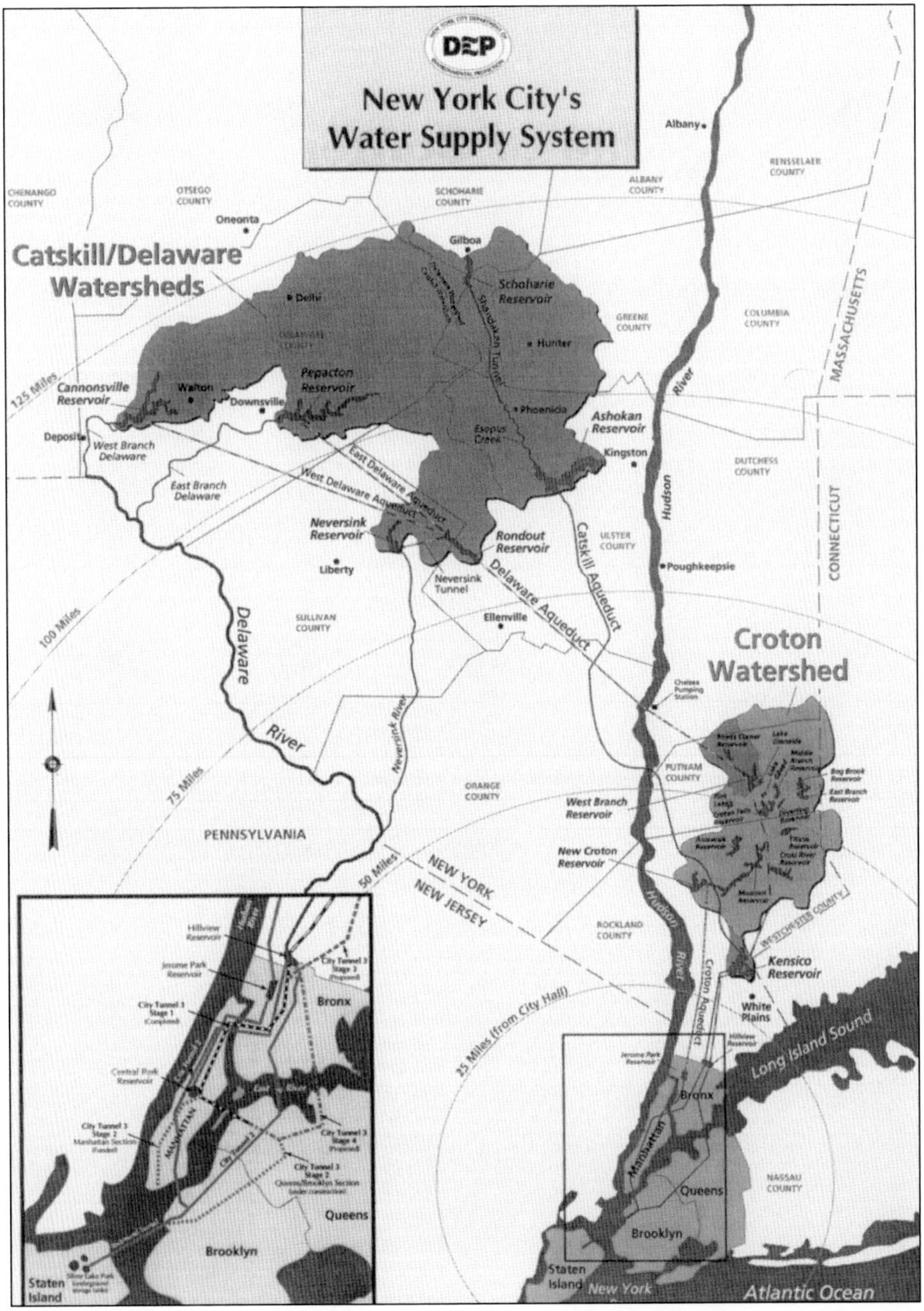

With the completion of the Cannonsville Reservoir in 1965, the New York City Water Supply System was complete. However, upstate communities began to lock horns with the city again in 1990 when the New York City Department of Environmental Protection issued much tougher rules for communities in the reservoirs' watershed. This led to the creation of the Coalition of Watershed Towns to fight the rules. After several years of negotiation, a memorandum of agreement was signed in 1997, giving the city a waiver from filtration while committing it to construct wastewater treatment plants and to provide "good neighbor" money to the communities affected by the regulations.

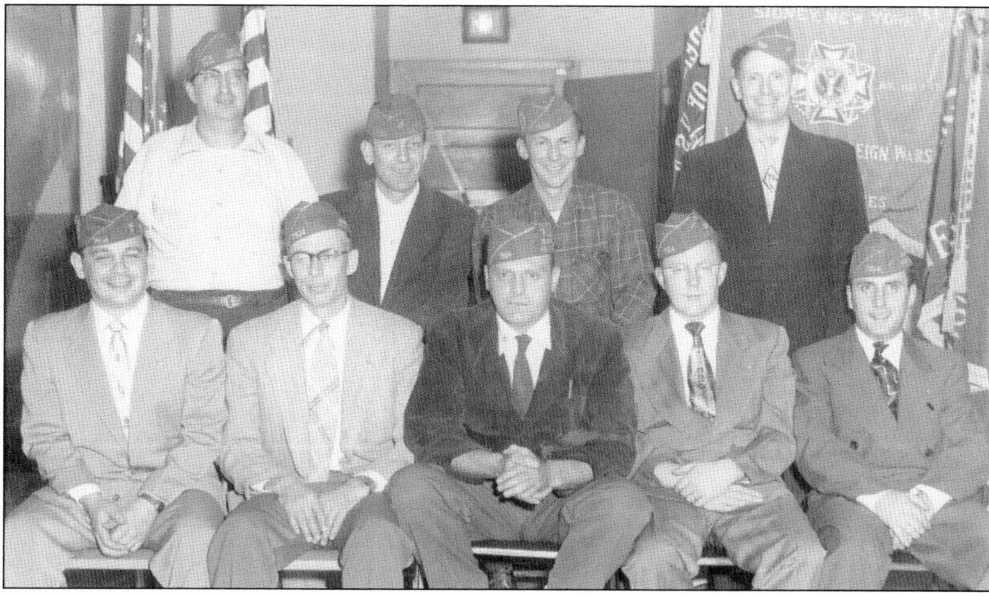

Recently installed officers of Veterans of Foreign Wars Corporal Arrandale Post No. 7914 of Sidney are pictured on April 21, 1955. From left to right are (sitting) Anthony Barber, trustee for three years; Albert Schumacher, junior vice commander; Dale Anderson, commander; Donald Warner, senior vice commander; and Richard Grow, quartermaster and installing officer; (standing) Salvatore Rossini, county council delegate; Harold MacDonald Jr., adjutant; and Carrol Bussey and Harry Fancher, county council delegates.

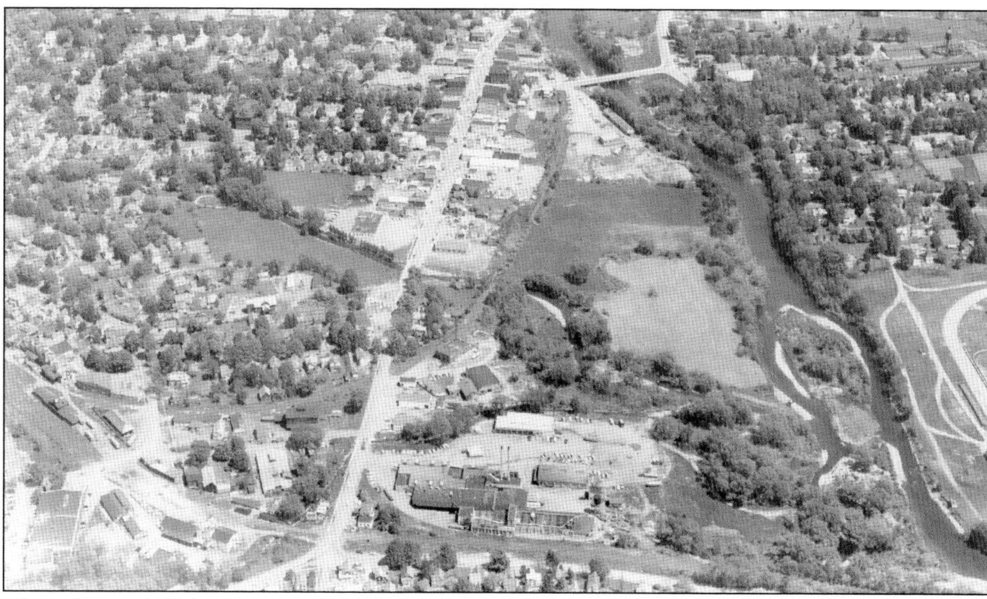

The village of Walton is seen from the air in the early 1960s. Clearly visible is the West Branch of the Delaware River running from north to south through the middle of the image. At far right are the Delaware County Fairgrounds, and at center is the new bridge carrying State Route 206 over the river. The main commercial thoroughfare visible is Delaware Avenue, and at the bottom of the photograph can be seen the creamery (today a Breakstones plant). Also visible in this view is the one-time course of the Ontario & Western Railway tracks.

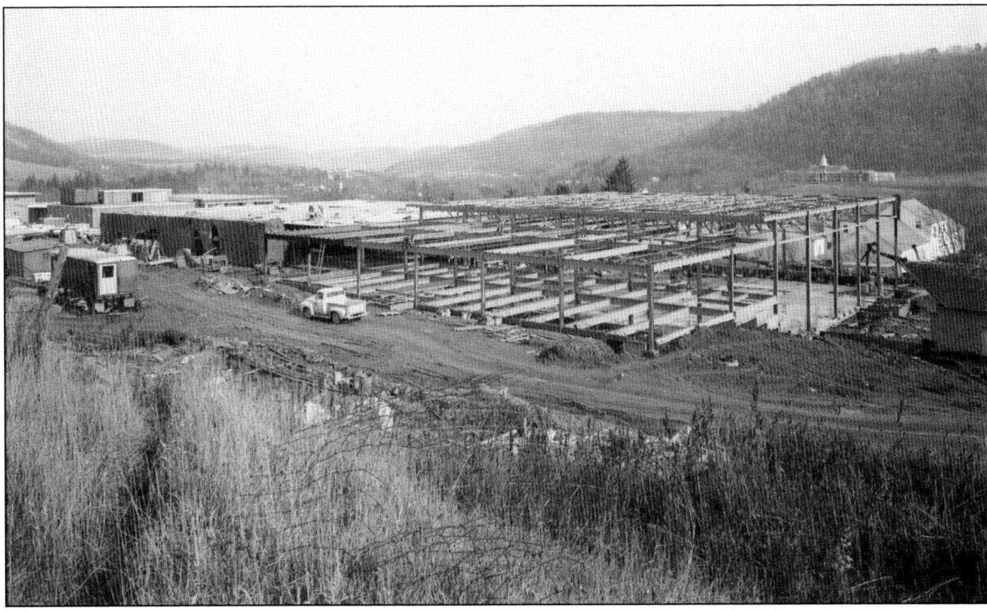

The county seat at Delhi has boasted of an agricultural college since the early 20th century. However, as with so many colleges during the 1960s, a wave of expansion drastically transformed the campus. Situated on a beautiful spot high over the village of Delhi, this image depicts construction at the SUNY at Delhi College of Agricultural and Technical on November 22, 1963. Just visible across the valley is the local high school, Delaware Academy.

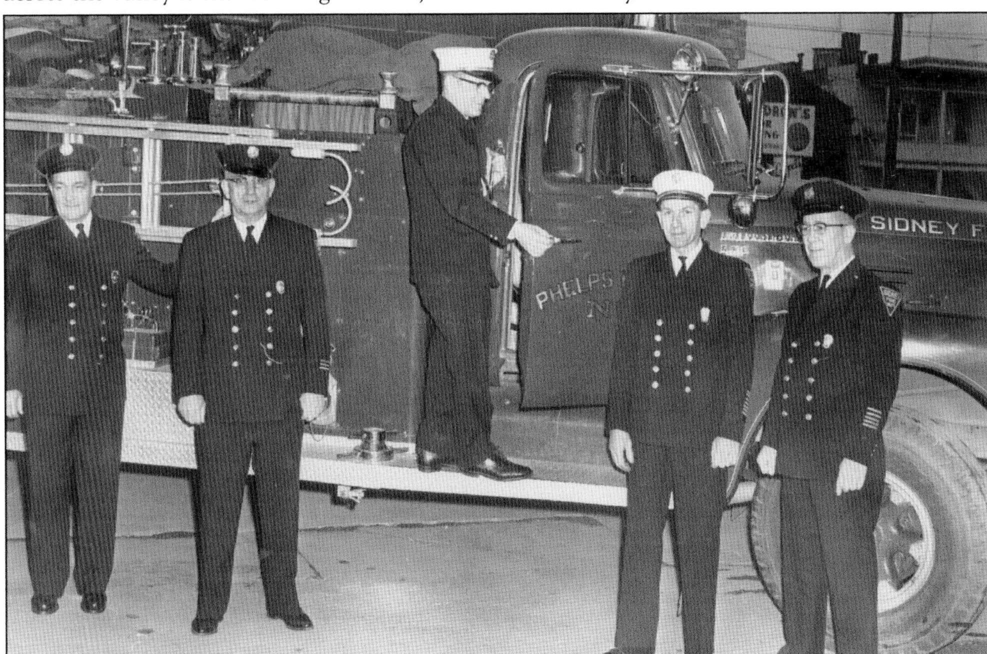

The new officers of the Sidney Volunteer Fire Department are inspecting the fire truck in front of the fire station in March 1965. From left to right are Lewis Parker, treasurer; Milford Ostrander, second assistant chief; Wesley Marr, assistant chief; Arthur Brown, chief; and Donald Fitzgerald, secretary.

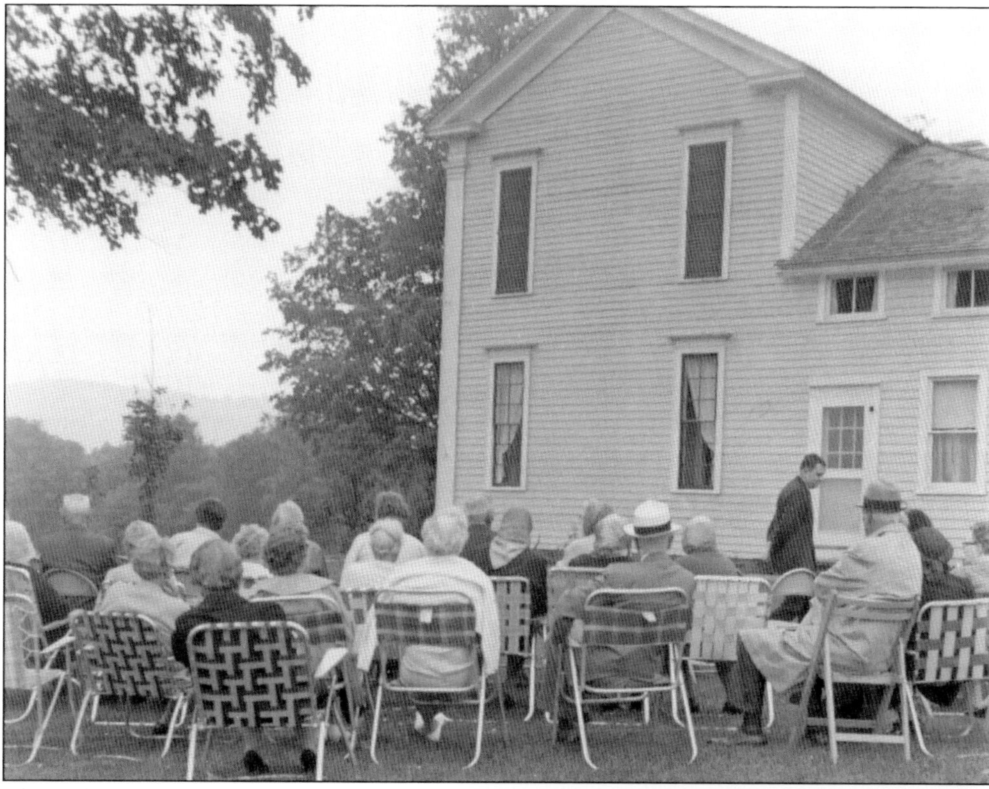

The Delaware County Historical Association (DCHA) was established in 1945 immediately after World War II. In 1960, DCHA acquired the historic Gideon Frisbee House in Delhi, generously donated to the people of the county by the Frisbee family. The house underwent considerable repairs and renovation during the mid-1960s so that by the time of this image in May 1967, DCHA was able to use it as its home.

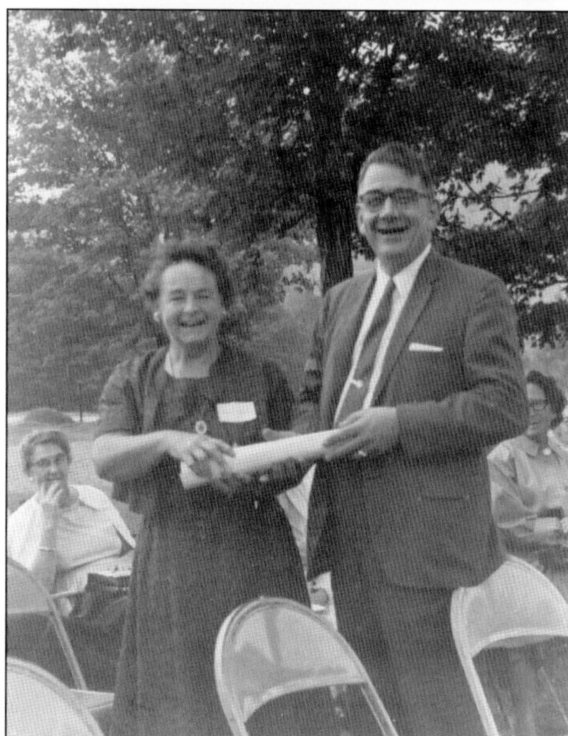

In May 1967, New York State assemblyman Edwyn E. Mason presents the first New York State Museum Charter for the Delaware County Historical Association at the Gideon Frisbee House in Delhi. Mason, of Hobart, by trade a lawyer, served as a member of the New York State Assembly representing Delaware County from 1953 to 1972. He was elected to the state senate in 1972 and served there from 1973 to 1978.

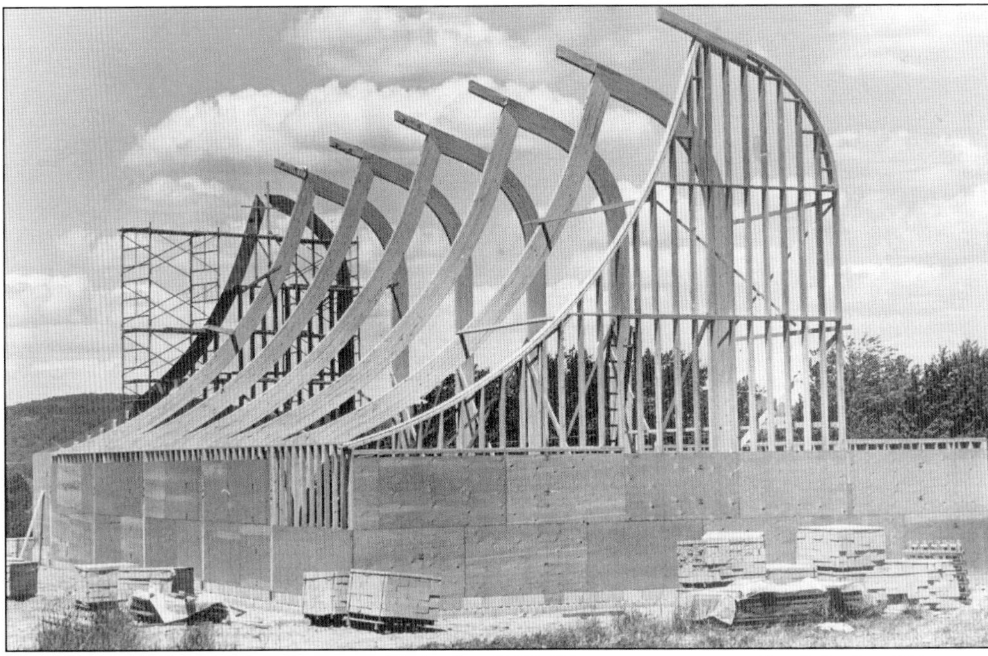

The Sidney Lutheran Church was established in 1952. The congregation utilized the local Veterans of Foreign Wars post and then built a new chapel. In 1966, a new church of contemporary design was constructed. This photograph shows the church during its construction. The newspaper noted that "the church is expected to be completed in the fall at a cost of $80,000" and that the "pulpit of the church is made of blue stone and weighs several tons."

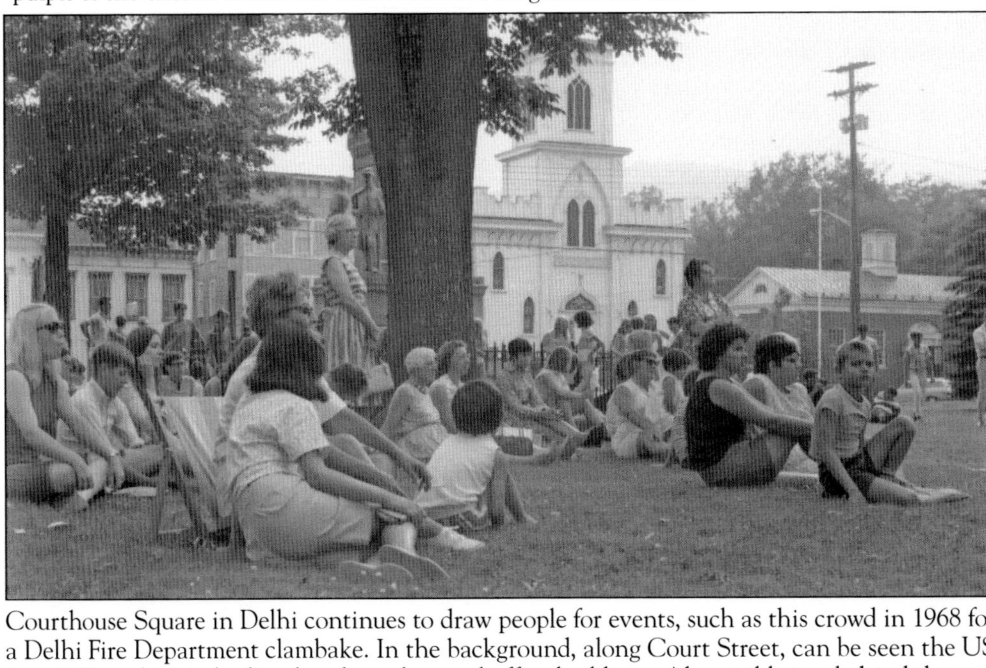

Courthouse Square in Delhi continues to draw people for events, such as this crowd in 1968 for a Delhi Fire Department clambake. In the background, along Court Street, can be seen the US Post Office, the Methodist church, and several office buildings. Also visible just behind the tree is the Civil War monument. Today, in the warmer months of the year, the square hosts a farmers' market, the Fair on the Square, and numerous other events. (Photograph by Bob Wyer.)

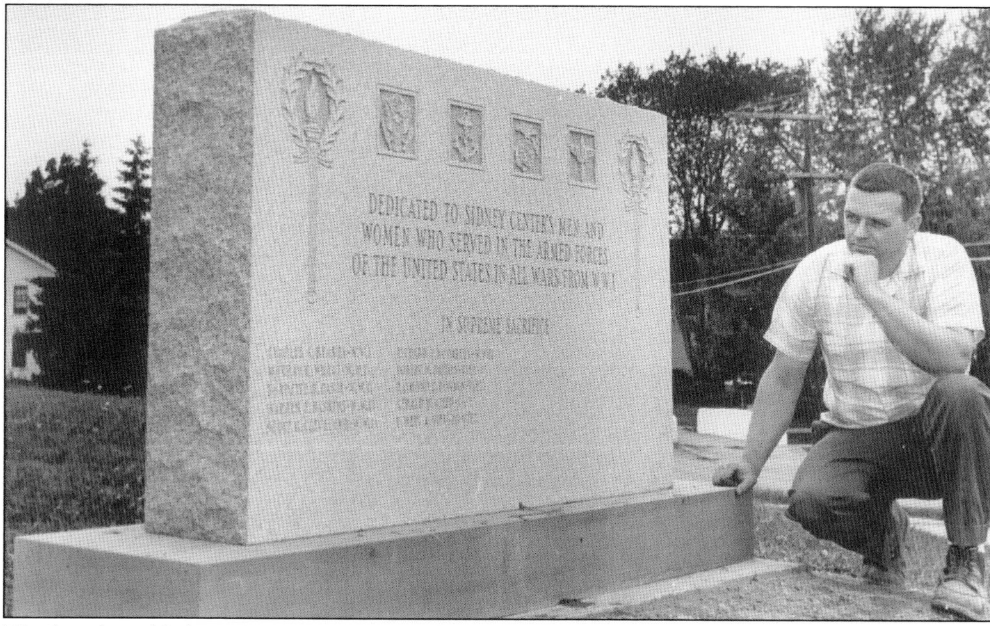

The hamlet of Sidney Center was particularly affected by the Vietnam conflict, with the loss of seven young men during the war. In May 1968, the community's veterans' monument already included four of those names. This photograph likely shows the monument being prepared for the addition of three more names of men who died in February and March 1968: Pfc. Robert A. Gifford, Pfc. Gerald W. Allen, and Sgt. Raymond C. Downin.

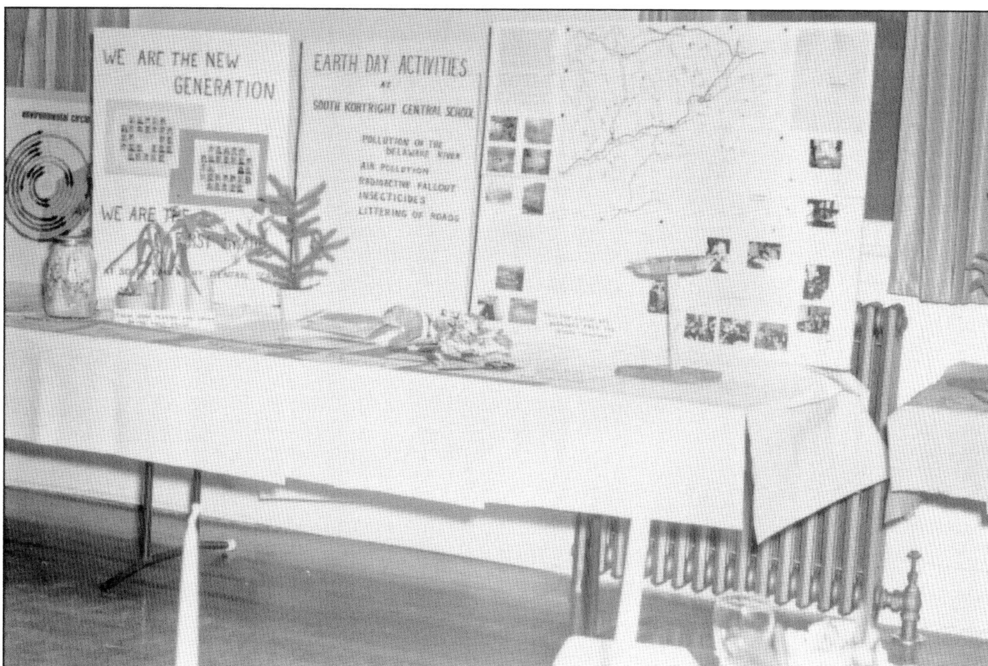

The nation's first Earth Day was held in 1970. Locally, communities across the length and breadth of Delaware County participated in the day's events. Pictured here is a display created by first graders and members of the Horticultural Society at South Kortright School.

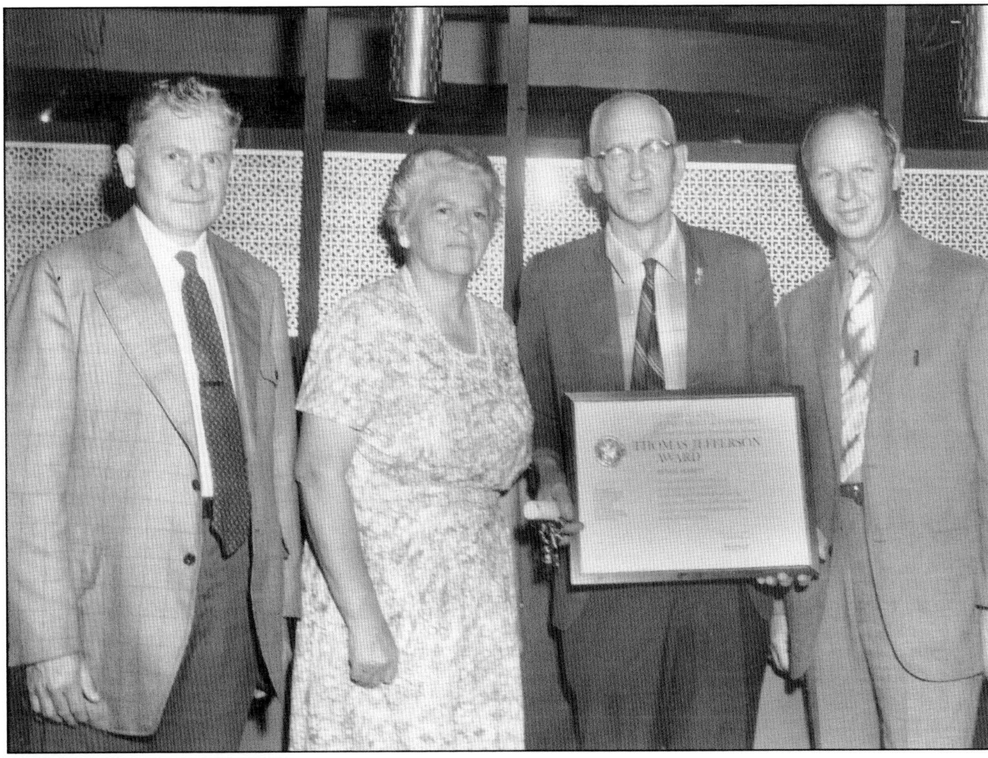

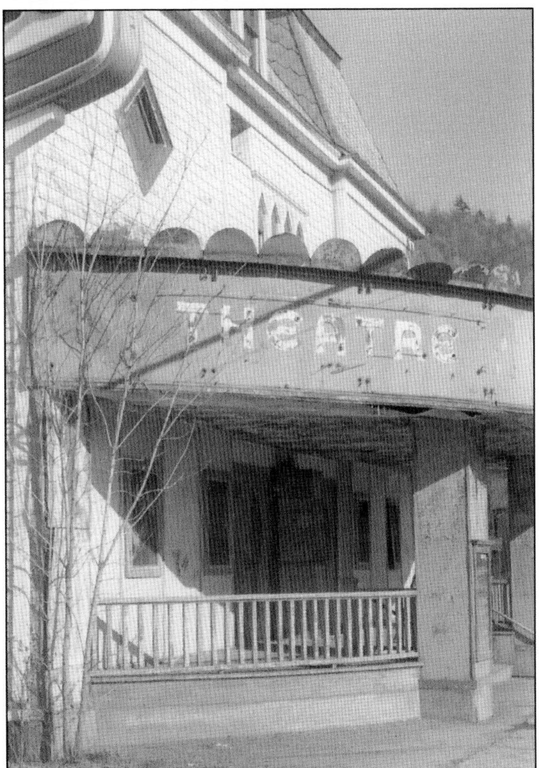

Walton's Arthur Bennett received a plaque in recognition of 30 years of weather watching for the US Department of Commerce National Oceanic and Atmospheric Administration in September 1971. This photograph shows Bennett at a testimonial luncheon. From left to right are Dr. Boyd Peck, a Mrs. Bennett, Arthur Bennett, and Herbert S. Groper.

Smalley's Theater in Delhi started as the Delhi Opera House in the 1880s. In the 1920s, it was purchased by William C. Smalley, who owned a chain of movie theaters. It was popular during the 1930s and 1940s when several well-known stars passed through town but saw business start to fall off in the 1950s. Smalley's closed in 1962. The building stood for another 28 years before it fell to the wrecking ball in November 1990. This photograph of a dilapidated Smalley's dates from about 1982.

While the county saw supermarket chain stores come into the area after World War II, some small stores continued to operate in communities for some time, including the Tremperskill Country Store in Andes, just south of the village. This image shows the store in 1972. The store still operates today, and it still sells gasoline.

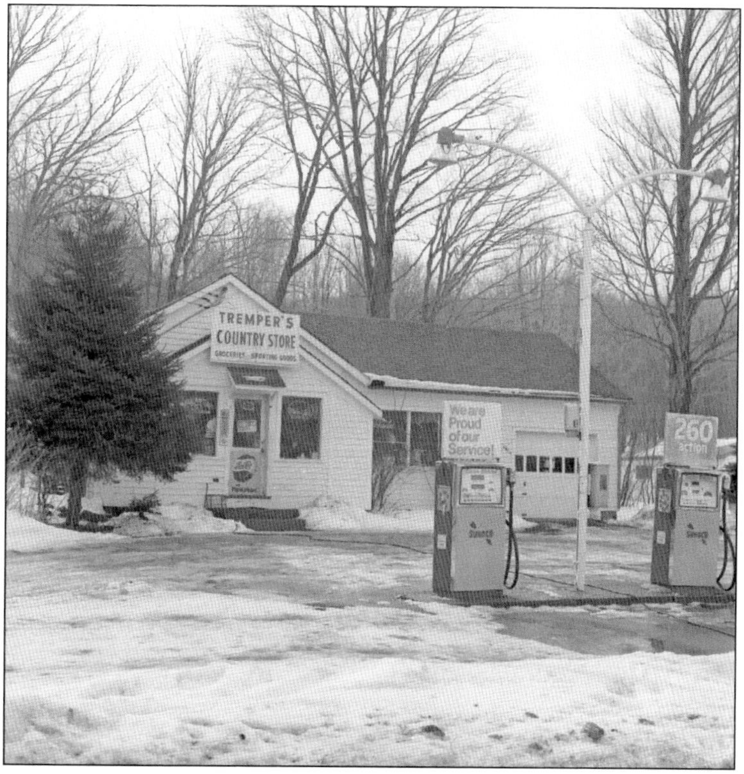

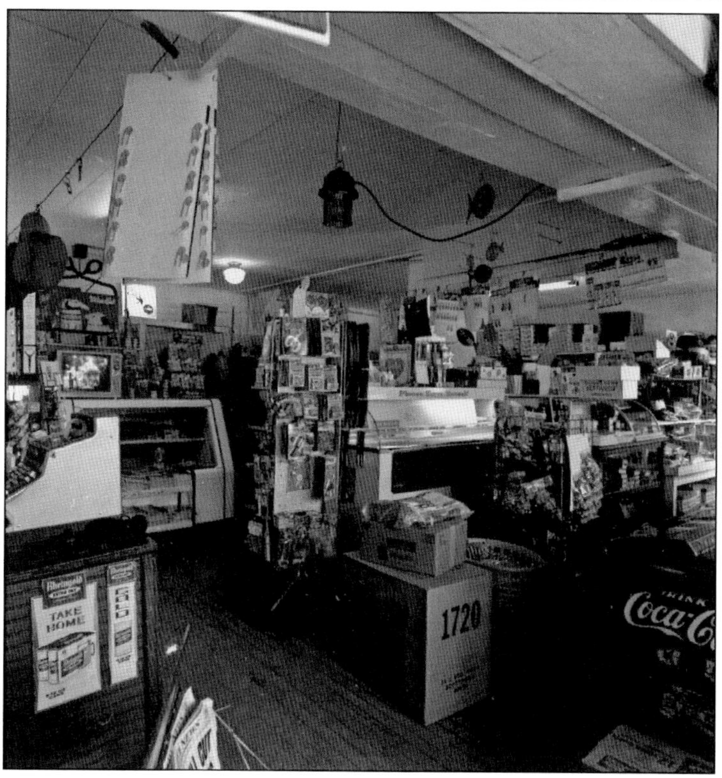

This is a 1972 view of the interior of the Tremperskill Country Store in Andes. Old-time stores, such as these, are a rarity in Delaware County today.

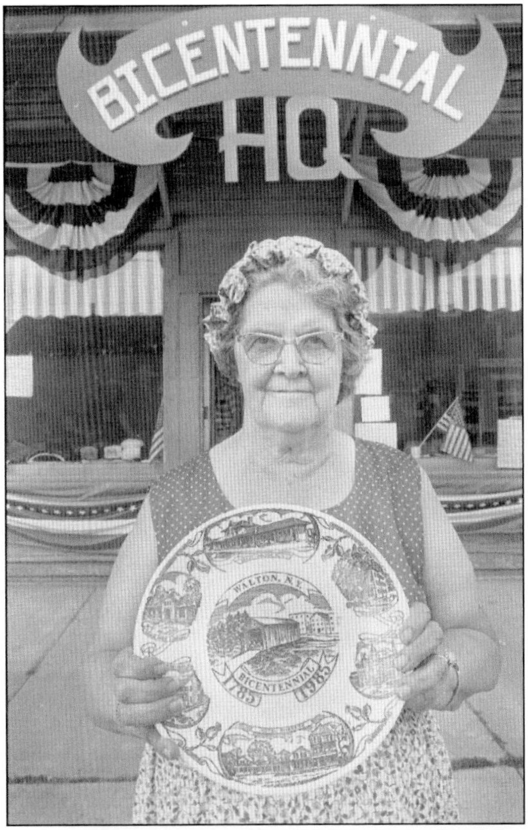

Most villages and towns in Delaware County are now at least two centuries old, and some are well beyond that mark. In 1985, Walton celebrated its bicentennial. In this July 11, 1985, image, Irene Birdsall proudly displays a commemorative Walton Bicentennial Plate in front of Bicentennial Headquarters.

Some of the 19 Delaware County supervisors attended a ceremony on Delhi's Courthouse Square marking Delaware County's bicentennial in 1997. From left to right are Donald Kerr, Tom Hynes, Lee Conklin, Frank Bachler, Eugene Merrill, Walter Johnson, James Eisel, Robin Turner, Joseph Hanley, Joseph Brown, David Anderson, Charles LaFever, Al Rosa, Gerald Mackin, and Jack Thomas.

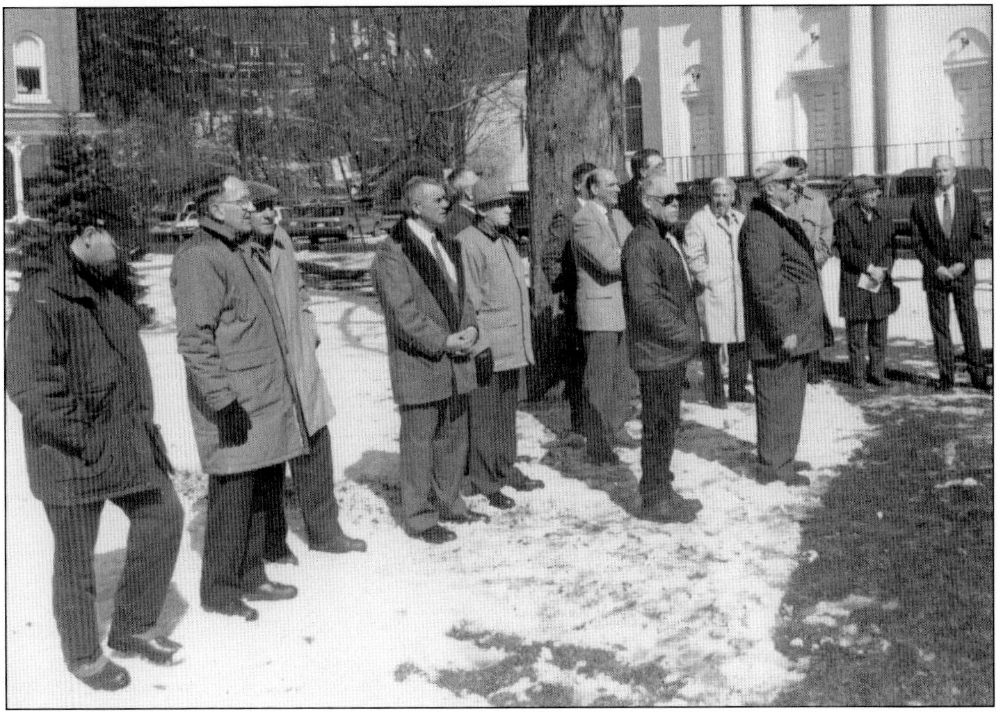

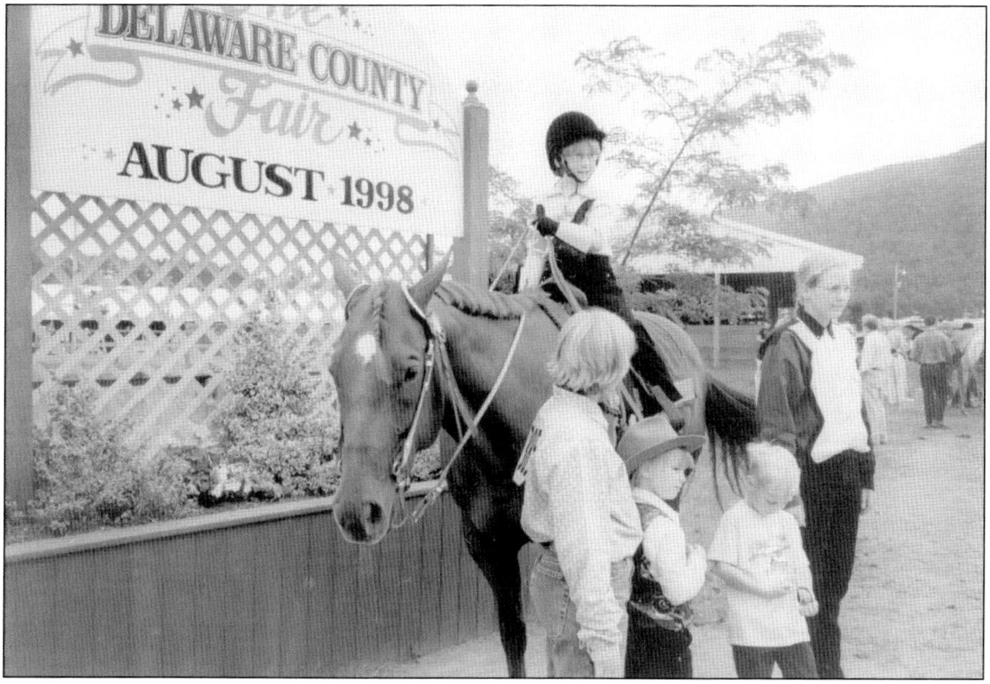

Young equestrians gather at the Delaware County Fair in one of the last such events to be held in the 20th century. Now, well into the 21st century, the county fair continues its tradition each August. (Photograph by Betty Hamilton.)

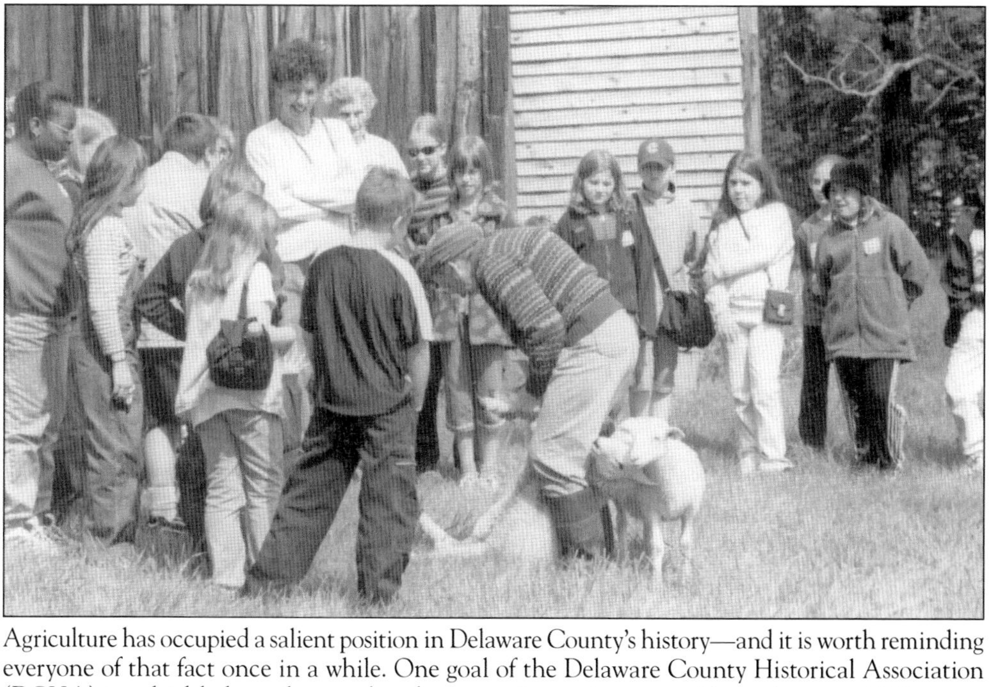

Agriculture has occupied a salient position in Delaware County's history—and it is worth reminding everyone of that fact once in a while. One goal of the Delaware County Historical Association (DCHA) is to highlight and remember the county's agrarian roots. Shown here is a 1990s scene from DCHA's always popular program for fourth graders, "Produce, Preserve, and Play." Local sheep farmer Elizabeth Philips of Treadwell demonstrates the art of sheep shearing.